THE WORLD OF WALTHER NERNST

The Rise and Fall of German Science

Nernst and Lindemann in Oxford, 1937.

THE WORLD OF WALTHER NERNST

The Rise and Fall of German Science

K. MENDELSSOHN, F.R.S.

MACMILLAN

First published 1973
THE MACMILLAN PRESS LTD
London and Basingstoke
Associated companies in New York Melbourne
Dublin Johannesburg and Madras

SBN 333 14895 9

Printed in Great Britain by
T. and A. Constable Ltd.
Hopetoun Street, Edinburgh

Dedicated to the Memory of
F. A. Lindemann, Viscount Cherwell

Contents

Preface

The idea for this book first suggested itself when, almost ten years ago, the Humboldt University in East Berlin asked me to deliver a memorial address on the occasion of the centenary of Nernst's birth. Since then I have been helped by discussions with my colleagues, too numerous to be mentioned individually, in trying to recall events of the past. I am particularly grateful to Nernst's surviving daughters, Mrs Edith von Zanthier and Mrs Angela Hahn, for a great deal of information about their parents and ancestors which they gave me both verbatim and in writing, and for making available to me notes made by Emma Nernst. They also supplied the material for many of the plates. Other illustrations were kindly provided by Lady Simon, Mrs L. Meitner-Graff, Professors G. Born, J. Eggert, O. R. Frisch, W. Haberditzl, W. Heisenberg and I. Prigogine, and Drs C. Bosch and F. L. Haber.

Oxford   K. M.
March 1973

1. Prologue

So this was Berlin—the city where I was born, had gone to school and studied. The window of the ultra-modern hotel looked out on to an enormous stretch of waste land where weeds had begun to grow on the brick dust. Incongruously this desert was criss-crossed by a network of streets, traversed occasionally by a bus which would faithfully halt at bus stops that had lost their significance well over a decade ago. With difficulty I tried to reconstruct familiar landmarks—department stores, café, cinemas, Griencisen's funeral parlour and that little Italian restaurant to which we had taken the girls who were now grandmothers. It seemed inconceivable that on this arid and sterile ground there had existed a large city, pulsating with life, with ideas and with confidence.

The centre of Berlin was dead, as dead as could be. It hardly required a concrete wall to convince the rest of mankind that this was the place where the two halves of the world were turning their backs upon each other. Out in the western suburbs the Kurfuerstendamm and on the eastern side the Stalin Allee, which had now again become the Frankfurter Allee, were each proclaiming themselves noisily as the only true, genuine, respectable and historically justifiable Berlin.

However, nobody is fooled, except perhaps the political pilgrims who come to wail at their respective sides of the wall in tunes of undeserved affluence or insincere class feeling, as the case may be. Berlin provides a wonderful forum for speeches, crises, emotions, examples of modern architecture and souvenir postcards but the dead city remains dead— which may be just as well. Nothing lives here but memories, and it was for memories that a small group of scientists, all now in their fifties or sixties, had gathered at the old university institute of physical chemistry. Walther Nernst taught here and impressed the stamp of his personality on a long line of pupils from all over the world. Now their surviving remnant had come to celebrate the centenary of his birth. For a few days the past came to life again. It seemed only yesterday, but then again so long ago, that the unimpressive looking little man had walked through these corridors or stood by the blackboard where suddenly, in the middle of a lecture that great inspiration had come to him which we now call the third law of thermodynamics.

However, it was not for Nernst alone that the students used to come to Berlin. In the 'twenties and early 'thirties discussion meetings were held

A

in Nernst's laboratory every Friday afternoon. One or two recent scientific publications, chosen for their topical interest, were refereed and discussed at each of these sessions. Usually the speakers were young

IM JAHRE 1905 ENTDECKTE
WALTHER NERNST
IM VERLAUF SEINER IN DIESEM
SAALE GEHALTENEN VORLESUNG
DEN 3. HAUPTSATZ
DER THERMODYNAMIK.
DIE HUMBOLDT-UNIVERSITAT
GAB 1964, IM JAHRE
DES 100. GEBURTSTAGES
DES GROSSEN GELEHRTEN,
DIESEM HORSAAL DEN NAMEN
WALTHER-NERNST-
HORSAAL

IN 1905
WALTHER NERNST
WHILE LECTURING IN THIS
AUDITORIUM DISCOVERED
THE 3RD LAW
OF THERMODYNAMICS.
IN 1964,
THE CENTENARY YEAR OF THE
BIRTH OF THE GREAT SCIENTIST
THE HUMBOLDT UNIVERSITY
NAMED THIS LECTURE ROOM
WALTHER NERNST
AUDITORIUM

Memorial tablet at the Physicochemical Institute, Berlin

scientists who had been given the task of making a *précis* of the papers and of submitting it to the meeting. They acted the less important parts while the main performance was put on by the audience, headed by a formidable array of Nobel Laureates. Besides Nernst there were Einstein,

Planck, von Laue, Schrödinger, Gustav Hertz, as well as Otto Hahn and Lise Meitner who in the years to come were to discover and explain nuclear fission. The first three rows were usually packed with scientists each of whom had a wide international reputation in his field, while at the back sat the young research students. Sometimes a distinguished visitor would speak, Heisenberg or Debye from Leipzig, James Franck or Max Born from Goettingen.

The Berlin 'colloquium', as this Friday meeting was called, was not the place for idle talk or polite circumlocution. The significance of reported observations or of new theories was discussed and analysed mercilessly but not necessarily dispassionately. Often the germ of a new idea would arise not so much from the reported paper as from the discussion which followed it. The men on the front benches had long passed the stage when one worries about one's reputation in the scientific world. All that mattered to them was physics, and physics was thrashed out among them, often with almost brutal frankness. Even such a notoriously mild-mannered man as Einstein would make his point at this gathering very decisively, and equally candidly admit a mistake. There was the occasion when he and Nernst argued an issue fiercely without reaching agreement. A little later at another colloquium, the same point came up with Einstein now offering an opinion very close to Nernst's original argument. This was too much for Nernst, to find Einstein now voicing his own original opinion without making the slightest acknowledgement of his conversion to it. Einstein's reply was classical and typical of the spirit of the colloquium: 'But really, my dear colleague Nernst, is it my fault that God created the world differently from what I thought three weeks ago?'

At the back the research students sat spellbound. This was modern physics in the making. Here the long hours in the laboratory or at the desk were turning into a living thing, the creation of new thought. Once a week they went to this school of hard criticism and clear thinking which impressed itself indelibly on their minds. That was what they had come to Berlin for.

Science was not the only thing worth while in Berlin. Opposite Nernst's laboratory, on the other bank of the Spree, was the Theater am Schiffbauerdamm where Brecht and Weill's *Threepenny Opera* created a controversial sensation. The plight of Germany's seven million unemployed rang through the uncompromising harshness of its songs. Berlin was gay and hard at the same time, fascinating and exciting. Within fifteen years it would be dead, rapidly turning into a myth.

How did it all happen? What created and destroyed this city and the country of which it was the capital? The venerable age of German civilization lets us forget too easily that there was nothing old or venerable about Berlin. When it was destroyed in 1945, it had been the capital of the German Reich for less than seventy-five years. When in 1933 Hitler came to power with the burning of the Reichstag, it had housed the German Parliament for not even half a century. The rise and fall of Berlin, its short but magnificent brilliance, sets it apart from the other great cities of the world. For a very limited but significant span of time it was the centre of scientific thought.

Within those fifty years of its history the temper of German scientific thinking passed through a succession of phases; from the staid, thorough and somewhat ponderous investigations of the late nineteenth century to the reckless, imaginative and daring exploits of the 'twenties. Each phase is an image of its time, beginning with the solid but limited concepts of the Prussian State, through the heady intoxication of a World Power and to the cynical uncertainties of inflation and depression. Every change left its mark and each new phase produced its characteristic contributions. In the story of the rise and fall of German science Nernst shall be our guide. He was born in the year 1864 when, after a lull of a century, Prussia embarked on a new wave of conquests which rapidly led to the new Reich. He died one year before the battles of Stalingrad and El Alamein dashed the hope of German domination of the world. Nernst was a son of Prussia, a true representative of the forces that created the new Reich. Apart from his scientific achievements, he was a patriot in the best sense of the word; he stood for all that was good and decent in this strange dynamic era.

The enigma of modern Germany, its dual personality of hard-working reliability and mad fanaticism, has its roots in bygone centuries. It is quite impossible to comprehend the events of the recent past without first talking about the historical changes out of which this vital expansion drew its strength. They are very different from those related by the carefully vetted history course of German school primers.

The Holy Roman Empire of German Nation, to give it its full name was created when at Christmas of the year A.D. 800 the Pope in Rome, crowned Charlemagne as 'Kaiser'. When more than eight centuries later it perished in the holocaust of the Thirty Years' War, its ultimate heir, Prussia, did not yet exist as a State. It was still the Mark Brandenburg, German colonial territory on purely Slavonic soil. Since 1415 it was ruled by the Hohenzollerns, first as Electors and after 1701 as Kings. The second of these created a large army which set the unique pattern for the Prussian State with all its merits and faults. Suddenly, after six centuries of colonial servitude the Slavonic population was drawn into a State organization. Unlike the development in other countries, the national consciousness of the Prussian was created not by becoming a citizen but by becoming a soldier. For the former serf, the command of his officer was the ultimate order which had to be obeyed without question. Complete obedience and a sense of duty which could never be evaded were the hallmarks that in due course set the stamp on all Prussian institutions, the officialdom and the schools.

The ruthlessness of this robot army was first demonstrated by Frederick II and more than a century later by Otto von Bismarck who created the Hohenzollern Empire single-handed. He came from the Markish nobility and the belief in the infallibility of the Prussian army remained the keynote of his policies. Born in 1815, he grew up on the family estate of Schoenhausen, a man of magnificent physique with an insatiable appetite for food, drink, women and power. His youth as a law student at Goettingen and Berlin was wild and disorderly. After entering the judical Government service at Aachen he went off without leave, in order to follow for some months an Englishwoman with whom he had fallen in love. Reprimanded on his return, he handed in his resignation and retired to look after the family estate. Through Johanna von Puttkamer, whom he married in 1847, he came into the circle of pietists who formed the *camarilla* under whose influence the king was at the time. Bismarck never held any strong religious views and there is every reason to assume that his pietist leanings merely served his political ambition. The next year already gave him an opportunity for an ambitious intrigue which, however, misfired badly and under the failure of which he had to suffer for the greater part of his career. When in 1848 an uprising in Berlin was at its height, Bismarck suggested not only that the childless king should abdicate but that his brother the heir presumptive, the much discredited 'Shrapnel Prince', also should renounce the succession in favour of his infant son. The latter would then have been an easy pawn in Bismarck's hand. As it turned out, Bismarck had not reckoned with Prince Wilhelm's spirited wife Augusta who crossed his scheme and bore him a grudge for life.

As a result Bismarck was somewhat discredited and when after the revolution the military clique regained power, he was not selected for high office in Berlin but sent off to the National Assembly at Frankfurt. His chances diminished further when in 1857 the king's insanity had reached such a pitch that Prince Wilhelm was made regent and under the influence of Augusta tried to introduce a new liberal era in Prussia. Augusta had not forgotten and in 1859 she arranged for Bismarck to be put 'in cold storage' by sending him as ambassador first to Petersburg and then to Paris.

Meanwhile Bismarck's friends in the military Markish nobility were biding their time, waiting for a chance of embarrassing the liberal cabinet. This came soon enough when in 1861 the War Minister, Albrecht von Roon, demanded a further great increase in the armed forces. The liberal Ministers felt, rightly, that this was nothing but an attempt to keep Prussia indefinitely as an authoritarian robot State, and they as well as the Landtag opposed Roon's 'army reform'. Wilhelm, who now was king, on the other hand had grown up with the army and however much he had listened to Augusta's liberal ideas, his loyalty was with his fellow-officers. Roon, feeling that he could count on the king's sympathy did everything in his power to aggravate the situation. Finally, when all prospect of a compromise had disappeared and the king had manœuvred himself into a hopeless position, Roon suggested to him that there was only one man ruthless enough to extricate him from the dilemma—the Prussian Ambassador in Paris.

Bismarck was just then vacationing in Biarritz, having a love affair with Madame Ekaterina Orlova, the wife of the Russian Ambassador in Brussels. The amour was going well, as we know from Bismarck's letters to his wife whom he kept informed about all details. Into this idyll burst a telegram from Roon, saying that the king had agreed to receive Bismarck. He hastily kissed Ekaterina good-bye and set out for Berlin where, on the 22nd September, he had his famous conversation with Wilhelm at the palace of Babelsberg. In it he assured the king that he felt capable of saving the crown, if necessary by instituting a dictator-ship, and, moreover, that he had great plans for the future of Prussia. Wilhelm made him Prime Minister and Bismarck kept his word; in less than two years the Prussian guns thundered at Dueppel, taking Schleswig away from Denmark. After another two years they spoke again, at Koeniggraetz, reducing proud Austria to an obedient satellite and in 1870, six weeks after the outbreak of a third war, the Emperor of France was taken prisoner. Bismarck's plan was working beyond the king's highest expectations and Wilhelm became content to follow the lead given by his unruly Prime Minister and faithful servant.

Bismarck's plan had been worked out during his years at Frankfurt. Like all successful schemes, it was an extremely simple one. The wars of Frederick the Great had convinced Bismarck that the Prussian army was a unique instrument for wielding power. It would fight bravely and relentlessly against the heaviest odds. It was insensitive to heavy casualties and could be relied on to obey orders however exacting or inhuman. Its officers' corps was absolutely loyal to the king. The identity of army and State in Prussia had been brought about by historical accident rather than by design but it had proved eminently efficient.

However, Bismarck's plan went further than the time-honoured scheme of a military dictatorship. He realized that in order to achieve the status of a great Power, the army must be backed by an equally efficient economy and that, in the nineteenth century, meant an industrialized society. What he needed was a guiding idea which would give meaning to the gigantic enterprise, and that he had found in Frankfurt. The Prussian concept of duty and service as the basic rights of the king's subject was well fitted for the army and the officials but the appeal of the uniform alone was unlikely to satisfy the intelligentsia and the businessmen, possibly in the long run not even the workers. In Frankfurt he had come across the nostalgic romanticism of the professors who by now had begun to write novels about the Middle Ages, soon to be followed by even more romantic ones about the still more distant past of the Goths conquering Rome and the splendid heroes of the Germanic prehistory. It was a most suitable ideology for the empire of which Bismarck dreamt, and a completely harmless one as far as current events were concerned. So he decided to roll it all into one, Frederick the Great, Goethe, Hermann, Schiller, Beethoven and the old Emperor Barbarossa who had disappeared into the Kyffhaeuser Mountain in about 1200, to emerge again when Germany was reborn. The time of the new empire had come and Bismarck was to herald it. The stage was set for the most glamorous spectacle of the century and the curtain rises on the Second Reich.

2. Founder Years

Walther Hermann Nernst was born on the 25th June, 1864, in the little West Prussian town of Briesen where his father was a judge. The family traces its ancestry back to the time of the first king of Prussia, when a Master Christian Nernst was a cooper and citizen of the little Markish town of Prenzlau, where he died in 1721. His son Johannes Christian Nernst, a carpenter, lived in the same town and died in 1769. Ten years earlier this carpenter's son, Johannes David, was born, the great-grand-father of Walther. Johannes David became a Lutheran pastor and married a pastor's daughter, Luise Schramm. He, too, lived for a time in Prenzlau where he preached at St Mary's Church. Of his six children the youngest Philipp, was Walther's grandfather. Both he and his elder brother, Hermann, fought in the war against Napoleon, and Hermann achieved distinction by bringing the news of the victory at Waterloo to Berlin. The story is told in the Nernst family that in the evening after the battle the Prussian commander, Marshal Bluecher, looked around among his young officers and then decided: 'Lieutenant Nernst, you have a young wife in Berlin, you will be our fastest courier'. With captured horses Hermann made the journey in five days and the *Berlinische Nachrichten* gave the news of his triumphal arrival: 'At 1 p.m. the bringer of this great news was escorted into the city by 24 trumpeters amid the jubilation of the citizens. While the courier made his report to the king and queen a salvo of 100 shots was fired by the cannon in the Lustgarten.'

Philipp was badly wounded in 1813, but 1815 saw him again in action in a regiment of dragoons. After the war he farmed, renting the Govern-ment estate of Potzlow, not far from Prenzlau, and bringing up a family of nine from two marriages. The fifth son, Gustav, read law and married Ottilie Nerger. Walther was their third child, but one of the older children died early and Ottilie, too, soon died.

Artisans, a pastor, a farmer and a provincial judge; the Nernsts were coming up in the world but no more so than might be expected of any hard-working, capable family in Prussia's expanding society. There is no record of hereditary genius or even of outstanding enterprise. It seems that Walther owed his brilliance to a lucky throw of the genetic dice. Indeed, there was little in his outward appearance which gave a hint of the acuteness of his mind or of his caustic sense of humour. He was a short man who grew bald early and who wore a pince-nez on a black ribbon. He was fond of the theatre and even wrote a play for the Berlin stage which only missed success by the company going bankrupt on the first day. For a time he toyed with the idea of becoming an actor himself and he realized this ambition to some extent by wearing throughout his life the mask of a trusting and credulous little man. His favourite expression of innocent astonishment could be underlined by a twitch of the nose which removed the pince-nez. There was also usually a note of astonishment in his voice and the outrageous and sarcastic comment of which he was master was never accompanied by a change in his voice nor by a smile. He just remained genuinely serious and mildly surprised. A story became current among his colleagues that one day God had decided to create a superman. He began his work on the brain and formed the most perfect and subtle mind, but then he was unfortunately called away. The archangel Gabriel saw the unique brain and could not resist the temptation to shape the body, but unfortunately, due to his inexperience, he only succeeded in fashioning a rather unimpressive looking little man. Dissatisfied with his efforts, he left his work. Finally, the devil came along and saw the inanimate thing, and he blew the breath of life into it. That was Walther Nernst.

Walther's father was promoted from the little town of Briesen to become judge at Graudenz, a fortified frontier town on the left bank of the Vistula. It was here that the boy went to school at the *Gymnasium*, the standard form of German high school. Although he finished school as the best pupil with a Latin essay and although he had ambitions of becoming a poet, the greatest impression was that made on him by the chemistry master, who had succeeded in rousing in the boy a deep interest in his subject. At home Walther was given the use of a cellar to carry out his own experiments.

Something has to be said about the German *Gymnasium* which derived its name not from the original Greek athletic schools in which the inmates exercised *gymnoi*—naked—but from the later development of this institution when it had become the debating forum of philosophers. Private schools were, and still are, almost unknown in Germany and the *Gymnasium*, the standard form of secondary education is run by the State or by the municipality under the supervision of the Ministry of Education. The teachers, most of whom had obtained a doctorate, used to have the title of professor. The school was invariably housed in a substantial edifice which was both imposing and forbidding and its aspect accorded well with the type and manner of education dispensed within its walls. Its main purpose was the unrelenting provision of staggering quantities of factual knowledge, under elaborate precautions which ensured that much of it was retained for life. The pupils' slang term for the schoolmaster was *Pauker*, that is, drummer, and a coarse variation of this word suggests that originally the drumming in of knowledge may sometimes have taken place on the boy's seat. As for the syllabus, it has to be admitted that it provided a reasonably well-balanced and extremely comprehensive form of general education. From Latin grammar to calculus and from electromagnetism to the history of art and architecture, there is hardly a field of human knowledge left in which the *Gymnasium* failed to instruct. After nine years of secondary education, preceded by three years of preparatory schooling, the whole curriculum works itself up into the fierce crescendo of a final examination, the *Abiturium* which has been described by Albert Einstein—who was a poor scholar—as the most exacting test ever devised by man. On the other hand, once this ghastly hurdle had been successfully negotiated, the road was wide open; the examination permitted entry into any German university.

It was in this type of school that the lives of Nernst and his contemporaries were moulded, who were destined to build the new Hohenzollern empire. The *Gymnasium* was a curious mixture of the old and the new. It combined the German reverence for scholarship with the code of behaviour of the Prussian army. However unjust or erroneous the punishment meted out to a boy might have been, he had to suffer it before he was allowed to complain to the headmaster—since it would be the same in the army. At the same time, it was made clear to him that he was punished because he had been found out rather than because he had committed the act for which he was punished. Discipline was fairly strict but no particular effort at 'character building' was made, with the emphasis on fitness obtained through physical jerks rather than through games. The old German tradition of scholarship was represented by the heavy syllabus and the retention of the Latin words for the forms, the examinations and most other terms referring to school life. The boys were never encouraged to help in running the school and such things as the prefect system were unknown, this again would have been contrary to the spirit of the army, which did not permit any individual initiative.

Accounts of the *Gymnasium* have often found their way into German literature. They appear in the writings of both Thomas and Heinrich Mann, the former describing it in the famous *Buddenbrooks* and the latter in his book *Professor Unrat* which became widely known through its film version *The Blue Angel*. However, the character of the German attitude to education is perhaps best shown in a short episode told by Bertolt Brecht:

It is the little boys' first day at school and when they are taken to their classroom it turns out that the number of seats is one less than the number of boys. So one of them moves about disconsolately until the teacher cuffs him behind the ear, saying: 'That will teach you not to be unlucky again'.

Since there is no indication of any scientific interest in Nernst's family, the Graudenz Gymnasium must be credited with having aroused the love of chemistry and physics in the future Nobel Laureate. The other great love which was to last throughout his life was kindled in him by his maternal uncle Rudolf Nerger, who worked the Government estate of Engelsburg which he had rented. There the motherless boy not only found a second home made for him by his aunt Anna and his five girl cousins but, above all, life in the country and particularly the shoot became his chief relaxation. Walther always went there for his holidays and for many of his week-ends. In spite of their monotony the great plains east of the Elbe hold a peculiar fascination. There are fields as far as the eye can see and vast pine forests, studded with lakes. In the hot summers the scent of resin fills the woods and in the severe winters the frozen lakes provide glorious skating. The little Prussian towns are sleepy, unexciting places with none of the architectural beauties of the old German cities in the west and south. The houses are sober and unimaginative buildings of strictly functional character, expressing perfectly the orderly Prussian spirit. The little brick churches are unadorned and the only outstanding buildings to be found here and there are unassuming little palaces built by a Hohenzollern prince or princess, or an old town gate with storks nesting on the towers.

When in the early nineteenth century the peasants were freed from the old colonial heritage of providing services for Prussian nobles, they had to buy this 'freedom' by selling most of their land. Through this device they became agricultural workers on the huge estates made up from the land over which they formerly had held some semblance of ownership. Usually the houses of the landed nobility also showed the unpretentious Prussian simplicity although they were usually referred to by the villagers as 'the palace'. The happiest times of Nernst's youth were spent on such an estate with the Nergers at Engelsburg, and when later he became famous and wealthy, he bought estates on which he spent every available hour of leisure. This love of the country he retained to the end and he died on his estate 'Zibelle' in the midst of the lakes and woods which had meant so much to him. Engelsburg and Aunt Nerger were never forgotten. When fifteen years later Nernst inherited a little money from his father, he gave it all to Aunt Nerger who had become a widow and found it difficult to run the estate. Although it was all the money he had, he insisted that it was a gift and not a loan. When finally Engelsburg had to be sold because the aunt was getting on in years, Nernst called his youngest daughter, who was born just then, Angela, in memory of the estate.

At home in Graudenz his father was in the habit of making Walther read to him in Latin until the former fell asleep. It also appears that Walther Nernst saw practically every production that went on to the stage of the Graudenz theatre and he assured me, half a century later, that some of the acting he had seen there outclassed in excellence anything in Berlin, London or Paris. Since this information was given, as always with a dead serious face, it was impossible to tell whether he meant it or not.

Briesen, Graudenz and Engelsburg, the first two decades of Walther Nernst's life were spent in the quiet provincial atmosphere which was as yet untouched by the great events that were taking place at the same time. Eighteen sixty-four and the war with Denmark had only been the beginning. Austria had been forced into it as an ally but none of her wishes were to be considered at the peace treaty. Bismarck knew that this would lead to the break that he had wished to precipitate. Austria appealed to the other German States in order to have the matter discussed and this was the signal for Bismarck to order the Prussian Army to march into Austria. The war had two objects; to teach Austria a lesson and to show the German princes where they stood if they dared to oppose Bismarck. The campaign only lasted three weeks, which were all that was needed to defeat the Austrian troops completely. The German States who, had been on the side of Habsburg were paralysed with fear and terror and now their princes had to join a 'North German Federation' in which Prussia called the tune.

The federation was nothing but a transitional phase which lasted until Prussia had dealt with the only serious opponent who still remained in Europe: France. After a short respite of less than four years Bismarck provided the generals with the opportunity they were longing for. Moltke's lightning tactics had worked well against Denmark and Austria, they could now be tried against the strongest army in Europe. As has already been mentioned, the Prussian war machine scored a termendous success; after only a few weeks' fighting the French army capitulated at Sedan and Napoleon was taken prisoner. The war was virtually over. The Prussian army advanced on Paris, which was invested but not attacked. Bismarck knew that hunger in the capital and political dissentions would further weaken France and his calculation proved correct. While the Parisians were reduced to eating rats caught in the sewers, the Prussian High Command settled in sumptuous style a few miles outside the city walls, at Versailles.

It was here that the culminating scene of the drama was to be enacted; the foundation of the new German Reich. It was the most difficult task in Bismarck's career and one which only he dared undertake. However, he was now at the height of his power, much admired by all concerned and even more feared. Any lingering hope which the German princes might have entertained that unification could be a bargaining issue had to be dropped after Sedan. They were now only anxious that Bismarck should allow them to keep their titles and palaces, and were ready to render any service he should require in return for this favour. The time for this had now come. The only serious opposition which Bismarck encountered came from the German Kaisers whom he was about to create. The Hohenzollerns, King Wilhelm of Prussia and his son Crown Prince Friedrich, were doubtful and needed persuasion. Wilhelm had not forgotten the 1848 rising when he had to decamp hurriedly from Berlin in order to escape from German ideas of democratic freedom. The concept of old Prussia, dominated by the code of its army, was more to his taste than the grandiose and adventurous schemes which Bismarck was hatching. Now Bismarck could play his trump card. At his request the King of Bavaria, the most powerful German ruler of the most anti-Prussian State in Germany, wrote a letter to Wilhelm, beseeching him to accept the Imperial Crown of Germany. Wilhelm began to weaken at this display of patriotic loyalty but still had various reservations about the styling of the title which, however, were cut short by a 'spontaneous' acclaim on the part of the rest of the princes.

Bismarck's superb stage management had won the day and for a moment the ruthlessness which lay behind it seemed forgotten. However, even if the Germans forgot, the French did not. Pomp and circumstance had returned to Louis XIV's *galerie des glaces* but now it was an alien conqueror who had usurped the Palace of Versailles to proclaim the new German Reich on the soil of vanquished France. This act of crude bombast at the foundation of the Hohenzollern empire was to have its retribution half a century later when, after the downfall of the Hohenzollerns, Germany was forced to sign the peace of Versailles on the very spot so unwisely chosen by Bismarck for his triumph.

The victory bells of Sedan rang in that epic period called by the Germans *Gründerjahre*—the founder years. A foretaste had already been given by the 'North German Federation'. Business had begun to grow rapidly everywhere. Manufacturers on the Rhine built factories to supply the eastern territories of Prussia and the coal of the Ruhr valley furnished them with power and soon with chemical raw materials. The huge indemnity which France had to pay after the war provided capital for the development of industry and the building of railways. The sleepy German towns of Saxony, the South, and particularly the Rhineland, began to be seized by a wave of new enterprise. The constant drain of manpower emigrating to America ceased and instead the new German Reich began to attract industrial as well as agricultural labour from the Polish-speaking territories in the east.

During his school-days when young Walther Nernst's imagination was fired by the prospects of work in chemistry, more was involved than the love of pure science. Chemistry had suddenly become a thing of importance in Germany. It was a new word used together with such terms as progress, miracle and wealth. At about the time of Nernst's birth, a number of small firms had been founded, mostly in the Rhineland, which began the manufacture of dyestuffs because this was a flourishing industry in France and especially in England. They started merely by imitating work in those countries and usually employed less than ten workers. Three of these firms, the Badische Anilin und Soda Fabrik, Farbenfabrik Friedrich Bayer and Farbwerke Hoechst were soon to grow into formidable enterprises and eventually combine to form the huge I.G. Farbenindustrie. The rise of these firms in the new German Reich was truly meteoric. Within less than twenty years, and while Nernst was still a schoolboy, they produced half of the world's dyes. After another twenty years, at the turn of the century, the world's total production of dyes had doubled and by then the Germans manufactured well over eighty per cent of it. In addition they had created a gigantic pharmaceutical industry which made every other country rely on their drugs.

There were a number of factors which contributed to this unique economic explosion and the mentality of the founder years is not the least of them. Businessmen and workers alike were caught up in this great adventure of expansion which was backed by pride in their invincible army. For the better part of half a century, until World War I, Sedan Day was celebrated as a great national holiday, a proof of what by then was regarded as the rebirth of the old German Reich. Wagner, who had to flee as a political refugee after the 1848 revolution, returned to extol the greatness of the German past. It is significant that the *Meistersinger*, set in the Middle Ages, appeared in 1867 and that after the establishment of the Hohenzollern empire Wagner went back to the Germanic heritage of the Ring of the Nibelungen, glorifying the Rhine and the old gods of two thousand years ago. Germanic drinking horns and winged helmets became favourite items of decoration and innocent children began to be plagued for the rest of their lives with the most extravagant Germanic names. However, these emblems remained for the greater part nothing more than the outward signs of a relatively sober and hard-working nationalism and had as yet nothing of the heady and sinister intoxication of the Nazi age. It was merely that the German expansion under the wing of the Prussian army needed a grand historical background which a host of writers, artists and professors were only too eager to supply.

As it turned out, the combination of German romanticism with the qualities of the Prussian law-and-order State proved remarkably successful and provided much of the impetus in the founder years. Another important factor was the high regard in which scholarship had always been held in Germany. In fact, the miracle of the German chemical industry had its beginning in the German universities. Until 1828 it was generally believed that matter has two radically different aspects—the inorganic and the organic one. All minerals were placed into the former class whereas it was assumed that organic substances could never be formed out of the reactions between inorganic ones but required for their making the 'vital force' of living plants or animals. In that year Friedrich Wöhler succeeded in making out of inorganic materials, urea, a substance that was only known as a product of the animal kidney. This synthesis of an 'organic' substance in the laboratory presented chemists with the almost fantastic prospect that they might be able to create artificially all those substances which until then had been obtainable only as animal or vegetable products. Incredible as this possibility must have appeared to them, it was far surpassed by what happened in their laboratories in the next few decades. They soon found that not only could they artificially make many of the known organic materials but that the number of these was small compared with the enormous host of entirely new substances which do not occur in nature and which often had extremely useful properties.

In 1841 Wilhelm August von Hofmann was awarded the doctorate of the University of Giessen for a thesis on the derivatives of coal tar. He had done his work in the famous laboratory established there by Justus von Liebig the great chemist who became known for his application of chemistry to agriculture and for the production of the meat extract which, to this day, bears his name. Hofmann had intended to read law but, on coming to the university, had been impressed so much by Liebig's lectures that he decided to change his subject. He soon found that one of the substances obtained from coal tar was aniline which had previously been found in the distillation of indigo. Indigo, of course, was a highly priced blue vegetable dye and Hofmann was much intrigued with the possibility of obtaining artificial dyes from coal tar. Four years later he succeeded in preparing aniline from benzene, discovering at the same time that benzene is one of the chief constituents of coal tar. At that time Hofmann had moved to Bonn and it was in the same year, 1845, that Queen Victoria and Prince Albert came to Bonn for the celebrations held there in honour of the seventy-fifth anniversary of Beethoven's birth. The Prince Consort, who had been a student in Bonn, went to show the Queen his old rooms where he encountered Hofmann, who now used them as a laboratory. Both he and the Queen were much impressed by Hofmann's charm and personality. The Prince, who was keen on the development of science in England, was chairman of a committee for the foundation of a Royal College of Chemistry in London and Hofmann had, in fact, been suggested by Liebig for the headship. It seems that this personal meeting determined Prince Albert's choice and so Hofmann set up his new laboratory in London. He soon collected a host of students, mainly from England and Germany, whom he set to work on problems of his choosing. The question of the aniline dyes was among them and, by a curious chance, it achieved new importance at the hands of a seventeen-year-old student, William Henry Perkin.

Actually Hofmann had suggested that Perkin should attempt to make artificial quinine. Perkin used aniline as a starting substance, and while he did not obtain quinine, he discovered the first commercial coal tar dye—aniline mauve. Perkin's father, a builder, had only grudgingly agreed to his son dabbling in chemistry and he now saw a possibility of turning this fad into profit. Much against Hofmann's advice Perkin left the laboratory and set up in business with his father to produce aniline mauve on a commercial basis. Hofmann's advice was not altogether unsound since at first the new dye found little favour in England and only sold after it had become popular in France. Meanwhile Hofmann himself discovered other good dyes, the Hofmann violets, and then German competition began to cut into Perkin's business. He left the field to the Germans in 1874, retiring with a modest fortune to devote the rest of his life to pure research.

It must seem strange that the German manufacturers who themselves were starting in a small way should have been able to oust Perkin from his established position. The main reason was not only that capital became available to them—this could be obtained even more easily in England—but that they were able to back up their work with competent chemical research. Perkin had to rely almost entirely on his own expert knowledge, whereas the Germans could put into the field a considerable number of highly trained chemists. Besides the excellent chemistry schools at the universities of Giessen and Goettingen there were others of note, particularly those at Heidelberg and Bonn. At the latter was August Kekulé who, in spite of his French name, was a German, born in Darmstadt. Kekulé was a theoretical chemist who discovered the structure of the benzene ring, a revelation which came to him in a dream when dozing off by the fireplace. He saw chains of chemically linked carbon atoms winding along before his eyes until one of them grabbed its tail with its mouth forming a ring. Kekulé woke with a start and immediately set to work, applying his vision to the chemical formulae of the known carbon compounds. It did not take him long to realize that he had dreamt up the correct solution. The discovery of the benzene ring was an enormous step forward in the understanding of the structure of organic molecules. Significantly, after Kekulé's death his valuable books were acquired by the Bayer Chemical Company to form the nucleus of their research library—named after Kekulé—which eventually numbered a quarter of a million volumes.

Thus, the German universities played, from the very beginning, a most important part in German technological development. However, their contribution is only part of the story. In 1825 a *Technische Hochschule* was founded at Karlsruhe on the upper Rhine and soon similar foundations were established all over Germany until, at the turn of the century, there were about a dozen. The proper translation of the German term should be 'technical university' rather than 'college of technology', since not only administratively but also in their basic conception these institutions have full university status. The technical universities were created with the deliberate aim of producing in large numbers technologists of the highest standard and from the outset of their existence they stood alongside and never beneath the traditional type of German university. It is significant for their status that these German technical universities have had no difficulty in attracting Nobel Laureates for their professorships. The final degree is a diploma which corresponds in standard to the bachelor's degree of the honours course in a British university. An engineering doctorate given by these institutions was always regarded as somewhat superior to the doctorate of philosophy granted by the universities.

The technical universities have seen to it that German industry was supplied with men and women especially trained to undertake the large volume of developmental technological research which was to form the backbone of its rapid growth. Even more than in the science faculties of the traditional universities, emphasis was placed in the technical universities on close cooperation with industry by offering consultantships to members of the staff. In this way the transition from study to industrial work was facilitated because in his employment the student would, as often as not, retain personal contact with the professors who had taught him. All German firms of any importance, and particularly those in the chemical industry, set up research laboratories in which, as far as possible, the spirit and atmosphere of an academic institution was maintained.

This emphasis on sound and broad scientific research was typical for the management of German industry right from its beginning in the founder years. It was a unique feature which was not paralleled to any extent in other countries. For a long time it stood alone in the world and there can be little doubt that this research-mindedness was the significant factor, which even in the long run, permitted the German chemical industry to maintain its lead in an age that became increasingly competitive. At the turn of the century American firms were the first to follow the German example of research in industry, largely because many of them had started as branches of German enterprise, thereby inheriting the pattern rather than developing it from a basic decision. England and France decided to wait another half-century, until after the

Second World War; their industrialists too, though still very reluctantly, followed suit.

The question remains as to how the Germans succeeded right at the initial stage of their industrial expansion to hit immediately on this pattern which was to impart to their venture the capacity for a fantastic rate of growth. Some of the contributary reasons have already been mentioned; the psychological upsurge of the founder years, the ready availability of labour and the traditional regard for learning. However, against these must be set inexperience in manufacturing techniques, lack of raw materials and relatively meagre capital resources.

Possibly the last two shortcomings worked to their advantage. Much of the attraction of chemical processes is that a highly priced product can often be obtained from cheap raw materials, as was certainly true for the coal tar used by the dyestuff industry. In this kind of manufacture all therefore depends on scientific ingenuity and expert knowledge. In addition, the small size of the original enterprises usually meant that the chemist was not merely an employee of the firm but one of the founders. In this way a pattern of organization was established in which the scientist acted not only as an expert but also in a managerial capacity. It soon turned out that his combined interest in chemical reactions and their commercial application produced sound judgement in business matters. The little firms benefited and were not slow to realize the strength of their method. The pattern of scientific management which may originally have been partly accidental was generally adopted by German industries not only in chemistry but also in other fields. When in the 1930s the huge dye trust, I. G. Farben, had reached its zenith, its leaders were scientists and not accountants.

A typical example is the career of Carl Duisberg who rose to the chairmanship of the Federation of German Industry and became a friend of Nernst. Twenty years after its foundation the Bayer Company, with a share capital of 5·4 million marks, had 350 workers, one engineer and 14 chemists. They felt that, in order to remain competitive, they had to increase their scientific personnel and they hired three more chemists, who had just taken their doctorates. However, before setting them to work in their own laboratory, the company sent them back to university for another year's special research. One of these was Duisberg, whose father was a simple ribbon weaver. Like Nernst, Duisberg was stimulated by his chemistry lessons at school and, supported by his mother but much against his father's wish, studied chemistry. Again it was his mother who took the initiative when the question of a job arose. She had been to school with Friedrich Bayer, who later founded the chemical firm, and through her influence she secured a position for young Carl.

When Duisberg entered the company, its business had slumped and no dividends were being paid. With great clarity of vision he realized that the firm's future depended on its ability to develop new products since he felt sure that one or the other of these was bound to be a money spinner. With great determination and much courage he convinced the directors that the way out of the crisis was to establish a laboratory for basic research. Four years later the number of workers had already trebled when Duisberg, with one of the new chemists, Oskar Hinsberg, discovered that one of their dyestuff derivatives, phenacetin, had important therapeutical properties. This immediately led to the formation of a new division in the company, producing pharmaceutical substances of which Bayer's aspirin became the most important for many years to come. This was not the only triumph of the new research laboratory. In the same year another of Duisberg's colleagues invented alazarin blue.

Duisberg's position in the firm was admittedly strengthened by the fact that he had married the only niece of the childless managing director, but it would be unfair to attribute too large a measure of his success to this happy alliance. He had entered a company that lived by manufacturing the products of scientific discovery and his university research had taught Duisberg how science works and how discoveries are made. It was his scientific training that led him to the logical conclusion that, in order to prosper, the firm must create the atmosphere in which research could flourish. He also saw the need for the industrial scientist to be constantly aware of the company's commercial interests and its manufacturing capacity. The chemist Duisberg was in a much better position to assess the feasibility of large-scale production on the basis of pilot experiments in his laboratory than any businessman could. The firm soon learned that scientific management was the shortest and most economical way of making money.

German industry soon learned that as often as not good scientists also make good businessmen. Duisberg became the chief architect of the huge chemical combine. I. G. Farbenindustrie A. G. which had a share capital of 650 million marks and which was headed by men like himself and Carl Bosch, who received the Nobel prize for his work on ammonia synthesis. The scientific discovery on which this latter achievement was based had earned the Nobel prize for another German scientist, Walther Nernst. This, however, is a later chapter in our story.

The system of study at a German university makes it impossible to decide whether Walther Nernst read physics or chemistry. The basic idea, which remained virtually unchanged until modern times, was that a student sits at the feet of professors in order to learn and not in order to obtain qualifications on paper. When entering the university he made his own choice of the lectures that he wanted to hear and which might range over different faculties. It was not a rare occurrence that a man who came up to read law would be drawn into chemistry or medicine instead because he was stimulated by a brilliant course of lectures in those subjects. Often he might find it very difficult to make up his mind between two subjects and would study both. It did not matter all that much, since in later life he and others would regard his years at the university a worthwhile qualification, even if he had never sat for an examination. To some extent this attitude survived well into our century, when in any university the number of first-year students was very much greater than that in the later years. Any boy or girl who had obtained the *Abiturium*, the final examination at the *Gymnasium*, had the right to enter a German university without any further entrance qualifications. A great number of school-leavers did that and a high percentage of them would realize after a year or two that they did not wish to go on and obtain a doctorate in the end. Far from regarding their time at the university as wasted they, and any future employer, would consider these years of study as a valuable asset.

All this means that life at university was quite different in spirit from that at school, from which it would usually be separated by a year's military service. The absence of a rigid syllabus left the student all the freedom in the world in the pursuit of his studies. He alone was responsible for his progress and nobody in the university took any interest in how or whether he got on. As far as the university authorities were concerned, he was an adult human being who could live where and how he liked. All they did was to provide lectures. In later years qualifying examinations were instituted in some subjects but they were not meant to set up university qualifications. These, for instance, were examinations for chemists, set by the Institute of Chemistry or those held by the Ministry of Education to qualify students for teaching at a *Gymnasium*. The general principle was that study should remain a free academic pursuit which, when followed for some time, might result in the student submitting a thesis for a doctorate in one of the faculties.

This free and easy form of German academic life led to a feature which has always puzzled people in other countries, and that is the frequent change of university by one and the same student in the course of his study. Here, Nernst provides a typical example. His first semester was spent at Zürich. From there he went for a semester to Berlin, only to return for the third semester to Zürich. For the fourth semester he took up residence at Graz. After some study there he felt that it was time to work for his thesis, which he decided to do at Wuerzburg, where he settled for the next two years and obtained his doctorate.

Nernst was an enterprising man of a lively temperament and he may have moved about a little more than the average student, but even the latter would usually make at least one change. As we shall see later, the reason for Nernst's moves was not the wish to sample the atmosphere of these cities but to hear lectures in which he was particularly interested. The professors there did not simply teach standard courses of chemistry or physics, but they would put before the students their own particular views and theories. It was imperative for a man like Nernst that he should be able to enter into these current schools of thought which would enable him to form his own ideas on the kind of research work that he was going to do himself.

It is obvious that this extreme freedom of German academic life should have called for some form of organization into which the student could fit himself when he needed help in academic and personal matters. Such organizations had, in fact, existed since the Middle Ages. At that time students moved from university to university all over Europe and at each of them they entered groups of mutual assistance with others coming from their own country or region. These groups were called 'nations' and we find, for instance, that, during his studies in Bologna, Copernicus' name was listed there in the German nation. With the increase in the number of universities, the groups became regionally more defined as *Landsmannschaften*, that is, associations of fellow countrymen. Finally, at the beginning of the nineteenth century these associations reconstituted themselves as *Corporationen*, which have survived into the present day and are responsible for the image of the beer-drinking student with his coloured cap and *badolier* and his fencing scars.

A good deal of these trappings were a hangover from the old days of the wandering scholar who only too often was a swashbuckling, vagrant hoodlum in search of others of his kind with whom he could pick a quarrel. Drinking and sword fighting thus became the mark by which the student was known, an undeserved reputation for the great majority, whose real interests were their studies and who, for this reason, were much less in the public eye.

A student organization was then formed at the University of Jena and spread rapidly over the whole of Germany: the *Burschenschaften*. They set out to cleanse the universities of the hard-drinking and brawling loafers who had earned them an ill reputation. Their enthusiasm for a renewal of the old German Reich on a basis of democratic freedom and justice spread like wildfire through the country. The princes and their Ministers soon saw the danger which threatened them from the universities and suppressed the *Burschenschaften*.

In spite of all repression, discontent was smouldering beneath the surface only to break out again and again. It leapt up as a bright flame with the revolution in 1848 after which it was finally extinguished in the massacre at Rastatt. It was one of the darkest episodes in German history in which the revolutionaries were exterminated by the Prussian army under their commander the 'Shrapnel Prince', the future first Hohenzollern Kaiser of Germany.

Perhaps the best measure of the popular enthusiasm that sustained the founder years was the changed attitude of the students. The *Burschenschaften* had been revived and they now formed an ardent patriotic force, loyal to the Fatherland and to the Kaiser. After a quarter of a century Rastatt was forgotten and Wilhelm had turned from the Shrapnel Prince into a patriarch.

With the cleaning up of student life by the *Burschenschaften* at the time of Napoleon, the old Student Corps had fallen on evil days. It, too, attempted some kind of reform which, however, only consisted of the regularization of carousing and brawling into the so-called 'comment'. It is hardly likely that, in spite of lending new glamour to drinking and sword fighting, the Student Corps would have survived much longer, had it not been for the suppression of the *Burschenschaften* and the police supervision of the universities. The Corps had always been unpolitical, simply because its social life did not rise to the intellectual height of a political debate. It had now become the only safe organization for a student to belong to and for this reason was looked upon with favour by the State. The Prussian civil service in particular began to recruit for its higher ranks men who had been Corps students and could therefore be regarded as reliable. Soon this patronage began to lend a new aspect of respectability to the Corps. The roughnecks and drunkards were now joined by serious-minded young men of good family who went into the Corps not so much for the jollity of student life as for the prospect of entering the Prussian State service.

Nevertheless, the gaudy trappings and the comment had to be retained and many an abstemious civil servant recalled in later life with a mild shudder the quantities of beer he had been obliged to consume in the furtherance of his career. Not only did the Government recruit from the Corps but business and industry followed suit. Membership became a necessary qualification for those desirous of entering the Establishment. Fencing scars · graduated to a mark of social distinction. To be sure these were not the sign of duels but of a highly ceremonial procedure carried through with elaborate safety precautions. The combatants were heavily bandaged, leaving free only those areas of the face on which the scars were to be produced. Corps rules, in addition, specified that a doctor be in attendance who, as soon as blood was drawn, would see to it that the wound did not close up too well so that the victim was not cheated out of his scar. From now on it was apparent to all the world that its proud bearer not only had been to university but belonged to a Corps. Even so, rumour never ceased that some of the finest scars had been administered artistically by means of a razor, followed by rubbing some irritant into the cut.

The mediaeval pageantry of student life as practised in the Corps was part and parcel of the romanticism of the Hohenzollern empire. In addition, the Corps served other purposes. Careful social distinctions were made in admission to the different Corps. The most exclusive would only take sons of the old nobility as, for instance, the Bonn Borussia of which Kaiser Wilhelm II became a member when entering the university. In fact, there was a close resemblance between this choice and that of a suitable regiment in which the standing and tradition of a family would also play a decisive part. The freshman entering the Corps had first to serve an apprenticeship as a '*Fox*', in which he was attached to an older student, the '*Bursch*', whose job was to look after the newcomer and to advise him. It again is interesting to note the similarity to Prussian army parlance in that the student in these years would be called an 'active' member of the Corps. The same term applied to the years of the young officer spent in army service before he was placed on the reserve list. The student retiring from active life in the Corps became an '*alter Herr*', an old gentleman, who considered it an honour and a duty to help the young members of his Corps. The old gentlemen would periodically return to the university for commemoration festivities of their Corps and then would meet the young members looking for a job or other avenues of advancement.

It is significant that Nernst did not apply for entry into one of the Corps. He never was a social climber. This was not because he despised the advantages of helpful social connections but because the effort of climbing was alien to him. Only once was he persuaded to scale a mountain. This happened at the end of his first term in Zürich when his father and brother visited him and then took him along to ascend the Piz Languard. This experience in mountaineering sufficed for the rest of Nernst's life; he was already accustomed to achieving things without effort. To Nernst's mind the time and money spent on Corps membership were a shocking waste, leading to a worthless social status. He never changed his mind and later had nothing but sarcastic comment for his brother-in-law who was devoted to the life of his Corps. It is significant that Duisberg, too, took a poor view of the Corps and preferred to devote his time to student activities in such fields as natural history societies.

When Nernst finished his studies an epoch was drawing to its close. Gradually the founder years were giving way to a new era with different problems. The memory of the struggles that had led to the foundation of the new Reich was growing dim. The dynamic enthusiasm was replaced by a sense of achievement and solid prosperity. Germany was growing rich. In 1888 Kaiser Wilhelm I died and now Bismarck's days of power were numbered. He had convinced the Crown Prince that he was indispensable, thus making sure that he would remain in power in the new reign, but alas, when old Wilhelm I died, his son, too, was dying of cancer. Kaiser Friedrich's reign lasted only ninety-nine days, after which he was succeeded by Wilhelm II.

The young Kaiser was not bound to Bismarck by memories as his father and grandfather had been. In his eyes Bismarck was a patronizing old man who considered himself infallible although he had latterly made one mistake after another. The Chancellor was determined to stay at his post, if necessary against the Kaiser's wish, and forced a trial of strength in his usual tactless manner. Wilhelm called his bluff, asking Bismarck to hand in his letter of resignation. It arrived after considerable delay and was immediately accepted. From now on, the Kaiser declared, he would be his own Chancellor.

For the next thirty years the German scene was dominated by 'the Kaiser'. Whatever other forces were at work, his decisions were vital and he set the pace for many of the new developments, including those of science and technology. Nernst, himself, was his frequent guest and had ample opportunity for bringing the achievements and requirements of German science to the Kaiser's notice.

What kind of man was this Kaiser who set his stamp so firmly on the 'Wilhelminian era' of Germany? During his reign he was more in the news than any other mortal yet few people took notice of his death twenty-three years after his abdication. Within this short period the memory of him had faded away, leaving hardly a trace. Contemporary writing allows one to choose from anything between a divinely gifted monarch of immense wisdom to a stupid and bloodthirsty king of the Huns. In fact, he was neither.

When in 1858 Queen Victoria's ambitious daughter married Prince Friedrich of Prussia, it was clear that his father, the Shrapnel Prince, would become king in succession to his mentally deranged and childless brother.

Young Victoria's first child was born in 1859; it was a boy, the hoped-for successor to the throne. His birth had been difficult and it took an hour before the child showed definite signs of life. His left arm had been dislocated and remained paralysed for life.

His tall and handsome father appealed strongly to the romantic sense of the Germans of the new Reich. They connected his name and the reddish beard with the legend that the Kaiser Barbarossa would return from his enchanted sleep in the Kyffhaeuser Mountain to rule again over a strong Reich. Those who were closer to him thought otherwise, since they knew him as a well-meaning but weak man, who was torn between the opposing influences of his wife and Bismarck. Bismarck's success with the fair sex evidently did not extend to Queens. He had made an enemy for life of the old Kaiser's consort and now he had fallen out with Victoria. When later he disapproved of Wilhelm, he put the blame on her, crudely saying that 'the English mare had spoiled the Prussian stud'.

Victoria was a strange woman. She preferred her younger children to Wilhelm and when one of them died, she kept a wax figure of the dead child in the bed by which she would sit for hours. The handicapped eldest boy built up a resentment against his mother and her preference for English life. His great wish was to prove that he could overcome his disability, and proving himself became second nature to him. Lack of maternal love and understanding seems to have made him a somewhat lonely boy who failed to make contact with others at the *Gymnasium* at Kassel or at the university at Bonn. He developed and maintained a high regard for his headmaster at Kassel, Hinzpeter, on whose advice he acted shortly after his accession, in his attitude towards the socialists. Instead of training the Prince in time for his duties as ruler, he had been attached to a regiment in Potsdam, where he lived surrounded by the Prussian officers' corps. This was the old Kaiser's wish and was shared neither by Bismarck nor by the Crown Prince. In fact the latter went so far as to describe his son as 'immature', 'overbearing' and 'lacking in education'. This was only two years before young Wilhelm's coronation.

They certainly had made a mess of the upbringing of Germany's future ruler. The army worked on him through the old Kaiser, his mother Victoria through the Crown Prince and Bismarck for his own ends. It is hardly surprising that young Wilhelm listened to them all and in the end to nobody. In framing the constitution Bismarck had allowed great powers to the monarch because in this way Bismarck, standing behind the throne, would be all powerful. Now Wilhelm was going to wield this power by himself because he felt that it had been bestowed upon him by the grace of God. All considered, he made not too bad a job of it for most of his reign.

Liberalism and the Prussian generals continually fought for his soul and quite often liberalism gained the upper hand. Sometimes the Kaiser's freedom from prejudice was surprising. The question of anti-Semitism which was later to assume such monstrous proportions is a good example. Religious anti-Semitism, a heritage of the Middle Ages, had been ebbing away in Europe in the nineteenth century. In its stead there arose a school of philosophers, led by Nietzsche, who attacked Jewish culture and thought as being inferior to a Germanic race of supermen. It is amusing and perhaps not insignificant that this idea of Teutonic superiority should have originated with a man whose own Slavonic descent was unmistakable by the number of successive consonants in his name.

The doctrine of superiority always finds followers, particularly when the qualifications for exclusiveness can be obtained without much effort.

Not to be a Jew is fairly easy for most people. However, in the founder years and in the Wilhelminian era the Germans were so successful that very few of them required the added comfort of attested Teutonic lineage, and anti-Semitism did not gain much ground. On the contrary, even people who had anti-Jewish prejudices would have considered it bad manners to practise them actively.

Nevertheless, anti-Semitism was the type of creed which appealed to political adventurers and in 1880 Germany had her first experience of one of these. He was Adolf Stoecker, a court preacher, a man of limited intellect but boundless ambition. Stoecker was a member of the Prussian parliament and tried to have legislation introduced which prevented Jews from entering the State service and, if possible, exclude them from citizenship. However, the attempt was roundly denounced by Crown Prince Friedrich and the Crown Princess who described anti-Semitism as shameful and a disgrace to Germany. In addition, leaders of the German intelligentsia, such as Hofmann, Virchow, Siemens, Mommsen and many others, signed a manifesto in much the same spirit. Having failed completely, Stoecker had to bide his time, which was not long. When, a few years later, it became clear that Friedrich was a dying man, he began to work on young Wilhelm, counting on success because of the strained relations between the Prince and his parents.

Wilhelm had married Augusta Victoria of Schleswig Holstein, a homely girl of simple and pious tastes, who was forever promoting the building of churches. Through her friends the Prince became acquainted with Stoecker's ideas of a Christian Social movement which was to win over the workers from the Marxist heresy. At first Wilhelm seems to have been enthusiastic, but in spite of his wife's leanings and of his opposition to his parents he soon not only turned away from Stoecker's anti-Semitism but expressed his disapproval by dismissing him.

In fact, as time went on, the Kaiser's circle of acquaintances numbered many outstanding Jewish businessmen and scientists whose achievements for Germany he regarded highly and to whose advice he was ready to listen. It is significant that when in the First World War, owing to a miscalculation by the General Staff, an acute shortage of war materials occurred, it was a Jewish engineer and industrialist, Walter Rathenau, who was called in to find a remedy for the situation. Another Jewish friend of the Kaiser, Albert Ballin, the chairman of the Hamburg–America Line, committed suicide when he learnt of Wilhelm's flight to Holland in November 1918.

In fact, the German Jews had never looked back since, in the eighteenth century, Moses Mendelssohn had led them to emancipation. In 1812 Prussia had taken the lead in Germany in giving them citizenship and equality. Assimilation often took the form of baptism but even those Jews who retained their faith became fully integrated members of German social life. At the turn of the century one-third of the Jewish marriages were mixed ones. A certain amount of anti-Jewish feeling existed in the Prussian officers' corps, but even there members of the aristocracy would frequently marry, usually wealthy, Jewish girls.

The matter was different in Austria where Stoecker's Christian Socialist ideas met with much greater success. The reason for this was the inhomogeneity of population in the Habsburg empire where the German-speaking section was in the minority. The ruling class was almost exclusively recruited from this, turning the majority of the Austrian Emperor's subjects, such as Czechs, Poles, Hungarians, Bosnians, Serbs, Moravians, Croats and so on, into second-class citizens. All these were made to feel their inferior status acutely and they therefore found solace in the distinction of not being Jews. Hitler's Nazism was simply an importation of his own typically Austrian brand of anti-Semitism into Germany.

It is quite remarkable how the Jews, immediately upon emancipation, began to play an important part in the intellectual and artistic life of Germany. Moses Mendelssohn who, as a young man, had secretly to learn German, became not only one of the outstanding philosophers but also a champion of German literature. He exerted a strong influence on young Wilhelm von Humboldt, who later became the prime mover in the foundation of Berlin University which today bears his name. His brother Alexander, the famous naturalist, was a close friend of Moses' son Abraham, the founder of the banking house and father of the composer. Abraham provided Humboldt with a little laboratory at the bottom of his garden, which consisted of a hut, held together with copper fittings. The object of this iron-free structure was to make in it very sensitive measurements of the Earth's magnetic field. In the evenings the sound of music drifted into the laboratory from the near-by summer house where Felix Mendelssohn and his sister Fanny were practising. One of Humboldt's young co-workers, the mathematician Dirichlet, succumbed to the romantic surroundings and married Felix' youngest sister Rebecca.

Another of Alexander von Humboldt's friends in Berlin was the young and vivacious wife of the Jewish physician Marcus Herz. She was good-looking, flirtatious and collected around her a circle of artists and writers, in short she created in Berlin a *salon*. The saying went: 'If you have not seen the Royal Theatre and Henrietta Herz, you have not seen Berlin'. Humboldt kept up with her a lively correspondence, using the Hebrew alphabet in order to fox the censor. Another of his literary friends was also a Jewess, the famous Rachel Levin. She married Karl Varnhagen von Ense, a member of the Prussian diplomatic service and a well-known historian and writer.

Perhaps the most telling appreciation of the Jewish contribution to the Berlin intellectual life comes, if grudgingly, from Theodor Fontane, the chronicler of the Mark Brandenburg and bard of the Prussian Junker. In 1890 he wrote to a friend: 'As regards our nobility which I love sincerely, I had to realize that all freedom and culture, at least here in Berlin, come to us through the wealthy Jews. It is a fact which at last, one has to admit'.

A few years earlier an important discovery had been made by Heinrich Hertz, a young Jewish pupil of Helmholtz. He demonstrated the existence of electromagnetic waves, providing thereby the basis for all types of radio-communication. At about the same time Eugen Goldstein from Gleiwitz in Upper Silesia elucidated the nature of cathode rays and Paul Ehrlich laid the foundations of antibiotic therapy. It was only the beginning of the Jewish contribution to German science which soon was to be followed up by men like Einstein, Haber and Willstaetter. The Jews contributed only one per cent to Germany's population but one-third of her Nobel prizes.

3. A Place in the Sun

His studies took Nernst to Zürich, Berlin, Graz and Wuerzburg. These apparently aimless meanderings from university to university acquire a very different aspect when one takes a look at the professors who taught at these centres. In Berlin there was Hermann von Helmholtz, the acknowledged leader of physics in Germany who had made fundamental contributions to almost every aspect of the subject. In Wuerzburg Friedrich Kohlrausch broke fresh ground with his researches on the electrical conductivity in liquids and in Graz Ludwig Boltzmann had founded a school of thought which applied statistics to the phenomena of heat. All these men stood in the forefront of research and Boltzmann in particular was the pioneer who introduced the atomistic concept in physics.

As a matter of fact physicists, at the end of the nineteenth century, had no doubt that matter was composed of atoms but many of the most outstanding ones were extremely reluctant to accept interpretations of the known physical phenomena based on the existence of atoms. Their reasoning, which today seems remote and unrealistic, had a very sound basis. Essentially all evidence for the existence of atoms, so they argued, comes from the observation of chemical reactions. These showed that in the vast number of combinations and decomposition of the multitudinous forms of matter about ninety substances stand out as being immutable. All others could be explained as being compounds made up of these so-called elements. The next logical step, taken first by the English schoolmaster John Dalton in 1803, was to regard each element as being made up of constituent particles which conferred on it its characteristic properties. Accordingly, the nature of the particles must differ from element to element and, in addition, they must be indivisible since an element, by definition, is a substance that cannot decompose. Hence, these basic constituent particles of the chemical elements seemed to correspond closely to a philosophical concept introduced by Democritus three centuries B.C. He had postulated that matter cannot be subdivided *ad libitum* but that in the end a limit will be reached at which it becomes *atomos*, that is, indivisible.

While the atomic hypothesis had proved extremely fruitful in chemistry, it said nothing about the nature of the individual atoms but all evidence indicated that, measured on the human scale, they must be very small indeed. In 1865 Loschmidt succeeded in making an estimate of their size which eventually proved to be remarkably accurate. He deduced that the diameter of an atom is of the order of a hundred-millionth of a centimetre, which is far below the range of the most powerful microscope. The reluctance of the nineteenth-century physicists to introduce into their considerations invisible particles of an entirely unknown nature thus becomes understandable. The success of their science was founded on mathematical relations between quantities that were capable of accurate measurement, such as pressure, temperature or the motion of a visible object.

The strength of the scientific method called physics lies in its ability to make accurate predictions on the basis of laws expressed in strict mathematical terms. The immense success which the 'classical physics' of the nineteenth century had scored in this manner had established it as an extremely solid and seemingly impregnable edifice of natural philosophy. Moreover, it had been able to absorb a host of new discoveries without requiring any alterations to its original structure. There was every indication that it must be *right*. For quite some time physicists had become accustomed to the idea that, while many things were still awaiting discovery, none of the new facts would shake their proud and successful edifice.

Nernst and his generation, too, were convinced of the universal validity of classical physics, and far from doubting its infallibility they felt confident that the whole of chemistry could be subordinated to it.

By the nineteenth century the scientific amateurs had given way to the professionals and their experiments began to be carried out in university laboratories which had taken the place of the scientific 'cabinets' attached to princely residences. At the same time a fairly clear system began to emerge according to which the multitude of individual phenomena could be classified into groups that were consistent in themselves. The swing of a pendulum, the rotation of the planets around the sun and the trajectory of a bullet as well as the recoil of billiard balls could all be explained by Newtonian mechanics. The operation of these laws had allowed man to construct machines and instruments such as mining equipment and timepieces which were changing the pattern of daily life. Moreover, beyond their usefulness, the laws of mechanics impressed its practitioners by their universality, and a physical world picture began to emerge in which everything in nature seemed ultimately to be based on these laws. For the first time the idea of an integral creation was seriously considered and with it the wish arose to explain everything in nature on a common basis.

Admittedly there existed other groups of observations which in themselves were equally consistent and which permitted equally rigorous measurement and prediction as the laws of mechanics, such as light, sound and heat. Efforts were therefore made to reduce these phenomena, as well, to mechanical ones which, it was hoped, could then be expressed eventually in the formalism of Newtonian mechanics. In their explanation a language, and with it a pattern of thought, was employed that had been coined for the interpretation of mechanical phenomena. Light and sound were described in terms of vibrations and waves similar to the oscillations of a spring and the ripple on a pond. The immediate and far-reaching success of these theories created an immense confidence in the mechanistic world picture which helped to retain its concepts far beyond the time when its universality had to be given up. The observations in the field of heat, too, yielded with surprising ease to the notions of particle motion and vibration. Chemical changes, on the other hand, remained a subject apart, to which no key in terms of physics could be found.

Mechanics, heat, light and sound had by the end of the eighteenth century become the chapters of the book of physics which, except for a few odd phenomena seemed remarkably complete. One of the latter was electricity which made relatively rare appearances in nature in the form of lightning flashes and which could be conjured up in much smaller sparks in the laboratory. A weak force, just strong enough to attract or repel pith balls, and which had to be invoked by rubbing a glass rod with cat skin, was clearly nothing more than a fringe phenomenon that need not be taken too seriously. In 1785, moreover, it was brought into the realm of rigorous physical laws by Charles Auguste de Coulomb who measured accurately the force of electrical attraction and repulsion. He found a law of exactly the same form as Newton's law of gravitation which, if anything, only bolstered up further the universality of mechanics. Coulomb was equally successful with the other fringe phenomenon, magnetism. Here again the attraction and repulsion of north and south poles obeyed the same type of physical law.

To the non-scientist it must appear incomprehensible that the ever-present and immensely strong forces of electricity should have escaped detection for so long. The reason for this lies in a strange asymmetry of our physical world which, as yet, is far beyond our understanding. Electric and magnetic forces are polar, they have plus and minus, north and south, and with it they have attraction and repulsion. One pole, however strong, can be neutralized by the opposite pole so that, a little distance away from the pair, the net force is zero. As opposite poles, plus and minus, are piled up in equal numbers, their individual presence is hidden from observation. Gravity, on the other hand, is always attractive and as mass is piled up its effect on another mass is cumulative. Compared with electricity, gravity is an extremely weak force, a billion billion billion times smaller. We only feel it so acutely because the Earth has a fairly large mass and we are so near to it. Two smaller masses, say two bricks, hung up side by side will attract each other so weakly that the effect is imperceptible.

Electricity finally came into its own in physics during the first half of the nineteenth century. It all started with the well-known observation of an Italian doctor, Luigi Galvani, who noted that frogs' legs, which he required for biological experiments and which he had hung up on copper wires, twitched in a thunderstorm. They also twitched in fine weather when held between wires of different metals. It was an astonishing effect which immediately created great interest because Galvani and his colleagues at first suspected that electricity had been created by animal tissue. As it turned out, its real source was the two metals in contact with moisture and further experimentation led to the construction of 'Galvanic cells' such as are still being used in electric torch batteries. In fact, the most important result of Galvani's work was the development of these batteries which now provided a reliable supply of electricity for experimentation. Instead of the glass rod and the transient spark, the Galvanic cell delivered a steady current of electricity which, at the same time, was of low enough tension to save the experimenter from shock or electrocution.

Research into electricity increased rapidly and by the middle of the nineteenth century it had grown into a vast avalanche revealing the enormous importance of electrical forces in nature and their close connection with the phenomena of magnetism. The arc lamp, the dynamo, the electric motor and telegraphy heralded the beginning of an entirely new technology. Even more important for the shaping of a new world picture were the newly formed concepts of electrodynamics. Instead of being an entirely mechanistic universe, there were now two parallel worlds, a mechanistic and an electromagnetic one. There was no connection between them, except for the formal similarity between Newton's law of gravitation and Coulomb's law of electrical and magnetic attraction and repulsion. For the time being, and for more than half a century to come, this satisfying parallelism of the force equations produced among physicists a false sense of security and it increased their trust in the system of a classical physics. It seemed certain that, as yet unrevealed, a link must exist between the mechanistic and the electromagnetic worlds. However, when it was at last discovered by Einstein, far from strengthening the proud edifice built on the twin pillars, it shattered it completely.

There was nothing as yet to shake the confidence of the scientists in 1883 when Nernst set out on his studies. It is significant that less than three years later we find him in the main stream of contemporary research on the electrical properties of matter. However good the teaching at school may have been, Graudenz was a wretched backwater, untouched by any ripple of the latest results that were being obtained in far-away universities.

In order to get where he did in the world of current science, and as quickly as all that, a young man starting from scratch had to be of quite outstanding calibre. Nernst immediately showed he was and that he had learned in no time which way to go.

At Zürich where he went first, there was Heinrich Weber who had found some years earlier strangely low values in the heat content of some elements which disappeared when they were heated. Twenty years later Nernst used this almost forgotten research as a starting-point for his most famous work which brought him the Nobel prize. From Zürich he went to Berlin where Herman von Helmholtz, the most famous German physicist of his time, lectured on thermodynamics, the science relating heat with other forms of energy. Even a young man of Nernst's self-confidence could hardly have hoped that one day he would lecture in the place where the great Helmholtz stood and that his family would live in the adjoining official residence, lavishly laid out for the somewhat pretentious Frau von Helmholtz.

After another semester at Zürich, the next university was Graz and, while in Berlin Helmholtz had discoursed on well-established physical concepts, Nernst had now chosen to sit at the feet of the most celebrated rebel. Ludwig Boltzmann was a restless genius whose periods of brilliant activity alternated with times of deep depression. Born in Vienna in 1844, he had become professor at Graz in 1869 but after seven years he went back to Vienna, now as professor. Thirteen years later he was again in Graz, only to take up a professorship in Munich after another five years. Munich had held him for only four years when he accepted a chair in Leipzig. Here his stay was even shorter, a mere two years, after which he returned to Vienna in 1902. Four years later Boltzmann committed suicide while on holiday in the little town of Duino, near Trieste.

Boltzmann never doubted the validity of classical physics but he approached it in a most unorthodox way. He was keenly interested in mathematical methods and it was his introduction of one of these, statistics, into physics that led to quite new concepts which, in the end, proved extremely valuable. Statistics, as the name implies, is a method of handling numerical data which had first been applied in statecraft. It deals with the law of averages applied to large numbers, as, for instance, the average age or the average wealth of a given population. The data obtained in this way can never tell us how old or how wealthy one particular individual is but they give very accurate values for the community as a whole. An agent selling life insurance is never sure that his latest client might not be run over by a car the very next day. However, by insuring a large number of people, and knowing their average expectation of life, the company can be pretty sure of a profit. It is highly improbable that all their customers will be dead within a week.

B

Operating with these closely connected concepts of averages and probability brought Boltzmann brilliant success and the most acrimonious criticism of many of his senior colleagues. For many years the camp of physics was to be divided into those who accepted and those who rejected the statistical heresy. Nobody suggested that the statistical approach was actually wrong, the opinion was rather that it was bad for physics and might drive it in the wrong direction. Quite apart from the aversion which the purists had against the introduction of 'vague' probabilities into the 'absolute' laws of physics, Boltzmann's large numbers, of course, referred to atoms; and nobody had seen atoms.

The laws governing the volume of a gas whose pressure and temperature were changing had been established long ago through the experiments of Boyle and Gay-Lussac, and most physicists were quite happy with such concepts as pressure and temperature which could be defined and measured accurately. Boltzmann now chose to express these data in terms of the average velocity of the atoms and its square. While to the older generation this appeared as an unnecessary and dangerous departure from reliable precedent, the young ones, and Nernst among them, were intrigued by the thought of reducing conventional and man-made quantities to the behaviour of the ultimate building bricks of nature. Even better, there loomed ahead the possibility of finding a common language, based on atoms, between the worlds of physics and of chemistry.

Nernst came to Graz during Boltzmann's second period there. At first he was disappointed because Boltzmann did not lecture that year on theoretical physics, giving the beginners' course instead. However, he suggested that Nernst should collaborate in research with one of his former pupils, Albert von Ettinghausen. Boltzmann also provided the subject for the thesis, an investigation on the combined effect of magnetic field and heat flow on the electric current for which he had theoretically predicted the result. Nernst had now reached that all-important stage in the career of a young scientist when he passes from book learning to research. Until then all his studies, lectures as well as practical classes, had dealt with established knowledge but from now on he had to go beyond it and his aim had then to become the discovery of the new fact. It is by no means certain that the best student will become a brilliant researcher and apart from a sound knowledge of his subject the necessary qualifications are rather different. The fact that a man is good at answering examination questions does not ensure that he is equally competent at posing questions on the nature of the physical universe by means of experiment or theoretical investigation. The receptive mind need not be an inquiring one at the same time. For the young student who sets out on a research career, it is a shot in the dark and only experience can tell whether he is going to be the right man for the job.

Research, like any other job, has, of course, to be learned. Even the most gifted and successful scientist knows that the sparks of genius and the moments of inspiration are few and far between. The rest of his life will be devoted to patient work, careful planning and perfection of those techniques which he has to master for the exploration of his chosen field. Insight and intuition, while needed in his endeavour to penetrate into the unknown, are never more than vague guides, and inevitably he is forced to follow up many paths which eventually lead nowhere. Finding the right path, having been able to ask the correct question are rare events. The rest is frustration, often lasting for years, which has to be borne philosophically and with fortitude. Nernst was fortunate in finding in Ettinghausen an ideal teacher who, with great equanimity, would announce after some failure: 'Well, the experiment was not successful, at least not entirely'.

On the occasion of Ettinghausen's eightieth birthday, more than forty years later, Nernst recalled with particular gratitude his teacher's superb ability to master 'that most important chapter which is left out of the textbooks—irritation physics'. Nernst was forever impatient. As soon as he had an idea, he wished to see it tested and the preparation for the required experiment always constituted a sore trial for his nervous system. He admired Ettinghausen's ability of relieving the nervous strain during a long and complicated experiment by good-natured asides and by telling an anecdote here and there. When much later, in his Berlin days, Nernst tried to live up to his teacher's example, he met with only qualified success. The occasion was an experiment involving helium gas which at that time was still a rare and costly substance. The laboratory's precious stock of it had to be transferred from a container into the apparatus and the procedure was carried out by some of his assistants while Nernst supervised it personally. He realized too late that by breathing down their necks he was making them unduly nervous and in order to relax tension he told them about his recent exploit of shooting a dangerous wild boar. Unfortunately, however, his account became so dramatic that the man connecting the transfer pipe broke it and the gas escaped. Nernst immediately remembered the rest of Ettinghausen's recipe and called out aloud: 'Gentlemen, take a deep breath, there are two thousand marks worth of helium in the air'.

Ettinghausen, who was fifteen years Nernst's senior, had enough experience in the handling of research to guide the impetuous young man with authority. At the same time, he was still young enough to have the full grasp of current problems and he had not yet moved into the stage where administration and other commitments limit the time and attention which a professor can devote to individual research students. He also sensed early his pupil's great ability and remarkable powers of concentration, giving him enough free rein to make original contributions. The result was that the work not only proceeded rapidly but Nernst widened it so that it led to the discovery of an effect which became known under the names of both authors.

After only one year's work the discovery of the new effect had provided Nernst with the material for his doctoral thesis. However, when he submitted it in 1887, he had already moved on from Graz to the University of Wuerzburg to work with Friedrich Kohlrausch on the passage of electricity through liquids. This subject, in which he was to become the world's foremost authority, was evidently chosen under the influence of Boltzmann's atomistic outlook.

Investigations on the electric current which could now be produced so very conveniently by the use of galvanic cells had, for some time, deflected interest from the function of the cells themselves. Making bigger and better batteries became a necessity not only for research but also for the budding electrical industry, but it was more or less a trial-and-error exercise. The general pattern was always the same. Two different metal plates, the 'electrodes' were dipped into water in which a salt or an acid was dissolved and then a current would flow from one electrode to the other when they were connected by a wire. Thus, electricity was evidently produced by some chemical reaction taking place in the cell. This observation could have served as a valuable pointer to the role played by electricity in the make-up of matter but for the fact that the existing data were hopelessly complex and confusing.

Another approach was made towards the middle of the nineteenth century by Davy and Faraday at the Royal Institution in London. They reversed the function of the galvanic cell by dipping two similar metal plates, say copper, into a solution of, say copper sulphate, and then they passed a current through this cell. They found not only that the solution was conducting but also that the current caused a chemical change which they called 'electrolysis'. It consisted of metallic copper being dissolved at the positive electrode and deposited on the negative one. In other words, metallic copper in solute form had been transported by the current from one plate to the other.

Faraday now found an important clue; the amount of copper moved in this way was always exactly proportional to the quantity of electricity which had passed through the cell. He concluded that the current must be carried by positively charged atoms that were repelled by the positive electrode and attracted to the negative one. Equally, a negatively charged current of particles must at the same time be propelled in the opposite direction. He coined the name 'ions' for these charged atoms. The realization that single atoms could be electrically charged was the first step into an entirely new field—electrochemistry.

By now the Germans with their newly acquired interest in chemistry began to take up the research on ions. Hittorf in Munster and later Kohlrausch in Wuerzburg discovered that the ions did not form electric chains as had been thought but that they moved freely in the liquid, very much like atoms or molecules in a gas, as had been postulated by Boltzmann. Suddenly, a number of hitherto unconnected branches of physics and chemistry seemed to converge towards a common explanation, although nobody was very clear about what this interpretation would be like and where it might lead. It was at this stage of events that Nernst came to work with Kohlrausch in Wuerzburg.

When he arrived there in the autumn of 1886, he cannot have suspected that the next academic year would essentially shape his career. His two tasks were to complete his thesis on the work done in Graz and to learn about ions from Kohlrausch. At the same time a stout young man from Sweden with an impressive moustache made his appearance there; his name was Svante Arrhenius. He was five years older than Nernst and had obtained his doctorate at Stockholm with a very revolutionary thesis on ions. He had completely disregarded the current assumption that the ions were atoms which became charged when the electric current was switched on. Instead, he postulated that the salt when dissolved in water never existed in the form of atoms or molecules in the first place but that it spontaneously 'dissociated' into positive and negative ions, even when no current was present. To take a specific example, ordinary table salt, $NaCl$, made up of equal numbers of sodium and chlorine atoms, was to be dissolved neither in the form of $NaCl$ molecules nor as separate Na and Cl atoms. Instead the particles in solution were positively charged Na^+ and negatively charged Cl^- ions. If true, Arrhenius' theory would indicate that the forces of chemical binding were electric ones.

This bold suggestion, which completely broke with the generally accepted opinion of the time, could only be taken by a young man with a fresh mind that had not yet been moulded into the rigid pattern of contemporary teaching. One frequently finds that the crucial step out of the groove of existing theory is taken by a brilliant young man who has been taught the method of investigation up to the latest results, but who has not yet been indoctrinated with current theories. Newton's law of universal gravitation is perhaps the most famous example. He had to leave Cambridge because of the plague, immediately after taking his bachelor's degree, and returned home to ponder in an apple orchard the fact that the moon does not fall on to the earth.

Newton, who was a naturally secretive person, did not mention his theory until many years later. Arrhenius published his ideas immediately, stirring up inevitable and authoritative opposition. In fact, his thesis was adjudicated 'not without merit', a class too low to allow him to take up an academic career. He was saved by an offer from Wilhelm Ostwald in Riga who described himself as a convinced 'Ionian' and wanted Arrhenius to work with him. Under this external pressure and with bad grace the University of Uppsala offered him a lectureship. In the following year he obtained a travelling grant to go for a while to Ostwald and now he had come from Riga to Wuerzburg.

Arrhenius' influence on Nernst was decisive. He talked with enormous enthusiasm about Ostwald and his researches in the new borderline field of physical chemistry, so that Nernst decided to go to Riga as soon as he had obtained the doctorate. It was Arrhenius' enthusiasm rather than his new theory which impressed Nernst because, if Arrhenius talked to him about his thesis, as he probably did, Nernst did not take it in. In fact, when early in 1887 Arrhenius gave a lecture in Wuerzburg on his theory, neither Nernst nor even Kohlrausch grasped its meaning. It clearly was too far removed from current thought to strike a cord, even in a friendly and interested audience.

However, things began to change with the next arrival, Ostwald. Wilhelm Ostwald, who was then thirty-four, was a most colourful personality and already a world-famous man. He was possessed of an incredible vitality which kept him going at a remarkable rate of activity right up to his death at the age of almost eighty. His writings fill between 20 000 and 25 000 pages and, besides physical chemistry, deal with colour perception, monistic philosophy, types of genius, a synthetic world language and formulae for happiness. In addition he was a painter and a musician. He was descended from a family of German artisans who had emigrated to Russia. Although he was an outstanding pioneer of his science who gained the Nobel prize in 1909, his chief influence was that of a leader. When he was fifty, thirty-four of his pupils had become professors and the journal which he had founded, the *Zeitschrift fuer Physikalische Chemie*, had become the foremost source of information in his field throughout the world.

Ostwald had come to Wuerzburg in order to find brilliant young scientists for his new laboratory in Leipzig. At that university the only chair of physical chemistry in the world had become vacant and Ostwald had been appointed to it. There was now no need for Nernst to go to Riga. Ostwald immediately recognized the young man's ability and offered him an assistantship at Leipzig which Nernst accepted with enthusiasm. After obtaining his doctorate, he and Arrhenius spent one more semester at Graz with Boltzmann and Ettinghausen and then both of them moved on to Leipzig.

Ostwald received the Nobel prize for his work on catalysts, substances which by their mere presence promote chemical reactions. He seems to have been himself a unique human catalyst. Until their arrival in

Leipzig, Nernst and Arrhenius had worked side by side without really understanding each other's way of thinking. It was Ostwald's stimulus and his grasp of the essential problems which brought out the latent ability of the two younger men. Using these great gifts of analysis and coordination, Ostwald made Leipzig the centre of physicochemical studies in the world. Perhaps his laboratory might have maintained this position later in the face of severe competition, had he not resigned suddenly at the age of fifty. His interest had shifted to philosophical problems which led him to regard energy as the basis not only of physics but of all human activities and peculiarities. He became weary of experiments, lecturing and administration. Finally, he made a religious funeral service arranged by the university for a colleague who had been a free-thinker, the reason for his resignation.

Nernst's first paper from Leipzig leaves no doubt about the grand strategy that he had mapped out for his attack on the physicochemical problems. It was a brilliant combination of Boltzmann's atomistic ideas with the traditional type of thermodynamics developed by Helmholtz and Clausius. He realized with remarkable insight that electrochemistry offered an opportunity to bring these two lines of thought together.

One of the most important quantities in chemical reactions, or indeed in any physical process, is the 'free energy'. This is the amount of useful work, as distinct from heat, that can be derived from the reaction. When petrol is burned in a motorcar engine only part of the liberated energy can be used in propelling it while the rest has inevitably to be discarded as waste heat. All the quantities involved are measurable as mechanical work, heat and temperature. The atomic processes taking place do not enter the thermodynamic consideration. Since an electric current can also be used to create work or heat, the formulae of thermodynamics may be applied to it.

This is where Nernst started his work. In addition to the thermodynamic calculations applied to electrochemical changes, he also brought in atomistic concepts, based on the behaviour of particles, such as ions. For instance he regarded the chemical action of an acid on a metal plate as a liberation of ions to which he applied the well-known thermodynamic formalism describing the evaporation of steam. Just as the rising pressure of steam can push a piston, so the growing concentration of ions can do work. This work might, for instance, manifest itself in driving an electric motor attached to a galvanic cell. He carried out experiments and then put the measured quantities into his calculations. Further experimental checks proved that he was correct. The missing theory of the galvanic cell had been created. It was the result of an ingenious idea, elegant calculations and a lot of painstaking work. It also established Nernst as one of the foremost scientists in the wider field of physical chemistry.

In the German academic system the position of assistant allows the young scientist to supervise practical classes and it enables him to do research. It does not entitle him to lecture. In order to enter the academic career leading to a professorship he must first submit to his university a thesis of advanced original work and defend it before the assembled faculty. Only if the faculty accepts the thesis as of sufficient merit and only if the candidate is able to hold his own against criticism raised and questions asked, will he be promoted to a lectureship. The exercise is called 'habilitation' and is used to bar entry into the academic career for competent but unoriginal men. Failure to become a lecturer does not end their career which, with successive promotions, leads to positions which usually carry a fair amount of administrative duties.

After only two years in Leipzig, and using the theory of the galvanic cell as his thesis, Nernst was made a lecturer. It was now clear that he would not remain much longer in the benevolent but large shadow of Ostwald. He took a temporary assistant's job for the summer of 1889 in Heidelberg, where a lecturer was required until Bunsen's successor was appointed. In the following year he left Leipzig for good to take up a lectureship at Goettingen. There were a number of attractions which had made him accept this offer. The position was at the physical and not the chemical laboratory. Riecke, the professor had promised Nernst not only a sub-department but also, in the not too distant future, an assistant professorship. Finally, Goettingen had a very high reputation among German universities and it was a pleasant place in which to live.

The University of Goettingen had been founded in 1734 by the Elector Georg August of Hanover, who later became King George II of England. Early in the nineteenth century it became famous for the outstanding collaboration between the mathematician Karl Friedrich Gauss and the physicist Wilhelm Weber. Besides their fundamental contributions to the theory of electromagnetism, they also invented the electric telegraph. However, in 1837 professors and students turned out in revolt when King Ernst August of Hanover revoked the liberal constitution which had been granted four years earlier. Seven professors, Weber and the brothers Grimm among them, were dismissed and university life received a blow from which it was slow to recover. Then, in 1866 Hanover was annexed by Bismarck and the Prussian administration set to work immediately to restore the fame of the university. Foremost scholars were attracted by the excellent conditions which the Prussian Ministry of Education offered them at Goettingen.

The creation of outstanding centres of learning, particularly at the universities of Berlin and Goettingen, was a conscious policy, consistently applied during the founder years. By the time Nernst arrived in Goettingen a new age had been ushered in by the young Kaiser who had sacked

Bismarck and stated that the motto for his reign was 'full steam ahead'. The time of consolidation was over and Germany wanted a place in the sun. Her pulse was beating faster and stronger in the desire to become as great a nation as any other. There was a special prize for those things in which she could be better than others, and scholarship was one of them. The German achievements in science and learning were successes after the Kaiser's heart and he spared neither effort nor his own money to further them. Wilhelm got on well with the professors and by his patronage he introduced a new note into the life of the top echelon of the academic world. Quiet scholarship and the esteem of one's colleagues were one thing but to be singled out by the Kaiser as his confident and adviser was a very different kettle of fish. Men like Nernst were lifted out of their narrow academic atmosphere into the great world of affairs.

Since the German universities are State institutions, the professors are officials and are appointed and employed by the Ministry of Education, not by the university. When a vacancy occurs, the faculty has the right to submit to the Minister three names and it is customary for the top candidate to be offered the professorship. Whether he is going to accept it will, of course, depend on the conditions offered, and that is a matter for the Ministry. The man who essentially single-handed built up the international reputation of the universities of Berlin and Goettingen was Friedrich Althoff, Permanent Secretary at the Prussian Ministry of Education from 1882 to 1907. He was typical of the higher civil service of the Wilhelminian period; efficient, single-minded in his devotion to duty and unbelievably autocratic. The universities were his department and he ruled over their affairs as an enlightened despot.

It is likely that when Nernst came to Goettingen, Althoff had already opened a dossier on him in the Ministry files and that the confidential reports before him marked out the new lecturer as one of the coming men. Otherwise Riecke on his own could hardly have been so specific about the assistant professorship. Nernst had no longer to wait than one year. The University of Giessen offered him a chair in 1891 and Althoff promptly produced the assistant professorship at Goettingen in order to keep him there. After another three years Munich invited Nernst to become Boltzmann's successor, which was a most tempting suggestion since in the German federal monarchy, the capital of Bavaria, too, had impressive cultural ambitions. If Althoff wanted to keep Nernst in Prussia, he now had to make an effort that would go a bit beyond his own departmental responsibility. Nernst's price was the creation of a new chair of physical chemistry at Goettingen, and to go with it an electrochemical laboratory. Althoff could produce the new chair from the funds at his disposal but for the laboratory he had to get the money from the Ministry of Finance —and that would take time. Nernst, who was certain that he held the whip hand and who always knew how to drive a bargain, forced Althoff into an unheard of act. It was the promise, to be given in writing, that should the laboratory in Goettingen not materialize, Nernst would get a chair of physics at Berlin. Althoff yielded, possibly because he had every reason to believe that the Minister of Finance would play, as indeed he did. That was in 1894 and Berlin had to wait another eleven years.

Emma Lohmeyer was one of the prettiest girls in Goettingen. In addition to the bloom of youth her face showed intelligence, a happy disposition and a keen sense of humour. Like Nernst, she was a child when her mother died. Father Lohmeyer was professor of surgery and also ran a private clinic in a house which, at the same time, contained the family's flat. He was a man of many interests, who had mastered the piano and the cello to such perfection that he often played with the famous violinist Joachim, the close friend of Brahms. Brahms himself came frequently to Goettingen. Later in life Lohmeyer took to collecting carpets which he acquired in embarrassing numbers and sizes. He also spent a good deal of money on paintings of somewhat varying merit.

When Emma was six she lost her mother and a housekeeper took over. There were two older sisters, Meta and Frida and a younger brother, Wilhelm. When Meta was sixteen she took over the running of the household and four years later, when she got married, Emma, now herself sixteen stepped into her place. The Lohmeyers lived well but were not wealthy, particularly since a fair amount of money went into carpets and pictures. Trained by her domestic duties Emma got accustomed to rising early and working hard, habits which she retained throughout life.

She first met Nernst at a dance given by Professor Schulz, a Goettingen theologian. Nernst had come to Goettingen a few months earlier and taken lodgings with a Mrs Heumann. He was not dancing but stood by himself and Emma went to talk with the shy newcomer. It then turned out that the quiet demeanour was due entirely to a grave distrust concerning the state of his dress suit. It had been torn and Mrs Heumann had repaired it but, he felt, not to the extent that he could risk a dance. Possibly the incident appealed to Emma's sense of humour and in the following year they saw a good deal of each other, mostly taking walks in the university park. As winter came there were more dances, a sledge party and the engagement. They were married in 1892, when Emma was twenty-one, and set off for Cassel on the first day of their honeymoon in great style, with a coach and horses. On their way to Italy they stopped over at Graz to visit Ettinghausen.

A further mark of Nernst's friendship for and his gratitude to Ettinghausen was the dedication of his famous textbook to his old teacher which appeared in the following year. He called it *Theoretical Chemistry* with the sub-title 'Under the Aspect of Avogadro's Rule and Thermodynamics'. This addendum is significant because it testifies to Nernst's belief in Boltzmann's atomistic ideas and, in a subtle manner he dissociated himself from Ostwald who was dead set against regarding atoms as a permissible concept in physical chemistry. In 1811 Count Amedeo Avogadro of the University of Turin had postulated that equal volumes of any gas, at the same pressure and temperature, must contain the same number of atoms, and he thereby forged a link between the chemical atoms and thermodynamic quantities. Nernst's book became, for many years, the standard text in physical chemistry and it went through no less than ten editions. Only when, in the 'twenties, he himself was turning to other fields, was the book replaced by others, written characteristically by his own students Arnold Eucken and John Eggert.

The book was translated into English, French and Russian and gained wide popularity. Nernst once made a point of telling me that Edison had wrongly been called an unsound scientist. In evidence, he recalled that Edison had argued with him over some point and had tried to prove it from a passage in *Theoretical Chemistry*. Nernst finished by saying 'He had my book on his shelf; you see, he was no charlatan'.

In the same year that the book came out the first Nernst child was born. It was a boy, whom they called Rudolf, after Uncle Nerger. Nernst, who had hoped for a daughter, was possibly disappointed, which may explain why Emma made Rudolf her favourite. However, Nernst did not have to wait for long, the girl he wanted so much was born a year later. This was in 1894 when on the 22nd October a letter arrived from Munich, inviting Nernst to become Boltzmann's successor, which led to Althoff's intervention. The direct consequences were the newly created chair of physical chemistry in Goettingen and, even more important, the electrochemical laboratory. It was the first great success in the life of the young couple. The 22nd October became the date of the annual family feast and the new arrival was called Hildegard Elektra.

For the electrochemical institute the Ministry acquired the splendid mansion which had been built in 1866 for the first Prussian curator. It was quickly remodelled into research and teaching laboratories so that it could come into use for the summer term of 1895. The official opening ceremony took place on the 15th June and it was graced by the presence not only of the great Althoff but of the Minister of Education himself. The director's official residence on the upper floor of the laboratory had just been finished, so that the Nernsts were able to entertain their guests in style.

Throughout these years work on a great number of problems set by Nernst was going on at an ever-increasing rate, and soon there were as many as forty research students working for the doctor's degree. They came not only from German universities but from other countries since

Nernst was now world-famous. It was not only the work on related problems that forged them into a happy group of young men with common interests. Nernst, and especially Emma, saw to it that there were parties, outings and entertainments to be enjoyed by all.

Three more children were to be born, Gustav, named after his grand-father, in 1896 and four years later another girl. She arrived in February on a day which was mild with the promise of spring and Nernst noticed the first flowers emerging from the melting snow. He called her Edith Primula. Finally, there was a third daughter in 1903. Aunt Nerger, who had been a second mother to Nernst, was getting old and the estate of Engelsburg, where he had spent the happiest hours of his youth, had to be sold. Its memory was to remain in the family through the name of the youngest girl, Angela.

By then the life of the Nernsts had changed completely. For all his brilliance, his success in having a new chair created for him and getting a new laboratory would have been impossible ten years earlier. It was the new Wilhelminian era with its sense of enterprise and its growing wealth that enabled Althoff to build his empire of scholarship. It was not the only empire which was being created to ensure Germany's place in the sun. In 1884 the Deutsche Kolonialgesellschaft had been founded in Berlin to finance the acquisition of territories in Africa.

The African territories, Samoa and part of New Guinea, became the emblem of German expansion and the pride of the nation but they were an economic liability rather than an asset. The real weapon of world penetration was the export trade which was based on a fantastic growth of German industry. Since the foundation of the Reich the production of coal and iron had grown more than fourfold and that of steel twenty times. Apart from the fast expanding chemical industry there was an even larger growth in electrical technology. The firm of Siemens–Schuckert had become one of the leading manufacturers in the world and its size was soon matched by the Allgemeine Elektrizitaets Gesell-schaft, the A.E.G., founded by the Jewish financier, Emil Rathenau. It is significant that Rathenau was not an economist but had an engineering training.

The universities were not passed over in this upsurge of expansionist enterprise. They, together with their technical sister institutions, pro-duced the scientists and engineers needed by industry. In addition, enterprising professors, like the mathematician, Felix Klein, in Goettingen, set up small instrument factories which became the nuclei for another type of industry of precision engineering.

Nernst, too, was drawn, not at all unwillingly, into this vortex of technology and quick profits. In his studies of ionic conduction, he had turned to a peculiar class of solid electrolytes, substances which at normal temperatures are insulators but which, when heated acquire the ability to conduct electric current. Glass, in fact, is a simple example of this type. Once the temperature region of electrical conduction is reached, so much heat is being supplied by the current itself that no further external heating is required.

Apart from the electric arc lamp which is not suitable for indoor illumination, the only form of electric lighting known in the 1890s was the newly invented carbon filament lamp of Edison's, the German patent rights of which had been acquired by the A.E.G. Its light was not very bright and the lamp requires a vacuum which, at the time, was difficult to provide. It occurred to Nernst that if a solid electrolyte with a very high melting-point could be found, this would make an excellent bright lamp. After various trials, he was satisfied that a mixture containing cerium oxide would do the job. He first tried to interest Siemens in his invention but it seems that they were too hidebound to experiment with novelties and unwilling to spend money on the development research. After the initial tests for which Nernst had come into their Berlin laboratory, Siemens decided not to go ahead with the project. Possibly there was an additional reason for their reluctance. Nernst had immediately taken out a patent on his invention and it is quite possible that the price which he asked for it may have discouraged the firm. He next turned to the A.E.G. who, being a young company, were more adventurous. Moreover, the chairman, Emil Rathenau, was impressed by Nernst's personality and sense of enterprise. This type of professor was a man after his own heart. One of the company's directors, Mamroth, was sent to Goettingen and discussed details with Nernst, including finance. The A.E.G. acquired the patent and took over the development. Nernst got his price, a million marks a truly staggering sum.

Close personal relations with the inventor were maintained during the development, which was in the hands of the director of the A.E.G. Lighting Division, Dr Bussmann, who passed on the work to his two sons-in-law, both former pupils of Nernst. The final product was one of the most ingenious pieces of equipment ever designed. About twice the size of an ordinary light bulb, it contained the little cerium oxide rod which was the light-emitting filament, a preheating element and a third device which prevented overheating of the filament. On switching on the current the element started immediately with a dull glow needed to heat the filament. After about a minute or less the filament had become hot enough to pass current and then in the space of a few seconds emitted a white-hot light of great intensity. However, before the temperature could rise high enough to destroy the filament, the built-in regulating mechanism had come into play. The time required for preheating made the Nernst lamp somewhat cumbersome in use but, owing to the high operating temperature, the illumination produced per unit of electric power was far superior to Edison's lamp. Even so, the lamp was fairly expensive to manufacture, a disadvantage which became dominant when the production of evacuated glass envelopes for ordinary bulbs became much cheaper.

In the end, Siemens had been right in refusing the patent. When, a few years later, the metal filament replaced the carbon thread in Edison's lamp, the days of the Nernst lamp were numbered. In fact, the inventor himself accelerated the obsolescence of his creation. Shortly after selling the patent, he set a young American research student to investigate the effect of gas on an incandescent metal wire. This was quite clearly the next step towards the gas-filled metal filament bulb as we know it today. Moreover, it was a step on the right road because, when after his studies the American joined the General Electrical Company, he perfected the bulb as a brilliant commercial success. His name was Irving Langmuir and he not only became the firm's scientific director but followed in Nernst's footsteps by being awarded a Nobel prize.

Nernst had refused to consider royalties for his invention and insisted on a large cash payment. It would be difficult at this stage to assess his precognition of the scientific development leading to the gas-filled filament bulb which inevitably would outdate his own lamp. If, as Langmuir's doctoral thesis suggests, Nernst fully realized the technological trend of events, he was wise to sell his patent outright when he did. It was a business transaction and, as such, not less ethical than any other successful speculation in the world of commerce.

Certainly the Nernst lamp was a superbly finished invention which in the few years its glory lasted, made him known far beyond his scientific circle, if for no other reason than that the A.E.G. gave the invention the widest publicity. The Kaiser was much amused when Nernst demonstrated to him that the new electric lamp could be lit with a match and blown out like a candle since the cooling stream of air was sufficient to render the oxide rod non-conducting. It did its job as a prestige stunt when at the Paris World Exhibition the German A.E.G. pavilion outshone those of any other nation by its dazzling illumination with Nerns lamps.

Throughout his life Nernst was fond of talking about the meteoric career of his lamp, pointing out that some inventions are just too beautiful for this world. In his lectures he used to mention that the little blemish of preheating was not too serious. Fortunately, he said, another great invention, the telephone, was installed in Berlin at the time when his lamp came on the market. This made it possible for the brokers at the Stock Exchange to ring up home when business was finished and ask their wives to switch on the light. His delight in the financial coup which he had landed is clearly shown by the story which he told after visiting Edison in 1898. Edison, who was always proud of his ability to turn scientific discoveries into money-making inventions, complained that the A.E.G. had paid relatively little for his patent rights and he was amazed to learn how much Nernst had extracted from Rathenau. In reply Nernst shouted into the old man's ear trumpet: 'The trouble with you, Edison, is that you are just not a businessman'.

The Nernsts had been living in the moderate comfort of a university professor's status. Now they were rich. At about the same time that he sold the patent, Emma had inherited a tidy sum of money from her maternal grandfather, who owned a sugar factory. They could now spend money rather freely and perhaps nothing gives a better idea of their society than the manner in which they enjoyed their wealth. They entertained, later on their estate and sometimes a trifle ostentatiously, but not more so than the rest of that buoyant enterprising world in which they lived. They indulged in some luxuries, such as motorcars which, too, were manifestations of enterprise at that time and not yet a necessity. Above all, however, there was Nernst's work, his laboratory full of young and promising people.

One of the first things he did was to give 40 000 marks of his own newly acquired wealth for the enlargement and equipment of his laboratory. The acceptance of this donation was signed by the Kaiser personally on the 10th October, 1898. Nernst's research was increasing all the time in scope and size and the new extension of the institute provided more space for research students who, in addition to the professor's inspiration, now also profited from the money he had spent on apparatus. Thus, a fair share of the Nernst wealth went into the research school, and not just by providing for their work. Emma kept open house for all the young men, and soon also for young women. Miss Moltby, an English girl whom Nernst had accepted as a research student in his laboratory, was the first woman to obtain a physics doctorate in Germany. One of the favourite entertainments were the Nernst feasts, outings into the pleasant countryside near Goettingen to which the students were sometimes conveyed by motorcar since Nernst was an early enthusiast and at times owned as many as four cars simultaneously.

The first car was bought in 1898 and it was followed by seventeen others. Nowadays the successive possession of eighteen cars during a lifetime is not necessarily a record but it was certainly most unusual in Nernst's time. As far as Goettingen is concerned, Nernst's was the first car and soon became a well-known, but not always appreciated, feature of town life. These early vehicles were, of course, highly temperamental and noisy. The children's cry: 'Nernst is coming', soon became the signal for their comrades to rally to the sight and for their elders to scatter in disgust from danger. Nernst remembered, with special fondness, an early steam-driven model which Emma distrusted because the boiler was under the seat. When driven fast and in suitable wind, long flames would issue from the rear of the vehicle and the farmers whom it passed on the country roads had to steady their horses and hurriedly crossed themselves.

Nernst was never interested in sport, which he considered a shocking waste of time, and his attitude to the motorcar was essentially that of a scientist who welcomes technological advance. To him, his cars were the emblems of a modern age in which he regarded himself, rightly, as a leader. The mechanism and, above all, the basic principles involved fascinated him. The internal combustion engine and his work on chemical reactions at high temperature soon met and it is impossible to say whether the car or his experiments with hot filaments were the starting point. He began to study the explosive nature of the oxidation of petrol and even published a paper on this subject. Being Nernst, he also thought straightaway about improvements. He concluded from his studies that the heat of combustion could be enhanced by the judicious injection of nitrous oxide into the cylinder head and got his trusted mechanic, Oscar Schlueter, to connect a supply of this gas to the engine. The first trials were made in secret because Nernst contemplated a spectacular demonstration.

Near Goettingen there is a small hill which served as a favourite place for quiet walks because it was too steep for the ascent of vehicular traffic. One Sunday afternoon, as the burghers and professors went in numbers on their customary promenade, they saw and heard, to their surprise, Nernst approaching this steep incline in his motorcar. As he reached the perilous gradient, he opened the nitrous oxide tap and, furiously hooting and with redoubled exhaust noise, he ascended the hill before the increased heat injured the engine.

The other hobby to which he devoted time and money was shooting. The happy childhood days with Aunt and Uncle Nerger at Engelsburg were never forgotten, with the memory of fields and woods where he had been introduced to the excitement of the shoot. Although he sometimes went for larger game, the long wait and careful preparation were not really to his taste and he preferred wildfowl and hares. As soon as he could afford it, he rented the shoot for a stretch of the Goettingen town forest which was near and allowed him to go out even for a short time. Even so, his claim that he could go and shoot a hare while the soup was already on the table was a mild exaggeration.

An account of Nernst's time in Goettingen would be incomplete without mentioning the Café N. The beginnings of this episode are not quite clear. One of the finest town houses, formerly belonging to the Graetzel family, had been turned into the 'Hotel and Café National', but it seems that it did not do too well. It was then taken over by a lady who found that she, too, encountered difficulties, requiring more cash than was at her disposal. She turned to Nernst, who found it impossible not to yield to the lament of a lady in distress, particularly when she was a dazzling blonde, and he advanced her a mortgage. However, even this chivalrous support was in vain and the professor found himself in the possession of a hostelry. Being Nernst, he not only accepted the unusual challenge but was determined to succeed where his predecessors in the restaurant business had failed. With the aid of an efficient manager and under his supervision, the hotel began to prosper and became generally known as the 'Café N.' After Nernst had moved to Berlin, he used to stay always in 'his' hotel whenever he had business in Goettingen. However, in the end he could not be bothered with it and sold the hotel in 1906 to a Mr Siegfried, who still ran it thirty years later.

One outstanding feature of the Café N was its illumination with Nernst lamps. It is not quite clear whether this was an improvement under his ownership or whether the lamps had been installed by the previous owner, who may have got in touch with Nernst in this way. Whatever the origin of the whole business, Nernst's chivalry was quite in keeping with his attitude to women in general. After examining a young lady for her doctorate, he admitted that it is sometimes difficult to assess their ability with complete objectivity. However sharp and cynical he tended to be in discussion with his colleagues, Nernst was invariably courteous and charming when talking with women, even if they were physicists. Unlike so many of his contemporaries, he welcomed women in the laboratory and there were indeed many among his pupils.

On the few occasions when his caustic wit was turned against the fair sex, the target was the managing variety. He once defended the second Mrs Einstein, who had the reputation of being a bit of a Press agent for her rather retiring husband. Einstein, a heavy smoker, was told by his doctor to lay off cigars for a while, but as soon as his wife had turned her back he sent the maid out to get him a box. When Mrs Einstein returned she could not but notice the thick smoke that pervaded the flat. However, she pretended not to notice it and instead looked at her husband with a worried face, saying that he appeared unusually pale and asked whether he felt all right. Einstein now got so worried that he really gave up smoking for a while. 'You see,' said Nernst sanctimoniously, 'she is an excellent wife, she saved his life.'

The other case concerned Lady Kelvin. At a reception Nernst and Kelvin met Mme Curie who in her young years was extremely good-looking. They asked her about the newly discovered radium and she told them that she had brought a sample along, but that the lights were too bright to see its glow. So the three of them squeezed into the space between double doors, but before their eyes had grown accustomed to the dark, there was a knock at one of the doors. It was Lady Kelvin, who thus showed that she was, as Nernst put it, 'a most attentive spouse'.

Nernst had come to Goettingen when he was twenty-six and he left for Berlin at the age of forty-one. Those fifteen years were the happiest and most fruitful ones of his life. Emma and the children had enriched his home. He had arrived as a promising but relatively unknown young man and left a wealthy and world-famous one. It was the invention of his lamp—and the brilliant disposal of it—that had been responsible for most of the outward signs of success, including the interest which the Kaiser began to take in him. Nernst never disguised his enjoyment of money, but he never liked wealth for its own sake. To him it simply meant independence, a state which he cherished above all others. The relatively modest circumstances of the Nernst family and the difficulties experienced by his beloved Aunt Nerger had taught him a lesson which he never forgot to the end of his days.

There was, of course, the other and, to him, more important side of his work, the research institute. Its output in the Goettingen years had steadily increased and the results opened up many pioneer inquiries, moving steadily into the field of chemical equilibria which had become the central problem not only of physical chemistry itself but also of its industrial application. Its final solution had to wait for the Berlin days, but all the work leading up to it had been done in the Goettingen years. It was a debt to that university which Nernst recognized by returning to Goettingen for the first publication of his great discovery.

4. The Summit

Goettingen had afforded Nernst a place in the sun, Berlin now provided him with the summit of his career. He was to remain there for more than a quarter of a century, but the supreme glory of his scientific achievement fell into the first decade of his stay, the years before World War I. It was also the period in which the Hohenzollern Reich experienced the short zenith of its power. The centre from which this power flowed, and to which everyone who wanted a share in it was attracted, was Berlin.

One can hardly credit the Elector Frederick Irontooth of Brandenburg with prophetic foresight simply because five hundred years earlier he had settled on the little island in the Spree to fleece the honey and fur trade. Nevertheless, he had been proved right in the end and Berlin became the trade and traffic centre of Europe. It was now on its way to replace Paris as the capital of Europe.

Things began to happen when the railways came and replaced the slow road and river traffic by a vast flow of goods. With the railways came not only trade but industry and it is significant that Berlin's first large factory, the Borsig works, was established for building locomotives and rolling stock. It was soon followed by a rapid development of textile and light machine manufacture and finally by huge electrical works. To this was added the steady growth of administrative offices first for Prussia and then for the Reich. Berlin soon became the fastest-growing city in Europe and possibly in the world. The population, which in the middle of the nineteenth century had numbered less than half a million, had now risen to more than four million and it was this fantastic development which gave it its characteristic stamp of endless streets full of tenement blocks in which the working population was housed.

Some idea of the crowding in these tenement barracks is provided by a comparison of the average numbers of people living in one building in different cities. In 1920 this figure for London was 8, for New York 15 and for Berlin 76. Trees in the streets, balconies and window-boxes were the only relief in the endless asphalt desert. By the beginning of the twentieth century, the older blocks of flats had fallen into a sad state of disrepair and provided hopelessly congested areas of the most miserable slums. Every Berliner knows the work of the grim caricaturist Heinrich Zille who created the type which was characteristic of a large proportion of the four million; men with a cynical dry humour, women whose figures were a shade too opulent and hordes of cheeky precocious children.

The western suburbs, too, were built up with tenements, but of a much superior character. There was usually only one court of back flats which had an open entrance, while that of the front flats was locked and invariably had a little notice, saying, '*Aufgang nur fuer Herrschaften*'—entrance for the gentry only. Here there were small front gardens and many squares and small parks where the Spreewald nannies in their pretty costumes took the gentry's young for an airing. Still further out there were villas by a chain of lakes. The whole west was separated from the east by the Tiergarten and, in fact, Berlin was pretty much a divided city, even before the wall was built. The proletarian quarters were backed by a factory belt and, fairly close to the centre in the south-east there was a feature no other capital city could boast, a parade ground of well over a square mile in the middle of a metropolis.

Most of all this has become a thing of the past. The centre with its fashionable department stores, its business houses and its public buildings is now a divided stretch of waste ground and many of the tenement barracks, too, have disappeared. In 1930 Werner Hegemann, in his well-known book on the building of Berlin wrote: 'On orders of the President of Police the open country was packed within a few decades with miserable tenement barracks, which now will take centuries to remove'. He could not have foreseen that fifteen years later the job would be done by the R.A.F. and the Soviet guns in about one week.

When Nernst arrived in Berlin, Prussian simplicity was being replaced by the most garish ostentation. The Tiergarten was marred by an avenue exhibiting the long line of statues of all the Hohenzollern in white marble and the sober Brandenburg Gate was overshadowed by the enormous and hideously ugly Reichstag building. Even the small but dignified old cathedral opposite the palace was dynamited to make room for a gigantic baroque monstrosity without which it was impossible for the Kaiser to worship God in a manner befitting his status. By sheer size it completely spoiled the aspect of another set of buildings, unequalled in any city, the museum island. It was composed of a group of Greek temples, laid out in harmony and loosely connected by colonnades which housed the National Gallery and the Old and the New Museums.

Having had a late start, Berlin could not outshine the famous picture galleries of Munich or Dresden, but the collections of antiquities could rival most museums in the world. Hand in hand with the rise in science and technology, archaeology and the study of the ancient world had advanced rapidly. It all started with Heinrich Schliemann, the son of a poor pastor, who as a grocer's apprentice in the small Maerkish town of Fuerstenberg, dreamt of excavating Troy, about which he had read in the Odyssey. At the age of fifty, after having become rich with cotton and tea, he realized his dream and amazed the world by the golden 'treasure of Priam'. After his death in 1890, the Kaiser supported from his personal funds the continuation of the work by men like Doerpfeld and Koldewey. The latter spent twenty years and about three million marks of the Kaiser's and the German Oriental Society's money in excavating Babylon. At the same time the German Amarna Expedition dug up a sculptor's studio in Egypt which contained the head of Nerfertiti.

The centre of Berlin's intellectual life, the university, was founded in 1810, in the midst of the Napoleonic wars. Their defeat at Jena had convinced the Prussians that in order to regain power, basic reforms had to be introduced. Under French occupation and surveillance, modernization of the Prussian army was out of the question and clearly had to wait for better times. Meanwhile the progressive forces persuaded the Prussian court that the country would remain backward unless an educated élite was created who could act as leaders in a modern State. They pointed to the fact that Napoleon's armies were successful because they were backed by the spiritual force of the French revolution. This was the atmosphere in which Friedrich Wilhelm III yielded to the advice of his Minister of Education, Wilhelm von Humboldt, to found a university in Berlin which would bear the King's name. The King's decision had been made under the pressure of circumstances and not from conviction, and more than a century had to pass until, in 1946, the name was changed to that of the true founder: Humboldt University.

The building chosen by Humboldt which to this day houses the main auditoria and offices of the university, was the palace built for Prince Heinrich, the brother of Frederick the Great. Centrally situated in Unter den Linden, its solid and sparsely adorned façade provides the traditionally forbidding Prussian aspect.

Science had been slow to develop at Berlin University. Originally the emphasis had been on the arts, theology and, in particular, on philosophy. The first rector, Fichte, was a philosopher whose famous *Addresses to the German Nation* made a strong appeal for patriotic renewal. His successor, Hegel, had not, originally, shared these sentiments. An admirer of the French revolution and of Napoleon, the defeat of Prussia left him cold but his attitude changed remarkably after he had accepted the chair of philosophy at Berlin as Fichte's successor. Unlike Fichte's patriotism, Hegel's brand was not democratic. He argued that through reason man must subordinate himself to the State because: 'All value that man possesses, all spiritual reality, he has through the State' which is 'the divine idea as it exists on Earth'. Unlike many of his colleagues, Hegel played along with the authorities and became very much the official philosopher of the Prussian military State. He discouraged personal responsibility except for those who by superior wisdom were destined to guide the State. They were 'world-historical personalities', a term which was seized upon by Bismarck half a century later. Although Hegel was a poor and uninspiring lecturer, his teaching and especially his dialectics gained him many adherents far beyond the borders of Prussia. Even after his death students came to Berlin to read philosophy under Hegel's successors and two of these were Karl Marx and Friedrich Engels.

In 1834 Heinrich Gustav Magnus was appointed the first professor of physics at Berlin and one year later he discovered the aerodynamic effect which bears his name. The new rifled guns of the Prussian artillery shot their projectiles much straighter than the old round cannon balls but they were deflected by wind in a most curious manner. Magnus solved the puzzle by showing experimentally that a hitherto unsuspected force acts on the projectile when it is spinning. He was a man of immense working capacity who turned his attention to a wide variety of subjects and was entrusted by the Prussian Government with a number of missions. There is a curious connection with the Nernst family. Magnus was the son of a Jewish merchant and was baptized into Lutheran Christianity by Johannes David Nernst, Walther's great grandfather.

Magnus instituted the function which was to become one of the most outstanding features of the Berlin Physics School, the weekly colloquium, a meeting at which new results and theories were discussed. It remained in being after Magnus' death and ultimately became the world's most important forum at which the progress of modern physics was debated. For the time being, however, physics teaching in Berlin had to be theoretical until, at last, in 1862, Magnus was given the money to set up a laboratory for his students. Unfortunately, the funds only sufficed for the acquisition of apparatus and Magnus had to make space for the laboratory by giving up some of his living rooms. His house, Number 7 Am Kupfergraben, miraculously survived the Second World War and is today the seat of the East German Physical Society. Vague promises of building a physical institute had been made for a long time but when Magnus died in 1870, it seemed still as far off as ever.

The physics chair was offered in succession to Gustav Kirchhoff, who declined, and then to Hermann von Helmholtz, both at that time professors in Heidelberg. Helmholtz only accepted after it had been agreed that he would receive a salary of 4000 thaler, that he would become the sole director of a large physical institute to be built forthwith and that an official residence would be provided in the same building. Even so, Helmholtz had to wait until 1878 for the new institute because the Franco-Prussian War delayed its planning and building.

In Heidelberg Helmholtz had held the chair of physiology, the field in which he had started his scientific career. His main interest was centred on sensory perception, in particular on hearing and seeing, and these studies led him gradually to pure physics. He was a man endowed with great intellectual power and a wide range of knowledge which allowed him to make important contributions to practically every aspect of nineteenth-century physics. Apart from his fundamental work in thermo-dynamics which had a direct bearing on Nernst's great discovery, Helmholtz fully realized the importance of the new field of electro-dynamics. Among his pupils were Boltzmann and Heinrich Hertz to whom Helmholtz suggested the research on electromagnetic oscillations which led to the discovery of radio waves. Others were Michelson, whose experiments on the velocity of light set the stage for Einstein and Wilhelm Wien who discovered the radiation law that preceded Planck's quantum theory. Both received Nobel prizes.

Through Helmholtz' work and influence Berlin became one of the world centres of physics research. His scientific eminence was matched by his success in Berlin society. His second wife, Anna von Mohl, had seen to it that the professor's official residence contained large and impressive rooms in which she could entertain in the lavish style that was becoming fashionable in the booming capital. Helmholtz' daughter Ellen married the eldest son of the inventor of the dynamo, the engineer and industrialist Werner von Siemens. Two years later, in 1884, Siemens gave half a million marks to the German Government for the setting up of a National Physical Laboratory with the proviso that Helmholtz was to be the director.

The site for the Physikalisch-Technische Reichsanstalt was chosen near the western end of the Tiergarten, opposite the newly founded technical university at Charlottenburg. This was to become Berlin's second scientific centre with a third one to spring up twenty years later at Dahlem. The first building to be completed at the Reichsanstalt was the director's splendid mansion and Helmholtz moved in forthwith in 1884. Here, too, Nernst and his family were to inherit, forty years later, the glamorous setting laid out for Frau von Helmholtz.

Helmholtz occupied the Berlin physics chair for a quarter of a century in which the foundations for the pre-eminence of the physics school were laid. Much of this rise was due to Helmholtz' reputation and to his forceful personality but he was also greatly aided by circumstances. His installa-tion coincided with the victory over France and the foundation of the new Reich, and life in Berlin began to assume a new aspect at breath-taking pace. In 1870 Kirchhoff could not be induced to give up his chair of physics at the ancient university of Heidelberg for one in the intellectual desert of Berlin. Only four years later he accepted the same position with alacrity—now in the glittering capital of a rising world power. Helmholtz had been largely instrumental in the creation of a chair of theoretical physics and Kirchhoff was the obvious choice.

Kirchhoff's world reputation rested on the discovery, in 1858, of spectrum analysis which he developed in collaboration with Bunsen and which permitted the identification of chemical elements by the light emitted from them. The method could be used to determine the composition of distant stars and led to the discovery of many new elements, the most striking of which was that of helium, first seen in the sun's corona during the total eclipse of 1869. Observation of the spectrum lines, the characteristic colours emitted from an incandescent gas, provides the most direct information about the structure of atoms and it became the foremost tool in its elucidation. In fact, the discovery of Kirchhoff and Bunsen can be rated the most important single step in the experimental foundation of modern physics.

Only a few months after this great discovery, Kirchhoff made another equally important one, the significance of which, however, remained hidden for many years to come. He found that when a body is heated, the emitted radiation only depends on the temperature, irrespective of the nature of the material. The surprising fact is that the substance concerned, whether a metal, a stone, or even a gas, should have no influence at all on the radiation given out. It points to the fundamental importance of the phenomenon of heat radiation and this was the clue which was missed at the time. Kirchhoff did not live to see the final explanation of his discovery which was to deal the death-blow to classical physics. It was left to his successor in the Berlin chair of theoretical physics, Max Planck, to formulate on the basis of Kirchhoff's radiation law the quantum principle.

Kirchhoff died in 1887 and it was, of course, Helmholtz who had to advise the mighty Althoff on the most suitable successor. It would be nice to think that with immense scientific intuition and prophetic foresight Helmholtz was able to pick out a comparatively unknown young man who would become one of the world's greatest scientists. Unfortunately this illusion is shattered by Planck's own account given in his short *Scientific Autobiography*. A scientific controversy had broken out between Wilhelm Weber and Helmholtz. It was a battle of the giants, the physics faculty of the ancient university of Goettingen against the upstart Berlin. Planck admits candidly that he had been waiting long years for a professorship, and in order to become better known he submitted a prize essay to the Goettingen faculty in which, however, he expressed opinions supporting Helmholtz. This lost him the first prize but, he said: 'Even though I failed to get acclaim in Goettingen, Berlin took note of me, as I should soon find out.' He meant, of course, the offer of the chair of theoretical physics there.

Planck has left us, at the same time, some interesting notes on Helm-holtz which are worth quoting verbatim.

In his whole personality, his incorruptible judgement and in his modest manner he represented the dignity and truth of his science. I was deeply touched by his human kindness. When in conversation he looked at me with his quiet, searching but benevolent eyes, I was seized with a feeling of boundless, childlike devotion. I would have been prepared to confide to him anything which affected me deeply in the certainty of finding in him a just and mild counsellor, and an appreciative or even praising word from his mouth gave me greater happiness than all the success I could achieve in the world.

This is a remarkable statement from a man like Planck who was notoriously reticent and undemonstrative. It gives some idea of Helm-holtz' impressive and magnetic personality, which goes a long way to explain the enormous influence he wielded.

When, in 1888, Helmholtz finally took up the presidency of the Reichsanstalt, he retained his chair at the university, occupying both positions to the end of his life in 1894. He was in his late sixties when he accepted this dual responsibility and his administrative duties did not leave him much time for scientific work. Indeed, physics in Berlin would have been in danger of suffering a decline but for the creation of a new institute of theoretical physics which was established at Planck's appoint-ment. In his quiet and unobtrusive, but persistent, way, Planck won the esteem and friendship of the younger Berlin physicists who soon found fresh stimulus in his beautifully clear theoretical teaching. Wien's outstanding success in finding, in 1893, a fundamental relation bet-ween the quality of heat radiation and temperature, clearly shows the mark of Planck's inspiration. After Helmholtz' death the director-ship of the Berlin Physics Laboratory passed in less than twelve years to Kundt, to Warburg and then to Drude, all scientists with a high repu-tation whose short tenure did not allow them to make outstanding contri-butions.

The beginnings of chemistry in Berlin, too, were slow. Eilhard Mitscher-lich who was appointed in 1821 was, like Magnus, an excellent scientist but he was hampered by having no proper laboratory in which to teach students. The only teaching opportunity was provided by a small research laboratory which belonged to the Prussian Academy of Sciences. Things only changed when in 1865 August Wilhelm von Hofmann gave up his positions as professor at the Royal College of Chemistry in London and Chemist to the Royal Mint and returned to Germany to become professor at Berlin. His great prestige and the urgent demand of the growing chemical industry induced the Prussian Ministry of Education to build for him, and without the usual delay, a large chemical laboratory. Even so, the almost unbelievable growth of the school of chemistry under Hofmann required, in 1883, the building of a second chemical institute, adjacent to Helmholtz' physics laboratory. While the work in Hofmann's laboratory was devoted mainly to organic chemistry in which he had made his name, research and teaching in the second institute, first under Rammelsberg and then under Landolt, was concerned with inorganic and physical chemistry.

Hofmann carried as much weight in furthering chemistry as Helmholtz in physics and between them they gave the university a new aspect in which the sciences contributed at a steadily growing rate to its prestige. Hofman exerted a strong influence well beyond the confines of his subject. During his rectorate in 1880–1 an attempt was made by followers of the Court Preacher Adolf Stoecker to organize an anti-Semitic group among the students. The leader at the university was the professor of modern history, Heinrich von Treitschke. The sequence of five successive consonants in his name testifies to his Slavonic descent, but in spite, or possibly because, of this he was imbued with the Teutonic heritage. In 1871 he had become a member of the first Reichstag and through his writing and university teaching he emerged as the foremost panegyrist of the Bismarckian State. To this he added a dose of anti-Semitism derived from Nietzsche's doctrine of the Germanic superman. Hofmann condemned him in no uncertain terms, forbidding any such association at the university and signing with most of the other professors the famous declaration condemning anti-Semitism.

Hofmann died two years before Helmholtz and the grand era of the creation of Berlin science came to an end. However, unlike the partial vacuum which Helmholtz had left in physics, organic chemistry retained continuity by the appointment of Hofmann's successor Emil Fischer, another member of the race of scientific giants. Meanwhile Hofmann's great laboratory had become far too small and a new chemical institute was built for Fischer. In order to strengthen the field of physical chemistry, he and Planck persuaded the Academy of Sciences to offer, in 1896, a position to the eminent Dutch theoretician, Jacobus Hendricus van't Hoff, which entailed a professorship at the university free from teaching duties. Van't Hoff had been the first to compare the behaviour of chemical solutions with that of gases, an approach which was to become so important for the work of Arrhenius and Nernst. Then he had turned to the question of the actual structure of chemical compounds as distinct from the formula written down on paper. He reasoned that within each molecule the constituent atoms must be arranged in some definite spatial configuration which he worked out for simple carbon compounds. However, van't Hoff's latest and most important work was concerned with the direction in which a chemical reaction proceeds and it paved the way for Nernst's ultimate solution of this problem.

This then was the new world into which Nernst moved from Goettingen. Instead of the small dignified old university town with its donnish provincialism there was the dynamic new-rich capital city, a strange mixture of commercial enterprise, ostentatious living and hidebound Prussian militarism. Its intellectual centre had become a citadel of scholarship strongly garrisoned with the *élite* of German learning.

However, before we turn to Nernst's life and work in Berlin one important incident has to be recorded. At the very opening of the new century, in 1900, Max Planck had read a scientific paper before the Berlin Physical Society. It was the sequel to the work of Kirchhoff and Wien on heat radiation and it contained the final answer to this fundamental problem. Planck's formula provided the missing universal relation between temperature, energy and quality of radiation. It fitted the experimental data perfectly but it was marred by what appeared to most scientists at the time as a slight mathematical blemish. The energy did not emerge as a continuous stream but as a shower of small individual energy parcels which Planck called 'quanta'. This was to be the end of classical physics, leading to the greatest revolution in science. As yet, nobody saw what had taken place and Planck, for reasons of his own, did not press the point. Nothing happened, and for another five years classical physics went on in its sedate and well-established way. Its progress was at last interrupted in 1905 by a scientific paper which, in an almost foolhardy manner, ascribed physical reality to the energy packets of Planck's formula. It did not come from one of the famous physics schools of the day but from a solitary amateur scientist, a young clerk at the Swiss Patent Office in Bern, whose name was Albert Einstein.

The translation to Berlin was the final step in a scientist's career and Nernst was unable to restrain his sense of theatre on this important occasion. He insisted on stamping himself with the hallmark of the modern professor and made the journey with his family by car. The picture taken at this dramatic departure shows Nernst in his driving fur at the wheel and the rest of the family bundled into the back of the open landau. The radiator was festooned with two spare tyres and, as an extra precaution, the institute's chief mechanic was esconced next to the driver. As it turned out, this was a wise move because the car broke down, providing the family with an additional, though not unwelcome, night's rest. An authentic report on the cause of the failure is non-existent but persistent rumour had it that on the previous day the discoverer of the theory of galvanic elements had charged his battery with the wrong polarity. In any case, the journey was successfully completed on the following day and the Nernsts settled down in their new home in the

Moltkestrasse, near the new Reichstag building and in easy walking distance of the laboratory. There was even a stable for garaging the car.

Nernst came to Berlin as the successor to Landolt, who had been the director of the second chemical institute of the university in the Bunsenstrasse. The building formed part of a whole block of scientific institutes on the banks of the Spree. The northern side, overlooking the river was the physics laboratory which had been built for Helmholtz. Adjacent to it, in the east, was Nernst's institute and the southern tract had originally been used as an engineering school. With the establishment of the technical university at Charlottenburg, it had been turned over to physiology and hygiene. Facing the west was Helmholtz' official residence. It had been a condition of Nernst's appointment that practically the whole of the second chemical institute should be turned into a new laboratory for physical chemistry and only the top floor was retained as a teaching laboratory for chemists. Bombing and shelling have reduced the physical institute and most of the surrounding buildings to rubble but Nernst's laboratory has miraculously escaped. It, too, was scheduled for destruction to make room for modern buildings and I like to think that in a very small way my own pleadings have helped to save it as a reminder of Berlin science at its zenith.

The main lecture theatre is on the first floor and it was here, in the middle of giving his lecture on physical chemistry, that Nernst suddenly saw the solution that had eluded him for so long. This happened shortly after his taking office in Berlin and all the preparatory work had been going on in his mind for many years. Possibly the change of environment was playing a part in the formation of a new thought. The problem itself was an old one, it concerned the prediction of chemical reactions.

The enormous changes in the fortunes of mankind produced by science and its applications have an extremely simple cause. It is the unique economy of the method. A designer who creates on his drawing-board a new aeroplane knows beforehand that it will be capable of rising into the air. Before the machine taxies out on to the runway for the first time, it is well known how far, how fast and how high it will fly and how big a load it will carry. This we take so much for granted that we completely forget how uncertain we are when trying to make predictions in other fields of human endeavour. We can send spaceships to the moon and send each other birthday greetings to the far corners of the Earth but we cannot predict next year's elections, next month's strikes or next week's stock market. In these and many other departments of our life we fumble by trial and error, and trial and error is an extremely expensive method of progress. Compared with these semi-instinctive exercises, the fraction of trial and error involved in science and technology is minimal.

The laws of mechanics can be expressed in strict mathematical form and their application heralded the beginning of the industrial revolution. They permitted, by means of levers, springs and gearwheels the transformation of power, but power itself had still to be provided mainly by man or horse. These were aided in a modest way by the exploitation of the mechanical forces in nature through wind and water mills. Large-scale technology had to wait for the raising of steam, the production of power from the burning of coal. Clearly the most important task now was to obtain for power production the same accurate predictability that had been achieved for the mechanical devices. This meant creating a strict mathematical framework in which the laws of motion were combined with the phenomena of heat.

The branch of science combining the laws of motion with the action of heat has become known as thermodynamics and its foundations were laid in the famous treatise '*Réflexions sur la Puissance Motrice du Feu*' published in 1824 by a young French engineer officer, Sadi Carnot. Thermodynamic formalism has proved to be of immense general usefulness and Nernst's application of it to the problem of the galvanic cell, mentioned earlier, was just one example. Thermodynamics is a large subject and its historical development is rather involved so that for our purposes it is easier to pick out those features which are needed for an understanding of Nernst's work.

In 1847 Helmholtz published a paper entitled '*Über die Erhaltung der Kraft*' which contains a clear statement of the principle of conservation of energy. Newton already seems to have realized that in all purely mechanical processes energy can neither be created nor destroyed but the importance of Helmholtz' paper was that heat energy, too, fulfilled this condition. He extended this principle of the conservation of energy to all other physical phenomena such as electricity, light, sound and so on, and due to its universality it became known as the first law of thermodynamics. It laid for ever the ghost of a '*perpetuum mobile*' and in fact the first law can be stated as the impossibility of constructing a machine which does nothing but produce energy.

When Helmholtz submitted this important and far-reaching work, he did not know that he had been anticipated twice over. In 1845 James Prescott Joule at Manchester had shown experimentally that the same amount of mechanical energy is always transformed into the same quantity of heat and still three years earlier Robert Mayer had deduced the conservation principle by calculation. Mayer was a medical doctor at Heilbronn and his interest in the subject had been aroused when, as a young man, he served as ship's surgeon on a voyage to Indonesia. He noted that the venous blood of injured patients was much lighter in the tropics than in Europe and concluded that the larger use of oxygen in the latter case was due to a greater loss of heat energy from the body.

The first law of thermodynamics states the equivalence of all forms of energy, but it says nothing about transformations from one form into another. It was quite clear already from Carnot's work that while mechanical energy can be changed completely into heat, the opposite is not true. When a train is stopped, the energy of motion has been turned into heat in the brakes but supplying this same heat energy will not accelerate the train again to its original speed. Instead of allowing for a complete transformation the turning of heat energy into mechanical work involves not only the energy itself but also the temperature. In order to make a heat engine work, a quantity of heat has to be supplied to it at a higher temperature and a smaller one discarded at a lower temperature. This difference as well as the absolute value of these temperatures then determines the maximum portion of mechanical energy that can be abstracted. All this shows that a fundamental principle other than the mere equivalence of all forms of energy must be operating.

In 1850 a former student of Magnus was appointed to a professorship at the artillery school in Berlin. He was Rudolf Clausius who in the same year presented a paper to the Prussian Academy of Sciences that contained a clear statement of the new fundamental principle which has since become known as the second law of thermodynamics. There are various ways of enunciating the second law. Following the type of statement which we used for the first law, the second one can be regarded as the impossibility of constructing a machine which does nothing except to change heat into mechanical energy.

For the time being it appeared that with these two fundamental laws, of conservation and transformation of energy, thermodynamics was completed. Nothing more was evidently required to make all predictions needed for the operation of power-producing machinery. In fact, things worked out remarkably well for the design of heat engines. Once it was realized that the amount of useful energy which can be extracted depends on the temperature, the advantages of superheated steam and of the internal combustion engine immediately became apparent. Ever since, this simple principle of 'the hotter the better' has governed the design of heat engines, and in the end the gas turbine which uses the hot flame gases directly is bound to win over the steam engine which first degrades their temperature to the boiling point of water.

Of course, the basis of all heat engines is chemical reactions, that is, the burning of coal, oil or gas. In these reactions which combine the elements carbon and hydrogen with oxygen, we are only interested in the energy that is given off at the combustion in the form of heat. The chemical products of this combination, carbon dioxide and water are useless and simply thrown away. However, there exists another, and equally important, aspect of chemistry in which the chemical product itself is all important while the energy involved is merely an attendant feature. One of the oldest examples is the extraction of metals from their ores, as for instance the liberation of the element iron from its combination with oxygen. The smelting of iron out of iron oxide takes place in a blast furnace and is brought about by a strong supply of heat. Here energy has to be added to the process, while in a heat engine it is abstracted.

It was from observations of this kind that in 1867 the great French chemist Marcellin Berthelot hoped to solve a problem which had already bedevilled the alchemists of the Middle Ages. In their endeavours to make gold they carried out a vast number of chemical experiments and soon noted that some substances combine with one another while others refuse to do so. The readiness of two substances to combine they described as 'affinity' and certain heavy oils, for instance, which will only form compounds with very few other substances they noted as being *parum affinis*: paraffin.

With the rapid growth of the chemical industry the prediction of chemical reactions, that means the measurement of affinity, became of paramount importance. Berthelot certainly succeeded in asking the right question, which is often the most important step, and he almost got the right answer. He asked why certain reactions, such as the burning of coal, will, once started, take place spontaneously, whereas others, like the reduction of iron oxide to metallic iron, do not go on by themselves. This, of course, is the old problem of affinity stated in more definite terms. Berthelot thought he had found the answer in the liberation or absorption of energy and concluded that: 'Those reactions take place spontaneously in which heat is liberated'.

While Berthelot's principle was evidently correct in the vast majority of cases, it must have been obvious from the beginning that there exist quite clear exceptions. Salt will readily dissolve in water but the mixture gets colder and heat, instead of being liberated, is consumed. To say that this type of process is different from a chemical reaction is no excuse in thermodynamics and the real reason why, in spite of flagrant failures, Berthelot's principle was so readily accepted is quite different. Very few scientists understood the full meaning of the second law of thermo-dynamics. The second law is, at the same time, thermodynamics at its best and at its worst. Its beauty and strength lie in its universal validity which can be applied to the metabolism of a living structure or to the nuclear energy production in the centre of the sun. Its drawback is the generalized formalism which makes it almost impossible to visualize the physical quantities with which it operates. All too often applying thermo-dynamics is like a deaf man playing the piano, who has to rely for his success entirely on striking the correct key at the right time.

Although Berthelot's principle quite clearly could not claim general validity and therefore was not acceptable in the formalism of thermodynamics, it is important to our story. The fact that it is wrong, but not very wrong, provided the most important step in Nernst's solution of the whole problem. As became clear later, the actual process of thought followed by Nernst does not provide the easiest way of understanding the significance of his achievement. However, in the interest of historical accuracy a rough outline of his original approach will be given before presenting the more fundamental aspect of his discovery as it was revealed subsequently.

It was the great merit of van't Hoff to have realized clearly the thermodynamic meaning of affinity. Again the two relevant quantities are those stated in the second law; the total change of energy involved in the chemical reaction and that fraction of it which could be transformed into mechanical work. Helmholtz had called it the 'free' energy and van't Hoff now showed that it was this free energy which provides a measure of chemical affinity. Its strict mathematical relation to the total energy had already been established in 1880 by Helmholtz and, independently, Willard Gibbs in America had come to exactly the same result.

Since the energy residing in a substance can be determined by direct measurement, it seemed at first sight that it should now be possible to calculate any chemical equilibrium. However, only too soon it turned out that this was not possible. The problem of predicting chemical reactions had still not been solved. The trouble lay in the mathematical form of the Gibbs–Helmholtz equation which allows the total energy to be calculated from the free energy while the reverse procedure is impossible. It showed that, after all, thermodynamics was not yet complete. Some so far unknown basic principle was still missing. At this place Nernst entered the field. He certainly was better qualified to tackle the problem than anyone else. His analysis of the electrochemical reactions leading to the theory of the galvanic cell had demonstrated Nernst's deep insight into and his brilliant command of thermodynamics. Moreover, the processes in the galvanic cell which occur at constant temperature had provided him with an important clue. In such cases, according to Berthelot, the free and total energies should be equal and, so argued Nernst, Berthelot's principle had been found to be almost right. He next looked for cases when it ceased to be valid and noticed that agreement got worse with increasing temperature.

Now Nernst had something to go by. The Gibbs–Helmholtz equation had shown that a relation exists between the two energies but it was not specific enough except for one temperature only, and it was here that Nernst picked up the second clue. He saw that on thermodynamic grounds the two energies must be equal at the absolute zero of temperature. Unfortunately this still did not solve the problem since, even with this proviso, for each value of the total energy an infinite number of values of the free energy can still be postulated. One more condition was clearly required and this missing link in the problem he suddenly saw in a flash as he lectured on the subject in his first term in Berlin. The difference between the two energies must not only disappear at absolute zero, it must also become vanishingly small as absolute zero is approached. This was the first formulation of what became known, first as Nernst's theorem and then as the third law of thermodynamics.

In this particular form the new law of nature was a revelation to Nernst but it will appear as such neither to the reader nor to the great majority of physicists. Nernst, who had been living with the problem of chemical equilibrium for years, of course, realized immediately that he had solved it but even he cannot have foreseen at that moment the far-reaching implications to which we shall turn later.

Nevertheless, he was fully conscious from the beginning, of the importance of his result for thermodynamics and, being Nernst, he did not hide his satisfaction. Some of his colleagues remarked caustically that when looking up the new law in Nernst's book they had to search in the index under 'm' for 'my heat theorem'. This certainly was the form in which he introduced the subject in his lectures. Einstein, who admired him and who said in Nernst's obituary that 'there was never anybody quite like Nernst' also noted that he tended 'to be childishly pleased with himself'. In fact, the boot was on the other foot. Einstein was in many respects a simple soul who would be taken in by the most transparent hard luck stories and was not very good at managing his own affairs, something that could hardly be said of Nernst. Nernst's blatant self-glorification was probably not at all childish. More likely it was part of the role that the playwright and actor in him had assigned to himself; that of a harmless, astonished and innocent little man, whereas in fact he was possessed of exactly the opposite qualities. He knew that drawing attention to one's achievements is often a necessity and by doing it in a completely outrageous way this useful activity could be camouflaged as an amusing eccentricity.

When lecturing on 'his' heat theorem, Nernst was careful to point to an interesting numerical phenomenon concerning the discovery of the three fundamental laws of thermodynamics. The first one had three authors, Mayer, Joule and Helmholtz; the second had two, Carnot and Clausius; whereas the third was the work of one man only, Nernst. This showed conclusively that thermodynamics was now complete since the authorship of a hypothetical fourth law would have to be zero. As usual, he was probably right although it is just possible that the form in which his theorem is at present accepted may not yet be the final one.

Once Nernst had enunciated the postulate of the merging of total and free energy near absolute zero, the next step was to test its validity by

C

direct experiment. The next eight years, right up to the outbreak of war in 1914, were devoted to this work. It was carried out with tremendous energy and Nernst was fortunate in being supported in this crucial period by an enthusiastic team of co-workers, some of outstanding brilliance. Foremost among the latter were Arnold Eucken and the brothers Lindemann.

Eucken, who later became professor in Breslau and then in Goettingen, was the son of the famous philosopher and himself a man of puritanical mind and frugal habits. In Breslau, the institute's mechanic, Klosse, was taken aback when, on a nice Saturday afternoon, he met his professor in the centre of the city, surrounded by an admiring band of street urchins. Eucken carried over his shoulder a strong pole on which was impaled the gleaming white pan of a water-closet. It transpired that it was being taken to the station to be conveyed to the professor's week-end cottage at the Zobten. When Klosse mentioned, embarrassed, a taxi or a lab-boy with a hand cart, Eucken retorted angrily that he was still sound enough in wind and limb not to waste money on luxuries. Eucken's textbook of physical chemistry which in due course replaced Nernst's *magnum opus*, was also a masterpiece of economy. In spite of being beautifully clear, the brevity of explanation made it difficult for the students to digest. The faint-hearted took refuge in the more chatty text on the same subject written by Eggert, another of Nernst's pupils.

The Lindemann brothers came from England. Their father, an amateur astronomer who had discovered a minor planet, was originally a civil engineer. Born at Langenberg in Alsace, he had come to England at the age of twenty and married an American widow with three children. She bore four more in her second marriage, a girl and three boys, Charles, Frederick Alexander and James Septimus whom they called Sepi. The Lindemanns had a joint annual income of £20 000 and were thus well off. The father was a friend of Nernst's and a great admirer of the Kaiser's positive attitude to science. He sent the two elder boys to study with Nernst and the younger of these, F. A. Lindemann, became Nernst's favourite pupil. Charles eventually gave up science for the army, but F. A. Lindemann stayed in physics, becoming professor at Oxford and in later life the closest friend and scientific adviser of Winston Churchill. A strange and somewhat withdrawn man, he was posthumously and undeservedly elevated to the role of sinister grey eminence by the pen of a novelist. The Lindemann boys stayed throughout the years of their doctorate research at the Adlon, Berlin's most expensive hotel, and spent a good deal of time playing tennis. They made up for it by working late at night, but even so, it irritated Nernst. Not being impressed by the Lindemanns' trophies, he burst out one day: 'Two grown men chasing all day long one little ball. Your father is so rich, why doesn't he buy one for each of you?'

The work on which all of them were engaged was research into the behaviour of matter at low temperatures. Nernst's original aim, of course, had been the prediction of chemical equilibria and he had achieved it by postulating the equality of the total and free energies near absolute zero. This now permitted the calculation of the free energy, and with it of the equilibrium, from the total energy. This total energy of a substance is, at any temperature, given by the heat contained in it and this can be measured in a straightforward manner. Let us say, the substance is first cooled to the absolute zero of temperature, then heat can be gradually added in measured quantities. Naturally this has the effect of raising the sample's temperature and in this way the total amount of heat which has gone into it at any given temperature can be determined. The number of calories needed to raise the temperature of the substance by one degree is called its specific heat.

Hence determination of the specific heat of various substances down to very low temperatures was the most important type of experiment needed to prove the validity of Nernst's postulate. Nernst had thought of a very elegant method for carrying out this research, and Eucken and F. A. Lindemann made the measurements. However, as heat is supplied to the sample it not only warms up, it also expands, and this increase in size accounts for part of the energy taken up by it. Accordingly, Charles Lindemann was given the task of measuring the thermal expansion at low temperatures. These three were by no means the only students engaged in this work. A host of others, many of whom became well-known scientists in later years, were busy with similar experiments in the Berlin laboratory.

As the results kept coming in, it became clear that Nernst's postulate was correct. The whole idea of the work can be illustrated by the simple example of an equilibrium involving one substance only, tin. This metal can exist in two crystalline forms, white tin which is stable above 19° C while below this temperature the grey form is stable. The transformation proceeds slowly but it is known that in countries with long cold winters, such as Russia, tin roofs tend to corrode by white tin turning into grey.

The 'reaction' which we have to consider in this simple case is that between the two modifications of tin, and we already know from direct experiment the equilibrium temperature, namely 19° C. Determining the specific heat of both white and grey tin from the absolute zero upwards and knowing its expansion coefficient, Nernst's theorem now allows us to calculate the difference in free energies between the two forms of this metal. The temperature at which this difference becomes zero then denotes the state of equilibrium. Measurement and calculation in this case yielded 22° C. This is even better than it looks because the reference point that had to be used was not the zero point of the centigrade scale but absolute zero, at $-273°$ C. This makes the calculated equilibrium temperature, measured in the absolute Kelvin scale, $(273 + 22) = 295°$ K which is extremely close to the true value of $(273 + 19) = 292°$ K; an impressive proof of the validity of the third law.

The tin equilibrium was, of course, only one of many examples studied. We chose it only because of its simplicity. Reactions involving several substances, and those extending not only to the solid and liquid but also to the gaseous phase, posed very complex problems. Nernst tackled these thermodynamic problems with great vigour and ingenuity, discovering elegant short cuts in the calculations. However, his attention was drawn more and more to new fundamental problems which at first had arisen more as side issues of his work on chemical equilibria. These new problems were all concerned with the true significance of the absolute zero of temperature.

The existence of an absolute zero of temperature had first been postulated in the early eighteenth century by Guillaume Amontons. He had made observations on the expansion of air when heated or cooled and deduced that at about $-240°$ C its volume would have shrunk to nothing. Since the volume of air cannot become negative, he concluded that there must exist a lowest possible temperature. More accurate measurements later showed that the true value of this rock-bottom of the temperature scale is at $-273°$ C. Amontons was probably the first to interpret heat as the motion of individual atoms and molecules, and accordingly he regarded absolute zero as the ultimate state at which all molecular motion has ceased. This view remained unchallenged until it was unexpectedly refuted by the third law of thermodynamics.

It soon became clear that Nernst's solution of the Gibbs–Helmholtz equation led to a strange but inescapable consequence concerning the nature of absolute zero. It was not the energy which becomes zero as this temperature is approached but a quite different physical quantity, the entropy.

The entropy concept was introduced by Clausius in his formulation of the second law of thermodynamics. It appears there in the form of a quantity of heat divided by the temperature and it is a measure of that waste heat which is 'lost' when in a heat engine heat is transformed into mechanical energy. The full significance of this quantity was eventually discovered by Boltzmann in his statistical interpretation of thermodynamics. He showed that the entropy is a measure of disorder on the atomic scale.

Thus the third law had transformed absolute zero from a state of complete rest into one of perfect orderliness. In due course this new concept was to single out the realm of low temperatures as a most unusual corner of our physical world. For the time being the problem of vanishing entropy gave an entirely new aspect to the attainment of low temperatures. It could be shown straightaway that with the disappearance of entropy, all cooling processes, too, must come to an end. While Nernst's theorem still makes it possible to approach absolute zero to an arbitrary degree, it does not permit its complete attainment. At the same time, this fact provides us with another and much simpler formulation of the third law of thermodynamics. It can be stated as the impossibility of designing a machine which allows absolute zero to be reached.

There are far-reaching consequences, affecting our basic concepts of temperature, which arise from this aspect of the third law. We cannot here enter into a discussion of the rather abstract problems involved but it must seem unsatisfactory to ascribe a fixed value to a temperature that cannot be reached. One possible way out of this dilemma would be to use a logarithmic, instead of a linear, temperature scale with the value zero for $1°$ K which would then bring the present absolute zero to minus infinity.

Another feature of this new dilemma involves serious practical issues. The third law permits, as we have seen, the calculation of chemical equilibria but it then turns out that this calculation requires measurements of the specific heat down to a temperature which can never be attained. Like the carrot dangled before the donkey's nose, the third law offers a solution which it then takes away again through another of its aspects. Thus, while in principle this horrible problem must forever remain insoluble, the situation is not quite as hopeless as it may appear at first sight. The measurement of the specific heats of white and grey tin which were mentioned earlier had been carried out down to about $12°$ K and, as the good agreement between the calculated and the actual transformation temperature shows, this was evidently good enough. Evidently, even if it is impossible to cool the sample to absolute zero, reliable estimates for the chemical equilibria can be obtained, provided it has been cooled low enough.

What has to be considered 'low enough' is an awkward question to which we shall have to return presently, but whatever the answer will be, Nernst realized immediately that he had to extend his measurements to the lowest possible temperature. The liquefaction of gases had proved to be an excellent means of attaining low temperatures. In 1877 Louis Cailletet had liquefied oxygen at $90°$ K, at the turn of the century Dewar had reached $12°$ K with liquid hydrogen, and in 1908 Kamerlingh Onnes had approached absolute zero to within one degree by liquefying helium. Nernst set out for Leiden to look at the large and impressive low temperature installations which Onnes had built up in the last fifteen years. He returned to Berlin, having firmly decided against following the Leiden example. It was not the very considerable expense involved that deterred him but the time that such a project would require. There can be little doubt that Nernst could have wrung the money out of Althoff or some other sources but the prospect of waiting years before he would see the experimental confirmation of his theorem was quite intolerable.

Nernst was forever impatient, a trait that contributed much to his success. Far from fitting the popular image of a scientist as a painstaking and meticulous individual he was, like so many of his colleagues, a highly emotional prima donna. His own study and laboratory always presented aspects of extreme chaos which his co-workers termed appropriately 'the state of maximum entropy'. His desk had to be approached by a circuitous path which led from the door through stacks of books, papers and articles three feet high. They evidently presented a filing system which he alone was able to use, and this he did most efficiently. When discussing some aspect of research for which he required documentation, he would wander to one of these stacks, attack it one or two feet below the surface and extract without fail the desired article.

In the laboratory he often did things with his own hands, not because he was gifted with superb manual dexterity but simply because he could not wait for somebody else to do it. Having soldered a couple of wires together, he simply put the hot iron on the wooden table—where it burnt a hole—in order to proceed without further delay to the next task. For a sensitive electrical measurement, he would fetch a galvanometer but instead of setting it up properly and levelling it, he propped the instrument on a few books which happened to be within reach and started taking readings. Being on a slant, the indicating light spot, of course, drifted to one side but Nernst simultaneously corrected the error by rapid, if rough, mental calculation which was incorporated in the result that he jotted down. He gladly left higher degrees of finesse to others, saying that, as far as he was concerned, no effect was worth investigating if it required more than ten per cent of accuracy.

Now low-temperature facilities were required in a hurry. As was shown by his lamp and many other examples, Nernst was a master in the brilliant design of simple apparatus. He sketched out a small and remarkably uncomplicated hydrogen liquefier which the institute's mechanic, Hoenow, built for him in a couple of months. Altogether the machine had only cost about £20 to make, and it worked. That is to say, the trusted Hoenow could make it work whenever he, as well as the machine, happened to be in the right mood. The trouble was that Nernst, although an experimenter of genius, was no perfectionist and once he was convinced that the equipment would work 'under ideal conditions' he left both equipment and achievement of ideal conditions to others. When I entered the laboratory twenty years later as a research student, things were still much the same. The first warning I received was to avoid

Hoenow, who by then had become a highly temperamental diabetic, on days when he liquefied hydrogen. Nor had the character of the liquefier improved in the intervening period. Moreover, unless great precautions are taken, hydrogen liquefaction can be hazardous, and on one occasion an explosion took away quite a few windows, a wall and Hoenow's moustache! He then confided to me that Nernst had originally intended to automate the whole process by attaching alarm bells to the controls. The idea was that Hoenow should go on with his other work while the machine quietly made liquid hydrogen by itself. This somewhat ambitious plan had to be given up at the first attempt since the bells started ringing furiously the very moment Hoenow took his fingers off the controls.

Nernst seems to have had an exaggerated and decidedly unrealistic opinion of his hydrogen liquefier because he got Hoenow to build a number of copies which were sold. I discovered one of these in the early 'thirties in the Clarendon Laboratory, and it appears that long ago Lindemann must have bought it off Nernst in an ill-advised fit of optimism. Needless to say, since he had not bought Hoenow with it, the machine never worked. What shocked me was that the Oxford machine bore the serial number 43 and I have been wondering since who had been the other forty-one gullible customers.

While Nernst was quite willing to take the credit as designer of a superb little hydrogen liquefier as a side issue, his heart was not really in it. What he wanted were low-temperature facilities to measure specific heats, and these he got in record time. As already mentioned, the results were furnished mainly by Eucken and F. A. Lindemann and they were so extraordinary that the interest of the Nernst laboratory swung away from chemical equilibria to an entirely new and strange aspect of physics: the world of very low temperatures.

It had been suspected for quite a long time that something was wrong with specific heats at low temperatures. In 1820 the French scientists Dulong and Petit had noted that, for equal numbers of atoms, the specific heat of most substances had the same value. A satisfactory theory for this observation was later furnished by Boltzmann who explained the heat content of a solid in terms of vibration of the individual atoms. However, in 1875 Heinrich Weber had found that the specific heat of diamond was much lower than the value postulated by Dulong and Petit but that the normal value was reached at higher temperatures. Finally, at the turn of the century Dewar, at the Royal Institution in London, had obtained some rough indication that, in general, specific heats at low temperature were much lower than expected.

Nernst had been a student in Zürich when Weber lectured on his unexplained observation with diamond and now the measurements of Eucken and Lindemann showed clearly that for all substances which they investigated the specific heats gradually fell to very low values as absolute zero was approached. In fact, their careful measurements indicated that the specific heats would probably vanish at absolute zero, a result which was quite incomprehensible on the basis of classical physics.

While these measurements were still in progress, and quite independently of the work at Nernst's laboratory, a theoretical paper was published in 1907 which postulated a vanishing of the specific heats at absolute zero. Moreover, the theoretical prediction of the rate at which this process was supposed to take place was in remarkably good agreement with the experimental values obtained in Berlin. There could be no doubt that the theory was correct. The author was Albert Einstein and, as in the previous paper two years earlier, his address was given as the patent office in Berne.

Like Nernst, but fifteen years later, Einstein had heard Weber's lectures in Zürich and the strange results mentioned by his professor had worried him ever since. In his earlier paper Einstein had explained the photoelectric effect on the basis of Planck's quantum theory and now he again invoked the quantum concept for the explanation of the decrease in specific heats. Einstein accepted Boltzmann's idea of atomic vibrations but he postulated that these vibrations cannot have any arbitrary value; they must be quantized. In Planck's radiation formula the energy has not the classically accepted form of a homogeneous stream which can be subdivided in an arbitrary fashion, but appears as a shower of discrete energy packets. In this atomistic concept of energy, the size of these quanta is connected with the wavelength of the radiated light and heat. It is given by the number of waves emitted per second, that is by the frequency, multiplied by a universal constant. On the scale of our ordinary experience, this constant is extremely small, a thousand times smaller than a millionth millionth millionth millionth of the quantities which we use in everyday measurement. It is of atomic dimensions, and this is the reason why our senses fail to reveal to us the quantum nature of light or of any other form of energy.

In his first paper Einstein had already gone much farther than Planck in accepting the physical reality of light quanta when explaining the photo-electric effect. He now took a further step in applying the same considerations to the vibration of atoms in a solid. Each atom, he argued, can only accept energy packets corresponding to its characteristic vibration multiplied by Planck's constant. As the temperature is lowered and the heat energy of the substance decreases, the stage must be reached when there is not sufficient energy available to provide each atom with an appropriate quantum. This means that less energy can be taken up by the solid; its specific heat therefore decreases.

Einstein's first application of the quantum principle had aroused only limited interest, chiefly because hardly anyone had as yet grasped the fundamental significance. Moreover, it dealt with light radiation, the subject on which Planck had originally developed his theory. Now things began to move. With his theory of the specific heats, Einstein had demonstrated the applicability of the quantum concept to a completely different field of physics and thereby emphasized its universal significance. Moreover, Einstein had now provided the essential idea in a subject in which a strong school of experimentalists, the Nernst laboratory in Berlin, was actively working. Nernst himself and his pupils, in particular F. A. Lindemann, immediately compared the Einstein formula with their results. They found that while doubtless the theory was basically correct, small discrepancies existed. For these they, in turn, proposed a quantum-theoretical correction, and thereby testified to their own belief in the quantum theory. Inevitably, physicists all over the world began to be interested in these new ideas. There was, however, one notable exception; Planck himself again made no comment.

Planck's silence, however, cannot be interpreted as disregard or criticism of Einstein as a physicist. In 1905, the same year in which his first paper on the quantum theory appeared, Einstein published another article with the somewhat vague title 'The Electrodynamics of Moving Bodies'. It contained the foundations of his theory of relativity and it was immediately hailed by Planck as the most outstanding advance in this field since the days of Maxwell. It was Planck who immediately recognized the genius of the unknown young man in the Swiss Patent Office but the praise was not awarded for Einstein's championship of Planck's own theory. His strange attitude arose from the contrast in the two personalities.

At that time Planck and Einstein were probably the only physicists who thoroughly realized the revolutionary character of the quantum theory. To Planck, the descendant of a long line of Prussian law-givers, revolution in any form was deeply abhorrent. He did not want as yet to talk about the quantum theory, hoping all the time that he might find a bridge between his disturbing brain-child and the established system of classical physics. Einstein, on the other hand, was a young rebel who actively disliked established attitudes, who avoided the bother of darning socks by the ingenious short cut of wearing shoes on his naked feet. The theory of relativity, on the other hand, which was to earn later for Einstein the scorn and abuse of his anti-Semitic colleagues, was rightly regarded by Planck as a continuation of classical physics.

Nernst, of course, was delighted with Einstein's application of the quantum theory to the specific heat problem. He began to realize that his heat theorem had a much deeper significance than being merely the missing link in the framework of thermodynamics. Why was it the entropy and not the energy that vanished at absolute zero? What was the nature of that strange remnant of energy remaining in the substance that could not be removed by any degree of cooling? An entirely new aspect of physics seemed to open before him and the key to it was, as Einstein had shown, the quantum theory. The world of very low temperatures promised to be quite different from the rest of physics because in it the quantum principle was going to take the place of the classical laws.

Unlike Planck, Nernst was not a conservative. He was for ever intrigued by novelties, whether they were motorcars or new theories and he always approached any issue without prejudice and with an astonishingly open mind. This was his great strength which contributed largely to his success. Far from being terrified by the quantum concept, Nernst now turned to it for the solution of a problem which had bothered him a great deal.

The manner in which he had been able to derive his heat theorem restricted the latter to solids and liquids but was not applicable to gases. Neither he nor anyone else could think of a mechanism by which the specific heat of a perfect gas could be made to vanish and some physicists tried to get out of the difficulty by pointing out that at absolute zero all real gases at least would have to condense in any case. Nernst, however, rejected any such suggestion as a subterfuge and the argument which he used is typical of the man. 'His' theorem, so he said, was a fundamental law of thermodynamics and therefore must be all-embracing. If nobody had any idea as to how the specific heat of a perfect gas could be quantized, that was just unfortunate since, in accordance with his theorem, such an effect must exist. He called this as yet unobserved phenomenon 'gas degeneracy'. It was discovered twenty years later.

Nernst and Planck, the two leading physicists at Berlin agreed, admittedly for different reasons, that Einstein was the most outstanding theoretician of the day and that he must be won for the capital. A special professorship at the Academy of Sciences, free from teaching duties, was offered to Einstein, and Nernst and Planck personally journeyed to Zürich in order to persuade him to accept. It was a difficult task, since Einstein was likely to be unimpressed by the magnificence of the post and he had weighty reservations.

After a remarkably inauspicious early career, Einstein had been offered, at the age of thirty, a lectureship at Zürich. This was three years after publishing his fundamental papers on relativity and the quantum theory. In the following year he had become professor at Prague and in 1912 at Zürich. Now, in 1913, he was asked to come to Berlin.

Born in Germany of Jewish parents, he had later accepted Swiss nationality. Whether he did this because it enabled him to get a job at the Berne Patent Office or because he preferred Switzerland to Germany in any case, is difficult to say. Probably both reasons played their part, and the glamour of Berlin left him fairly cold. Moreover, ten years earlier, immediately after landing the job at the Patent Office, he had married a Serbian co-student, Mileva Marič. Now the marriage had deteriorated and Einstein knew that Mileva would not come with him to Berlin permanently. It meant that he would have to part from their two sons.

After Nernst and Planck had done their best to induce Einstein to accept the Berlin professorship, he sent them off on a trip in the Alps while he made up his mind. Nernst later recorded with relief that on their return Einstein met them at the station, waving a white handkerchief, the agreed sign that he had decided for Berlin.

The special professorship for Einstein was largely of Nernst's making. It was part of an enormous scheme to strengthen science in Germany still further and especially, of course, in Berlin. It all started with the idea of a National Chemical Laboratory which, Nernst felt, was required as a partner for the National Physical Laboratory initiated by Helmholtz and Siemens. He was on good terms with the leaders of industry, who were quite prepared to finance the scheme, and he could also count on the Kaiser's support. It was here that Nernst was far more successful than even he had anticipated. The Kaiser listened to Nernst because he was a man after his own heart, a noted scientist with progressive ideas who would give a balanced opinion in a decisive manner. Also, Nernst was no sycophant and would talk to the Kaiser in a forthright and informal way which appealed to Wilhelm, who frequently asked him to meals at the palace.

Nernst's proposal to strengthen science further in Germany by a large Government laboratory was enthusiastically received. The Kaiser's imagination was taken up by the idea of creating a centre of research which would add further lustre to his reign. He was convinced that science and technology were going to be the most important aspects of the future and that it must be Germany's foremost aim to encourage them. It was this resolve, which the Kaiser had frequently expressed, that induced men like A. F. Lindemann to send his two sons to study in Germany.

The idea of the new laboratory was just the right thing for the Kaiser, except that it was not nearly ambitious enough. Nernst was not slow in sensing the Kaiser's mood and his wish to become patron of the new institution. To be worthy of Imperial patronage it had to be of a grand design, unique in its function and unparalleled anywhere in the world. This surpassed the wildest dreams of Nernst and his fellow-scientists, who were only too willing to work out the details. On the 11th January, 1911, the 'Kaiser Wilhelm Gesellschaft for the Advancement of the Sciences' was founded in Berlin with a capital of eleven million marks. Magnificent Kaiser Wilhelm Institutes for chemistry, physical chemistry and medical research were built immediately at Dahlem, a western suburb of Berlin. It is significant of the Kaiser's lack of anti-Semitism that two of the new directors, Haber and Willstaetter, were Jews. A third Jew was appointed in 1913 as director of the Kaiser Wilhelm Institute for Physics, the building of which, however, was delayed by the war. This was Albert Einstein.

In 1911 Nernst scored another success in the organization of science, this time on the international scale. He met in Brussels Ernest Solvay, a chemist, who in 1863 had invented a new process for making sodium carbonate which was named after him. By exploiting the method commercially he had become very wealthy and now wished to aid science in some general way. Nernst suggested that this could best be achieved by holding periodic discussion meetings among outstanding scientists, each covering one or two topical subjects. Such meetings, the Solvay Congresses in Physics and Chemistry have taken place at intervals since 1911 and have become famous throughout the scientific world. A group photograph of the first Physics Congress in 1911 shows practically all of the outstanding physicists of the time; among them Planck, Einstein, Sommerfeld and Nernst with his favourite pupil, F. A. Lindemann, in the background.

5. Glorious Times

Life in Germany in the last years before the First World War was good. The growing pains of the new World Power had been left behind in the last century. Wealth was increasing in a pleasant and orderly manner in a country that had been taking over the fundamental concept of law and order on which the Prussian State had been built. Progress rather than conservatism was the keynote, but progress of a regulated and evolutionary kind. It was still Planck's world and not yet Einstein's. The last two decades had revealed strange new phenomena such as radioactivity and the X-rays discovered by Roentgen. Awkward contradictions had arisen between new observations and established theories. However, even those who were clear-minded enough to see them, like Planck, remained convinced that all these difficulties would eventually be resolved harmoniously without changing the accepted ideas concerning the physical world.

Social life, too, was running in reasonably settled forms. The rich were rich and the poor were poor, but not terribly so. In between there existed a large and comfortable middle class, into which to rise was not too difficult and into which to fall was not too painful. It was a comfortable world.

The Nernsts soon found that the flat in the Moltkestrasse was too small for entertaining in the capital. In Goettingen their circle had been the university, the other professors and the students. Berlin social life was very different with its glittering mixture of art, finance, industry, and the higher civil service as well as the generals and the admirals. Nernst was not going to miss out on this; he loved company and had enough money to be able to entertain in style. In fact, very soon he acquired the reputation of being the most hospitable professor in Berlin. Needless to say, some of his colleagues, who were less affluent, did not fail to comment on the ostentatious surroundings and grand manner in which they had been entertained. Admittedly, it was well above the usual academic standard, even in Berlin.

The house, Am Karlsbad 26, which Nernst bought after his first year in Berlin, had been built in the founder years by a famous architect. Am Karlsbad was a small and quiet private street in the centre of the town. A drive leading through a small front garden brought the visitor to a porch of coloured marble. The door, opened by a caretaker, led into a hall completely covered in black marble with bronze caryatids. The walls of the large reception rooms were hung with tooled leather and had panelled ceilings with gold decoration. Nernst had installed his own lamps as well as a few of his competitor Edison's—the latter to provide illumination until the electrolytic elements of the Nernst lamps had warmed up. Altogether, the atmosphere was of a somewhat sombre dignity. The study upstairs had two large desks which, like the rest of the furniture in that room, were covered in Nernst's usual manner with correspondence, manuscripts and other papers through which only he could find his way. This chaos was in complete contrast with the domestic accounts that were kept most efficiently by his wife.

In fact, it was Emma's almost unbelievable capacity for hard work that kept the establishment going. Nernst loved the children, especially the daughters, and insisted on a close family life with common meals but he left all arrangements to his wife. She had not only to run a large household and look after the education of five children but also to be ready for frequent visitors and to entertain on a large scale. In addition Nernst dictated all his papers to her. She also had to inspect his shirts before they were washed since he had the habit of making notes on the starched cuffs and these had to be copied by her so as not to get lost. She got up at half past seven every morning, and saw the children off to school while Nernst had breakfast in bed and never got up before ten. On one isolated occasion he went to the laboratory at nine and naturally found none of his co-workers there. This enraged him so much that he immediately sent telegrams to all of them, reminding them of their duties. Living close to the institute made it possible for him to come home for lunch, which was followed by an afternoon nap. Afterwards he had two cups of coffee, one black, to wake him up, and one white to be enjoyed. The real work was done in the evening and late at night, since he never went to bed before two o'clock in the morning. There can be little doubt that the strange working hours kept by his student, F. A. Lindemann, throughout his life were a direct heritage from his teacher.

It seems that Nernst's ability to work hard and, at the same time, to enjoy life to the full, was amply shared by Emma. Early in 1914 they went to South America where he had been invited to give lectures at a number of universities. He had to learn Spanish and Emma checked his progress in the same way as she checked the children's school work. She evidently enjoyed the trip and made a number of notes for her children. The Nernsts were everywhere lavishly entertained, particularly by the large German communities. She records, however, that on the trip back through France the mood of their colleagues there was sombre with forebodings of war.

As if work, a lively social life and travel were not enough to fill their

days, the Nernsts had bought in 1907 the country estate of Rietz, forty
miles from Berlin. Rietz had well over a thousand acres of fields, meadows
and forest, added to which Nernst rented shooting rights over nearly
another thousand acres. Since his childhood days at Engelsburg with
Aunt Nerger, love of the country had been extremely strong in him. Now
that the summit had been reached and he could well afford it, he wanted
to enjoy the country again, together with his family. Week-ends and,
above all, the school holidays were spent at Rietz. The house was large
enough for the children each to bring a school friend. The boys were
now big enough to accompany him to the shoot. Throughout the summer
guests were entertained there and one of the main events was large
shooting parties in January. The two Lindemann brothers came often
and on one occasion, to their acute embarrassment, the younger brother,
Sepi, also turned up unexpectedly. The Nernsts had not known of his
existence and it was explained to them that this was the black sheep of
the family.

As in Goettingen, the Nernsts gave summer parties for the members
of the institute. On these occasions a special railway carriage was hired
to bring them from Berlin to the little station near Rietz. The last of
these parties took place on Saturday, the 1st of August, 1914. The care-
free gathering was interrupted by a 'phone call to Nernst from the local
district official who told him that war had been declared. Germany's
short golden age had come to an end.

While in the 'thirties everybody who knew Hitler's Germany realized
that war was inevitable, in 1914 it came as a surprise to most people.
There had been much talk of the possibility of war but nobody took it
very seriously, particularly in Germany. Nernst had been an exception
and had lost all hope that peace could be maintained when the Archduke
Franz Ferdinand was killed at Sarajevo. Possibly his contact with colleagues abroad had given him a more realistic assessment of the situation.

Whatever had been its cause, the outbreak of war took place in an
enormous upsurge of patriotism that swept away all political dissensions.
The socialists voted in the Reichstag for the increased army estimates
with only a few of their members, like Karl Liebknecht and Rosa
Luxemburg, opposing this measure. The Kaiser jubilantly exclaimed that
he knew no more parties, only Germans. In the heady atmosphere of the
first few weeks of the war, with the German armies thrusting deep into
France, Wilhelm's tendency to regard himself as the supreme and only
leader of a great nation had surpassed all caution. Years of unbridled
adulation now culminated in a spontaneous ovation of enormous proportions which the Berliners gave him at the outbreak of war. Again and
again he had to appear on the balcony of the palace to show himself to

the cheering crowds. In was on this occasion that he proclaimed 'I shall lead you forward to glorious times'.

The Nernsts, too, were caught up in the patriotic upsurge. The elder boy, Rudolf, who read law at Berlin and had done his military service in the Guards, immediately joined his regiment and went to the front on the 8th August. The younger boy, Gustav, who, much against Nernst's wishes wanted to make the army his career, had just entered his first year at Heidelberg University. He, too, was called up straightaway to the cavalry and then joined the newly formed flying corps. Neither was to return.

With the boys gone, Nernst himself felt that he also wanted to play his part and he took service in the voluntary drivers' corps. It was his first experience of the armed forces, since owing to poor eyesight, he had never done military service in his youth Now, at fifty, he was not going to stand back when the whole country went to war. His enthusiasm led to situations which, viewed in perspective, lent a lighter touch to his efforts. It was part of his preparations to acquire the proper military etiquette with which he had remained unfamiliar. And so he marched up and down in front of his house and, under Emma's supervision, learned to salute correctly. There was also a flurry at his departure from the institute for the war. The staff had come out into the Bunsenstrasse to wave good-bye when Nernst suddenly got out of the car again, calling for the storekeeper. He explained that he wished to take along a liberal supply of rubber bungs so that he could stop up the leaks if the enemy fired into his petrol tank.

His first task was to take documents from the General Staff in Berlin to the 2nd Army commanded by von Kluck which was thrusting deep into France. He set out on the 21st August and, on arrival at head-quarters Kluck retained him there for further duties. In the next two weeks Nernst took part in the breathtaking advance of Kluck's army which brought them close enough to Paris to see at night the glow of the city's lights. The French Government had left the capital for Bordeaux and total victory, similar to Sedan in 1870, seemed at hand.

Then something went wrong. The rapid German advance was followed immediately by an equally rapid withdrawal, in the course of which Nernst and his car came close to being captured by the pursuing French. Finally the German retreat and the French pursuit came to a halt, far from Paris, near Rheims and St Quentin, where both armies dug in for the coming four years. The *blitzkrieg* of the Schlieffen plan had misfired and the jubilant march to glory became bogged down in the mud of Flanders and at the fortifications of Verdun. As yet the average German did not realize what had happened, but when Nernst came home at Christmas he said, to the horror of family and friends, that the war was lost It was not defeatism or lack of patriotism which had prompted this remark but the cold critical analysis of a scientist. He went on devoting all his energy to the war effort, but it was not any longer with the hope of winning the war, only of staving off defeat.

After his return from the Marne, Nernst was called in as technical adviser by the High Command and so were a number of other outstanding scientists. The employment of professors in the war effort had not been the generals' original intention. It was forced on them by circumstances which they had not foreseen. By their indecision, first in France and then in Russia, they had succeeded in creating the one situation for which their strategists had no plan. Germany was now faced with a defensive war, surrounded by enemies whose strength was bound to increase in time and, what was even more threatening, with very limited resources.

This was the state of affairs which Nernst had so clearly analysed in his depressing Christmas pronouncement. For the next four years Germany tried in vain to reverse this trend and to regain the tactical initiative. All hope of achieving this now rested with science and technology. Although Nernst did not really share this hope, the attempt came astonishingly near success. However, these efforts entailed a terrible penalty. With every temporary success and with each new substitute for blockaded raw materials, the generals were able to drag out the war longer. And with each further day, week or month of losses in the field and of starvation at home the fabric of German social life was corroded until almost nothing was left of it. The basic concepts of duty, law and order, the foundation on which the Prussian military State had been built, were now being destroyed by the generals themselves.

The German General Staff had counted on a lightning war. When this failed, they had hardly lost any equipment but pretty soon they were going to be desperately short of ammunition. The scientists were asked to produce conventional forms of ammunition and, if possible, new types of weapons which would take the enemy by surprise. Here the idea was that surprise and its demoralizing effect might tip the balance between defence and attack and give Germany the chance to regain the initiative.

Nernst was to deal with both these problems, but his first assignment was concerned with a novel form of warfare, chemical weapons. Accounts of the use of smoke or of asphyxiating vapours go back to antiquity, but they had never really caught on with the military practitioners who always looked upon them as some sort of extra-curricular activity. Nevertheless, in desperation the High Command was now going to give chemistry a try. Nernst was asked to find some suitable substance that could be enclosed in shells and that would be released when these burst. It was a task of which he approved. As we know, he had not much hope of victory and he had already lost his elder son in the early days of the war. Nernst always maintained that war should aim at incapacitating the enemy and rendering him unfit for fighting without killing or maiming him. His ideal of humane warfare was a weapon which would temporarily paralyse but have no lasting effect. Trials were made with irritant powders and tear-producing agents but the military were not impressed. They wanted something stronger.

It is not known whether Nernst was unable or unwilling to think up a more lethal agent, but the project was taken away from him and handed to Fritz Haber, the director of the Kaiser Wilhelm Institute for Physical Chemistry. Haber had just solved another problem in record time, the provision of propellants and lubricants which would withstand the low temperatures of the Russian winter. He now turned his ingenuity and the great resources of his laboratory to chemical warfare. He and his collaborators soon realized that considerable quantities of a chemical agent which affected breathing would have to be released in order to have an appreciable effect in the open air. Chlorine was chosen because it could be stored in large quantities in the liquid form in pressure cylinders. Moreover, it is heavier than atmospheric air and, when re-leased, tends to blanket the ground rather than be dispersed upwards. Finally, it was readily available from German resources. All the necessary tests had been made and large supplies of chlorine had been assembled in the spring of 1915 when the scene was set for the first gas attack. Field tests had shown that gas was a temperamental weapon which required very special weather conditions for its use. Haber soon found out that when the blades of grass in the meadows showed any movement, the breeze was already strong enough to cancel any scheduled gas attack.

Although the High Command had ordered chemical warfare, the officers at the front were deeply suspicious of the outside expert who had been sent from headquarters to instruct them in the fighting of their battles. They were singularly unimpressed with the professor's secret weapon, for the operation of which he needed special weather. This kind of friction, which is common to all armies, did not make for easy coopera-tion on the part of the professional soldiers, as Haber was to find out on more than one occasion. The gas attack took place at Ypres on the 11th April when chlorine was released in three waves at intervals of seven hours. The result was devastating. There were fifteen thousand casualties with a third of them fatal. Haber had proved convincingly the use of chemical warfare to the military who were now duly impressed but had, of course, made no provisions to follow up their victory.

Haber later maintained that if, as he had advocated, the gas attack had been made on a greater scale and had been exploited immediately by a strong force of assault troops, it would have led to the breakthrough that Germany needed for winning the war. Whether this would have been the case is, of course, idle speculation. As it was, the element of surprise was lost and gas masks as well as gas counter-attacks simply contributed to the pattern of a war that remained as static as it had been before. Nevertheless, the generals felt that Haber's efforts at Ypres had shown promise and he was made director of the new Chemical Warfare Service of the Ministry of War. His whole laboratory at Dahlem was turned over to experiments on new and better poison gases and they can be credited with the two major innovations in this field, the use of mustard gas and of phosgene. However, when at the end of the war count was taken, it had to be realized that, once the surprise had been overcome, gas was not a very effective weapon. The total amount used by both sides was 125 000 tons and these had accounted for less than five per cent of all casualties. The fatality rate of gas was two and a half per cent compared to twenty-five per cent in the case of firearms.

At the Hague Conventions in 1899 and 1907 Germany had agreed not to use asphyxiating gases in warfare and the chlorine attack at Ypres was a clear breach of this undertaking. However, this was a minor point in a war which had begun by the breach of Belgium's neutrality. For Haber there was a macabre sequel to his decision to develop poison gas. His wife, Dr Clara Immerwahr, who was also a chemist, had pleaded with him again and again not to work on gas warfare. His answer was that his first duty was to his country and that no argument, not even the entreaties of his wife, could shake his resolve. On the evening of Haber's departure for the front, Clara committed suicide.

In spite of his great achievements, which earned him the Nobel prize, and in spite of outstanding academic success, Fritz Haber was probably not a happy man. A typical example of the assimilated German Jew of the Wilhelminian era, his main aim in life had been to serve his country which ultimately rejected and humiliated him. Born in 1868, the son of a wealthy dye-stuff merchant in Breslau, he grew up in a household that was essentially German and in which there was nothing much to remind him of his Jewish ancestry. His family had long given up Jewish religious practices and Fritz' grandparents had already testified their adherence to Germanic ways by naming his father Siegfried. Of course, they had Jewish relatives and mainly Jewish business friends but these, too, regarded themselves first and foremost as Germans.

Nevertheless, as much as the Habers and their friends had relegated their Jewish descent to an unimportant aspect of their life, they were occasionally and unpleasantly reminded of it. In spite of his considerable ability, Fritz Haber found it impossible to secure an academic job after obtaining a doctorate in chemistry at the technical university in Berlin. He tried a variety of industrial positions in Hungary and Austria, mostly in factories belonging to his father's friends, but he held none of them for long. In the end, he entered his father's firm as a scientifically trained salesman. Father and son did not hit it off very well and Fritz again tried desperately to get a university position. The assistantship at the chemistry laboratory at Jena which he finally obtained was not much more than the position of a glorified bottle-washer.

Possibly Haber was just unlucky. However, he was a gifted scientist and unlike Einstein, who had cultivated self-isolation, he had tried to sell himself as hard as he could. Anti-Semitism was not rampant in the Kaiser's Germany but it was often strong enough to hamper the career of a young and unknown man. Later, too, Haber, suspected that he failed to secure a professorship for this reason. One of his colleagues remarked on a similar occasion that before thirty-five he was too young for a professorship, after forty-five he was too old, and in between he was a Jew.

Haber decided on evasive action and got baptized, a course taken by many of his contemporaries. He had always tended to be a conformist. As a student he had shown that he could drink as heavily as any young German and had even acquired a smart duelling scar. One wonders, however, whether there existed any connection between this mark of distinction and an accident which he had when walking after a drinking bout through a glass door in his father's house. Even if he was a conformist, Fritz Haber was a highly intelligent man with a critical mind who must have been aware of this conflict in his life. Possibly, the insistence on his patriotic duty in the face of his wife's distress was one of those instances in which Haber had to prove to himself that, in spite of anti-Semitism, he was a loyal German.

When in 1915 the paths of Nernst and Haber crossed over the chemical warfare question, it was not for the first time. Seven years earlier they had a heated argument over a problem that was to become even more important for the war. It concerned the provision of nitrogen in compound form. Nitrogen is the most important constituent of plant fertilizers and its supply is essential for any form of agriculture. There is no shortage of nitrogen in the world since eighty per cent of the atmospheric air is made up of it. However, plants are unable to take up nitrogen in this form. They require it in the form of compounds, such as nitrates, which they can extract from the soil. The naturally occurring nitrates are in turn mostly the debris of organic matter and sustain plant and, with it, animal life on a moderate scale.

All this changed with the population explosion that began in the late nineteenth century. The soil of Europe, in particular, had become exhausted and its peoples had to rely on fresh grain supplies from the Ukraine and North America. Now nitrates had to be imported to make Europe's soil fertile again, the sources being guano and natural deposits in Chile. However, in his presidential address to the British Association in 1898 Sir William Crookes warned the world that these supplies were running out fast and might be exhausted within a generation. He called on his fellow-scientists to save the world from starvation by finding a method through which the nitrogen of the air could be 'fixed' chemically in compound form.

The first method used was the oxidation of atmospheric nitrogen in a powerful electric arc, developed by Birkeland and Eyde in 1904. It relies on an ample supply of cheap electric power which in Norway is available from hydro-electric stations but otherwise becomes very expensive in the case of a product required in huge quantities. A much more promising solution would be the direct combination of hydrogen and nitrogen to form ammonia. It had been tried by a number of scientists but led to no success because no method existed of predicting chemical equilibrium.

When Nernst had embarked on his thermodynamical considerations in order to discover the means of equilibrium prediction, the question of ammonia synthesis was one of the foremost problems awaiting solution. The thermodynamical way of looking at a reaction is a little more sophisticated than that usually adopted by a chemist. Instead of simply stating that two substances combine to form a third one, thermodynamics regards this state of affairs as an equilibrium between the reaction partners and the product. In many cases this makes little difference to the customary ideas. If a match is set to a mixture of hydrogen and oxygen gas, the reaction will run its course with explosive speed and water is formed with no appreciable traces of oxygen or hydrogen gas left. In other words, the chemical equilibrium is one hundred per cent in favour of the product. However, this is not always the case and the ammonia equilibrium is an example. Its very simple equation can be written as

$$3H_2 + N_2 \rightleftharpoons 2NH_3$$

and it means that three hydrogen molecules (H_2) and one nitrogen molecule (N_2) can combine to form two ammonia molecules (NH_3). However, the little arrows attached to the equality sign indicate that the reaction proceeds in both directions, hydrogen and nitrogen combining all the time while simultaneously ammonia is decomposing. The equation therefore describes an equilibrium.

What is important is to find out how much material there is on either side of the equation respectively. It if turns out that the concentration of ammonia on the right-hand side is minute, then the exploitation of the equilibrium must appear pretty hopeless. As we have seen, Nernst's heat theorem permitted this calculation, provided such data as the scientific heats of the substances involved were measured. In view of the importance of the problem, Jost in Nernst's laboratory investigated the ammonia equilibrium in 1907. One of the reasons for this research was a paper on the same question which had appeared three years earlier and had reported an experimental determination of this equilibrium. It now appeared that these values when used in the equilibrium calculations seemed to disagree with Nernst's theorem. The author was Professor Haber at the Technical University of Karlsruhe.

Nernst, in spite of his flair for making inventions and thinking up elegant experiments, was at heart a theoretician. His chief interest was in the fundamental laws of nature and any practical application of his work was developed as a side line. Haber, on the other hand, was first and foremost a chemical technologist. He was extremely well read in the theoretical aspects of his work but to him the command of theory was not an aim in itself. He had acquired it so that he could turn it to applications. He shared Nernst's burning interest in physical chemistry but for rather different reasons. What for Nernst was a key to the understanding of the works of God was for Haber a means of extending the works of man.

After the unsatisfactory job at Jena, Haber had obtained an assistantship at the technical university in Karlsruhe and in the atmosphere of this institution with its strong engineering bias, Haber began to show his genius. Only two years later, he presented his thesis for the lecturership and was accepted into the faculty. He wrote a number of books on electrochemistry and physical chemistry and his work began to attract able students who became the nucleus of his research school. In 1906, at the age of thirty-eight, he was appointed to a professorship. In the following year, at the annual meeting of the Bunsen Society in Hamburg, he had to face Nernst in a tough discussion on the validity of his ammonia data.

Nernst could be aggressive in a very forthright manner. He was only four years older than Haber but he was regarded as one of the world's greatest authorities in his field whereas Haber was still very much the coming man. Moreover, Haber was very sensitive to Nernst's accusation of slipshod measurement since in the previous year one of his students had published erroneous data. Nernst, on the other hand, was upset that Haber should defend data which threatened the acceptance of his new law of thermodynamics. In the end it turned out that the discrepancy was not very serious since the two rival experiments had been carried out under different conditions. However, the public disagreement in Hamburg had not endeared the two scientists to each other and while relations between them remained polite, they could hardly be described as cordial. Now and then one of them, and usually Nernst, would make a caustic remark about the other, and I remember attending a large scientific gathering at which both Haber and Nernst were on the rostrum, neither taking the least notice of the other's presence.

After the Hamburg meeting both Nernst and Haber went back to their laboratories to check their data and each found that they had been right. Nernst's experiments had been made, however, at much higher pressures than Haber's, and Nernst had a very good reason for this choice. The equilibrium equation shows that there are four gas molecules on the left side against only two on the right which means that the product, ammonia, occupies only half the volume of the reaction partners, hydrogen and nitrogen gas. Pressure will therefore favour the smaller volume, that is ammonia, and the equilibrium is shifted in the desired direction. Temperature, too, affects the equilibrium and the calculation showed that more ammonia would be produced at low than at high temperatures. Unfortunately, the speed of reaction at low temperature is slow and while the equilibrium was favourable, it would take far too long to make ammonia in this way to be technically feasible. Nernst decided, as Haber had done two years earlier, that nitrogen fixation by making ammonia was far from hopeful.

That is how things stood in 1907. Nernst was satisfied that his data had been correct and that his theorem had weathered the test successfully. Moreover, he was far too busy with the exploration of new avenues of fundamental research which the third law had opened for him. He therefore terminated his consultantship with the chemical works of Griesheim–Elektron on the ammonia synthesis since it did not promise an easy solution. In later years he readily admitted that he had lost interest in the problem too early but there was a limit to the investigations which even Nernst could carry out at one and the same time.

For Haber the challenge of pioneering an industrial process in the face of overwhelming difficulties was irresistible. It was exactly the task at which he was better than anyone else. He now had all the data required to calculate the lowest temperature at which ammonia was formed in reasonable quantity and the pressure at which this had to be done. The result looked fairly dismal. Technically the combination of high pressures and high temperatures is extremely difficult and even when pushing these conditions to the very limit of industrial feasibility and safety, the top output of ammonia was far too slow.

However, in many cases a chemical reaction can be speeded up by catalysis, a process on which Ostwald had worked and which had gained him the Nobel prize. It is a complex subject and quite different mechanisms can be involved, but the salient feature is always the same. An additional substance, the catalyst, is brought into the vessel in which the reaction is taking place and its presence greatly promotes the chemical change without, however, changing the catalyst itself. While many porous substances, as for instance charcoal, have quite generally a catalytic effect, a much higher yield can often be achieved by a more sophisticated choice in which more than one type of catalytic action is involved. Such highly efficient catalysts are very specific to the reaction under consideration and to the conditions under which it proceeds. Finding a suitable catalyst for the ammonia synthesis and matching it to the working condition was the kind of chemical technology in which nobody was more adept than Haber. After extensive trials he became convinced that, after all, nitrogen fixation could be made an industrially viable project. The way to it would clearly be arduous and expensive, requiring many large-scale trials, but the prize was enormous.

Using osmium and uranium catalysts, the reaction was found to be speeded up very considerably and one of the largest chemical manu-facturers, the Badische Anilin und Soda Fabrik, began to support Haber's research by retaining him as their adviser early in 1908. Then, in July 1909, Haber and his assistant R. le Rossignol were able to show con-vincingly by their laboratory experiments that success was in sight. Badische Anilin assigned to the project their most brilliant young chemical engineer, Carl Bosch, whose main tasks were to find an industrially more suitable catalyst and to design the high pressure reaction vessels operating at elevated temperatures. Both problems were solved in a remarkably short time. For many years, however, nothing was known about the suc-cessful iron compound catalyst developed by Alwin Mittasch, except that it certainly was different from the substance stated in the patent specifica-tion. The stakes were rather too high to allow for candour. In 1911 the whole process was sufficiently perfected for the directors of the Badische Anilin to decide on the building of the first Haber–Bosch plant with an annual output of 9000 tons of ammonia.

Nernst realized now that he had lost interest in nitrogen fixation too early and that Haber of all people had solved the problem which he himself had given up. However, Nernst could not help admiring brilliance and success when he saw it, even if, as in this case, the inventor was not his particular friend. He had been asked to present on the 1st October, 1913, a Jubilee address at the German Museum in Munich and had chosen 'The Importance of Nitrogen for Life' as his subject. In it Nernst drew attention to the growing shortage of naturally occurring nitrogen fertilizers in much the same way as Sir William Crookes had done fifteen years earlier. Now, however, Crookes' hope that science would find an answer to the dilemma facing mankind had come true and Nernst said: 'It appears that mass production of nitrogen compounds fixed according to Professor Haber's process is imminent'. In fact, the Haber–Bosch plant of the Badische Anilin at Oppau near Mannheim began to operate in the same year.

Crookes as well as Nernst had only mentioned the importance of nitrates as fertilizers. They are, however, equally essential for the production of explosives. It is doubtful whether the successful start of the Oppau plant in 1913 had any effect on the German decision to risk war a year later. The High Command, in any case, was counting on a short war and, as was to become clear soon enough, had made no serious plans for prolonged hostilities involving a blockade of necessary raw materials. When, after three months of war, it became clear that at both fronts the prospect of early victory had faded, the Haber–Bosch process suddenly acquired highest priority in the German plans. The stockpile of Chilean nitrates for explosives was rapidly running out and the position concerning fertilizers was, if anything, even more threatening. Even allowing for an ample supply of these, Germany was not able to grow all the food she needed. Without nitrates, serious starvation was likely to occur within one year.

But for Haber and the brilliantly organized German chemical industry, the High Command would probably have had to sue for peace within twelve months. The industrialists had shown more foresight and less optimism than the generals. With the prospect of war becoming more real, the Badische Anilin had decided, even before its outbreak, to set up a larger fixation plant at Oppau to produce four times more ammonia than the first one. By 1916 even the enlarged plant at Oppau was outdistanced by the mammoth installation set up at Leuna, which stretches for almost two miles along the railway line from Berlin to Frankfurt. The industrial success of the Haber–Bosch process destroyed the Allies' hope of forcing Germany out of the war at an early date by blockading the shipping lanes. In fact, their own demand for nitrates began to exceed the imports from Chile, and both Britain and the United States in 1917 made attempts to build nitrogen fixation plants which, however, remained unsuccessful. After the war the Haber–Bosch process came into use internationally and by 1930 over eighty per cent of the world demand for nitrates was satisfied from nitrogen fixation plants.

After the failure to gain a lightning victory in 1914, the war ceased to be a purely military operation and it now became necessary to mobilize the country as a whole. It became painfully clear at the same time that nothing had been planned for such a contingency. Industry had now to step in and it was, on the whole, with pretty bad grace that the High Command consented to cooperate with civilians. Prussian tradition and practice provided for civilians to receive orders but not to give them. The next four years were dominated by the dichotomy between military pigheadedness and civilian common sense with the generals winning every decision and losing the war.

The man whom the Kaiser had called in to coordinate the whole

German industrial effort was a Jewish industrialist and financier with a scientific training. Walther Rathenau was the son of the founder of the Allgemeine Elektrizitaets Gesellschaft, to whom Nernst had sold his lamp patent twenty years earlier. It seems that the considerable loss which the A.E.G. had made on this transaction left personal relations untarnished since Nernst and Walther Rathenau had remained close friends, each admiring the other's great ability. Rathenau certainly was the ideal man to act as coordinator, combining an excellent grasp of Germany's economic potential with sound judgement and immense personal tact.

However, it was now too late. Even worse than the shortage of munitions was the ever increasing shortage of food. The towns were naturally much worse off than the country and anyone who had relatives or friends on the land was privileged and envied. The usual Sunday outings of the townspeople turned into foraging parties at which trinkets and other treasured family possessions were bartered against bacon, butter and eggs. This new pastime enriched the German language by a term which became a firmly established standard verb: 'to hamster'. Nernst solved the food problem of his family in characteristic fashion. The raw material was provided by the shoot at Rietz and this was taken to the large municipal refrigerated storehouse in Berlin where he had rented private space. Thus, protected by paternal ingenuity, the girls grew up strong on game—in and out of season.

After the chemical warfare episode which, together with his service in France, had earned Nernst the Iron Cross, second class, he was entrusted with the development of explosives. Most of the work was done at the testing ground of Wahn near Cologne where he lived a good deal in 1915. Emma went with him. Nothing much is known about this work, except that with Marckwald he invented a new powerful agent, guanidine perchlorate. Some of the research was done at his Berlin laboratory, always in his usual impatient manner, filling his co-workers with admiration and horror for the off-hand way in which he dealt with new explosives. Usually the preliminary tests were done at the proving grounds at Spandau, ten miles away. However, on one occasion Nernst could not be bothered to go that far and instead packed the charge into a small disused well in the laboratory court. The bottom appeared to be filled with rubble and it was open at the top. This, Nernst argued, would direct the blast skywards without doing any damage. The firing took place just after noon while Rubens gave his daily lecture on elementary physics to an audience of about 300 students. They, as well as their lecturer, were duly startled, first by a terrific bang and immediately afterwards by complete darkness. The latter phenomenon turned out to be caused by dense clouds of dust which had been blasted into the lecture room. In his haste, Nernst had omitted to investigate the original purpose of the well, which in fact, was not closed at the bottom but opened into a number of ventilation shafts. This system of providing air for the lecture rooms had long been superseded by a more modern installation and the shafts were filled with dust and dirt that had accumulated in them since Helmholtz' days, forty years earlier.

Nernst's work in this time was chiefly concerned with the development of the trench mortar and again he spent some time at field tests on both the Western Front and the Eastern Front. In acknowledgement of his services he received first the Iron Cross, first class, and then the order *'pour le mérite'*, the highest decoration which the Kaiser could bestow. It was a closed order with a fixed number of holders, and Nernst always pointed out with pride that he was the successor to Count Zeppelin who had died earlier in 1917. This was the end of Nernst's war service and he returned to his academic duties.

The war dragged on and the Nernsts suffered another cruel blow when their other son, too, was killed at Verdun in April, 1917. Nernst wrote: 'Nothing is as good as physics to divert the mind from the present time which, in spite of the greatness achieved by our people, is nevertheless to be deplored'. It was the opening sentence of his famous monograph entitled *The Foundations of the New Heat Theorem*, and is dated 'December 1917'. He had fled from the miserable world of reality to find peace and solace in his scientific work, taking stock of past achievements. The book also was his farewell to the new world near absolute zero to which he had given meaning and content. Later his pupil, F. E. Simon, was to spend many years in clearing up numerous issues that Nernst had left unexplored, but as far as Nernst himself was concerned, he was completely satisfied that his theorem was correct. With beautiful clarity he set out the fundamental problem that had faced him, the solution that he had proposed and the proof of its correctness obtained from experimental evidence. Applications of the theorem to theoretical and practical problems of thermodynamics are discussed and above all he emphasized again the fundamental meaning of the new law in its connection with the new ideas of energy quantization. Only one real problem remained: no way had been found for applying the quantum theory to the motion of atoms in a gas. The 'gas degeneracy' predicted by him had not been found but Nernst was hopeful that at still lower temperatures than those which had as yet been reached, it would be found. That hope was still there when almost ten years later I entered the laboratory as a research student to start a doctoral thesis on the same old problem which still remained unsolved.

The copy of Nernst's monograph on my desk, which once belonged to Lindemann, looks more like a papyrus from an Egyptian tomb than a twentieth century scientific publication. Its pages are so fragile that they tend to crumble at even a light touch. The date of publication was 1918, the last year of the war and it is printed on a very poor ersatz paper. The ersatz glue which was meant to hold the spine together has fallen to dust. In much the same way the spine of everything else in Germany was cracking up. A nation of military robots down to the smallest child kept on unswervingly to follow the pigheaded orders of a leadership that had lost the war years ago but refused to acknowledge it.

When in 1917 Nernst wrote the dispirited introductory passage to his monograph on the third law, the death of his second son was not the only cause for his despair. A few months earlier he had an experience which depressed him as much as his personal loss. With Ludendorff in command of politics, it was clear that the Chancellor, Bethmann-Hollweg, had lost his battle against unrestricted submarine warfare and it was equally certain that, once this was declared, America would enter the war. With great clarity Nernst foresaw that a negotiated peace would become impossible and that the war must end with the downfall of the Hohenzollern monarchy. In the course of the years and with Nernst's frequent visits to the palace, the Kaiser had come to treat him as a personal friend. Now at the height of crisis, Nernst considered it his duty to put before the Kaiser his own depressing analysis of the situation as a warning of doom. He requested an audience which was immediately granted and which took place at Army Headquarters with Hindenburg and Ludendorff present. Nernst outlined the immense boost which the limitless American potential would give to the war effort of the Allies and he compared it with the rapidly dwindling German resources. The Kaiser and Hindenburg listened in silence when Nernst began to speak but Ludendorff interrupted him straightaway. He brushed aside Nernst's arguments as incompetent nonsense with which a civilian was wasting his time, a professor who was only able to make a fuss because the Kaiser happened to like him.

Soon enough Nernst's prediction was proved right. Inevitably, disaster followed disaster. Much against the Kaiser's wish Ludendorff had tried to mount an offensive in the spring of 1918 which he called the 'Kaiser battle', but it collapsed with enormous losses and on the 8th August, the black day of the German army, British troops broke through. Things now moved rapidly, hastened by the complete disintegration of the Austro-Hungarian monarchy and on the 29th September Ludendorff completely lost his nerve, informing the political leaders that the war was lost.

The standard history primer for German schools, issued six years later under the Weimar Republic, glosses over some of these events with a few glib phrases and remains silent about the others. Germany's young

generation was not to learn that her troops had been defeated in the
field and that the High Command had openly acknowledged the fact.
Instead, a legend was being created that the army, on the point of
ultimate victory, had been treacherously stabbed in the back by a
nefarious revolt at home.

6. Revolution

The military collapse, following years of disintegration of normal civilian life, inevitably encouraged some extreme left-wing politicians to try to establish a socialist State on Russian lines, hoping also to enlist help from the Bolsheviks. This, of course, was simply impossible. Germany was starving and so were the Russians. The Allies, the recent enemies, were the only hope for Canadian bacon and wheat and they clearly would continue the blockade if Germany chose to become a Soviet republic. Only one way remained to forestall such a disaster and that was to suppress these revolutionary intentions with the help of the army. That was the dilemma now facing the organized German Labour Movement, the Social Democratic Party.

It was in these inauspicious circumstances that the strange bed-fellows, High Command and Social Democrats, begot what was to become known as the Weimar Republic. Its relatively short life was a tangled period of events, dominated by political immaturity and the mixed blessings of proportional representation. To call the incidents preceding it a revolution is perhaps a trifle ambitious since what the Germans really wanted was not a new concept of society but peace and food.

Nernst, like many of his colleagues, bravely shouldered a rifle to defend the new State against anarchy. They themselves probably failed to realize that they were merely extras on the stage, whose presence was needed to demonstrate popular solidarity against the Communist danger but whose services as members of a fighting force were not seriously required. The High Command had a quite adequate supply of more efficient volunteers who were well trained in the liquidation of undesirables. It meant that the professors could soon return to their proper calling. In fact, they now had a much tougher job to tackle.

As it turned out a real revolution was taking place in science. Like any real revolution it had its roots deep in the past and its prophets had arisen in the midst of the old order. For more than ten years new discoveries had been threatening the well-established concepts of classical physics, but its practitioners had refused to admit that the foundations of the venerable structure were being undermined. Nernst was an exception because he had an unusually open mind and was habitually free from all prejudice, but even he and others who were equally prepared to accept new ideas failed as yet to assess their full meaning. However, in

Germany the war had played far greater havoc with the established social order than in the Allied countries and it was therefore not an accident that these new scientific ideas were taken up much quicker in Germany than elsewhere. Quite generally, people were more ready to accept new concepts, whether in political thought, art or science. Their old world had been destroyed. They were willing to give a new one a trial.

Two basically new ideas had been formulated in physics at the turn of the century, Planck's quantum theory of energy and Einstein's theory of relativity. Immediately after the war it was relativity rather than the quantum concept which aroused general interest and there are good reasons for this. First of all, Planck was a most unwilling revolutionary. As his very first paper on the quantum theory shows, he was fully aware of the far-reaching consequences to which his ideas led and these he regarded with horror. They threatened the basic concepts of classical physics which he had been teaching for decades and which he had come to accept as sacrosanct. We have already seen that he passed over in silence Einstein's application of the quantum principle. With equal perspicacity he saw that Einstein's theory of relativity, although revolutionary, was crowning rather than destroying the classical edifice. He therefore hailed it as a most worthy contribution to physics.

Einstein, on the other hand, did not mind being a revolutionary. He was a nonconformist by nature who wore his hair long and refused to have his suits pressed. Discussions with his first pupil, Otto Stern, also a future Nobel Laureate, who had come to work with Einstein in Prague, were conducted in a café which was attached to a brothel. Unlike Nernst, Einstein had been bad at school and only scraped through with difficulty. He did not distinguish himself during his studies in Zürich and was never considered for a lectureship. He even failed to secure a permanent position as a schoolteacher and subsisted precariously on temporary teaching jobs. He considered it a godsent opportunity when, through the kindness of the father of a former co-student, he was given an assessor's position at the Swiss Patent Office at Berne. The duties were not arduous and provided him with the kind of life he had been looking for, meaning peace and leisure to immerse himself in the unsolved problems of theoretical physics. To these he applied himself in complete isolation, which he kept up for several years during which the ideas were formulated that were destined to change the whole of physics. He later said that until he was thirty he had never seen a theoretical physicist, a statement which was qualified by somebody who pointed out that on occasion even Einstein must have looked into a mirror.

The main problem that intrigued Einstein was one which the leading theoreticians of the day, Lorentz and Fitzgerald, had found impossible to solve. It arose out of Maxwell's prediction of electromagnetic waves and their experimental discovery by Heinrich Hertz. Hertz' observations had left no doubt that Maxwell's idea of light being also an electromagnetic wave must be correct. In fact, the wave nature of light had already been confirmed much earlier by Young and Fresnel who demonstrated that rays of light interfere with each other in exactly the same way as trains of water waves on the surface of a pond. This immediately posed the question as to the medium in which the electromagnetic waves were travelling and which had never been observed. As a possible solution of the problem scientists had postulated the existence of an all-pervading substance: the ether.

Nobody had been able to think up an experiment by which the existence of the ether could be proved until at the end of the nineteenth century Albert Abraham Michelson found the solution to the problem. It involved the construction of an extremely sensitive optical device, to the perfecting of which he devoted the rest of his long life. The observation itself was a very accurate measurement of the velocity of light.

The original postulate required that the ether must be present everywhere, in empty space as well as in matter, and matter must be able to move through the ether without any friction. The Earth, too, in its orbit round the sun must move through the ether—at 112 000 km per hour. Just as the occupants of a fast open motorcar, even on a still day, will experience a strong wind, so the Earth in its motion through space should have a veritable ether gale blowing through it all the time. Since light is a wave motion in the ether, a flash of it produced by a terrestrial source should to an observer on Earth appear retarded when directed against the ether wind and speeded up in the downwind direction. This seemed to be a foregone conclusion on the basis of classical mechanics. However, Michelson's precision experiment left no doubt whatever that the speed of light was completely unaffected by the Earth's motion.

The only way out of this dilemma was proposed by Fitzgerald, who suggested that anything moving through the ether, such as the Earth and with it Michelson's apparatus, must be slightly shortened in the direction of motion. The degree of this contraction was assumed by Lorentz to be dependent on the ratio of the moving object's velocity to that of light. According to the mathematical equation proposed by him, the famous Lorentz transformation, the length of the object should shrink to zero when it reached the light velocity. However, even if this strange contraction phenomenon should exist, there was no explanation for it. This was the unhappy state of affairs in physics when the young revolutionary at the Berne Patent Office entered the scene.

Einstein discovered the flaw in physical thinking which had been missed by his illustrious contemporaries. They had considered time as an absolute, unvariable quantity. Instead of basing his ideas on classical

1 Walther and Emma Nernst (née
   Lohmeyer), 1892.
2 Emma Nernst with the three eldest
   children, 1899. Rudolf b. 1893, Hilde
   (later Mrs. Kalin) b. 1894 and
   Gustav b. 1896.
3 Domäne Engelsburg, 1904. Nernst and his dog Tyras with Frida and Edith Nerger
   (sitting), Aunt Anna Nerger (standing). At the window, Emma Nernst, and in the
   cart, the three eldest children.

4

4 Nernst's Hotel in Goettingen, the Graetzel House, which became known as the 'Cafe N'.
5 The Nernst family setting out from Goettingen for Berlin. The 'modern' professor had a motor car!

5

6   7

6 Rittergut Rietz. Nernst's country house.
7 The house am Karlsbad in Berlin where the Nernst family lived
from 1907 to 1922.
8 Nernst and Emma at the Hotel Burghof in Cologne. Nernst was
then engaged in the development of explosives during the First
World War.

8

9 The Solvay Congress at Brussels, 1911.

Standing: GOLDSCHMIDT, PLANCK, RUBENS, SOMMERFELD, LINDEMANN, DE BROGLIE, KNUDSEN, HASENOHRL, HOSTELET, HERZEN, JEANS, RUTHERFORD, KAMERLINGH ONNES, EINSTEIN, LANGEVIN.

Seated: NERNST, BRILLOUIN, SOLVAY, LORENTZ, WARBURG, PERRIN, WIEN, Mme. CURIE, POINCARÉ.

10   Portrait painted by Max Liebermann, 1912.

11   Max Planck, 1858–1947.

11

12

12   Erwin Schrödinger,
1887–1961.

13

13 Lise Meitner, 1878–1968.
14 Fritz Haber, 1868–1914.
15 Otto Stern, 1888–1969.

14

15

16 Max Born, 1882–1971.

16

17

17 Werner Heisenberg, b. 1901.

18 Max von Laue, 1879–1960.

19 Wolfgang Pauli, 1900–1958.

20 The Physical Chemistry Laboratory in the Bunsenstrasse in Berlin where Nernst became a professor in 1905.
21 Nernst giving a physics lecture to his students in Berlin, 1926.

22   Five Nobel Laureates: Nernst, Einstein, Planck, Millikan and von Laue at von
       Laue's house in Berlin, 1923.

23   Farewell Colloquium for Nernst, 1922, on the occasion of his leaving the
       Physico-Chemical Institute when taking up the Presidency of the Physical-
       Technical Reichsanstalt.
       From right to left, front row: Riesenfeld, Nernst, Marckwald, Noddack,
       Günther. Second row: Bennewitz, Eggert, x. Third row: x, Clara v. Simson, x,
       Bonhoeffer, F. (later Sir Francis) Simon.

24

24   Last picture of Nernst at Zibelle, 1940.
25   Nernst's country house at Zibelle where he spent his
     last years.

25

physics, Einstein started with the result of Michelson's experiment which he regarded as irrefutable, namely that the truly absolute and unchanging quantity is the velocity of light. The physical dimension of a velocity is a length divided by the time. Thus, with the same justification as postulating that a moving body is contracting, we can assume that the time, too, can vary according to the position of the observer. Einstein accepted the Lorentz transformation as correct and concluded that, since the length of the object could not become negative, the velocity of light must not only be invariant but also be the maximum velocity that can exist.

On the basis of this superb example of clear thinking, Einstein developed a new and perfectly consistent set of mathematical equations which was to replace Newtonian mechanics and which is known as the special theory of relativity. It describes a world in which the time takes its place on an equal footing with the three dimensions of space. This does not, of course, mean that Newtonian mechanics is utterly wrong. After all, it had proved its worth for centuries; but it is only an incomplete approximation, which is perfectly applicable when the motion observed is relatively slow and it breaks down completely for velocities approaching that of light; on the other hand, relativity is much more than a perfection of the classical equation. As we shall see presently, its new concept of the space-time continuum leads to completely unexpected and far-reaching consequences that could never have been derived from classical physics.

First of all, the fact that the propagation velocity of light also constitutes the limit for the motion of massive objects forges a link between the worlds of electromagnetism and of mechanics which did not exist before. A bridge had been formed between two vast fields of physical experience which till then had been completely independent. Secondly this common limitation of speed led to another fundamentally new link between mass and energy.

In order to propel an object, energy has to be imparted to it. A cannon ball is fired by the explosion of gunpowder in the barrel. More gunpowder has to be used to fire the bullet faster still and classical physics permits, in principle, the projectile to attain any desired speed, provided the propellant charge is made strong enough. Einstein's theory, on the other hand, does not allow velocities in excess of the speed of light and the relativistic equations of motion must see to it that this cannot happen. The classical formula relating the speed of a bullet to the propellant charge is simple in the extreme; it just equates this energy to the mass of the projectile multiplied by the square of its velocity. Since the energy can be raised to an arbitrary extent while the maximum speed must remain finite, the only way out is to allow for a change in the mass. In fact, relativistic mechanics requires the bullet to become gradually

D

heavier as it is speeded up until its weight becomes infinite at the velocity of light.

When Einstein first postulated this effect, its existence could not be proved by experiment since there was no means of firing projectiles with speeds approaching that of light. However, when the first observations on fast particles emitted in radioactive decay were made, it became clear that their motion did not obey the laws of Newton but those of Einstein. Since then the relativistic increase in mass has become a well-recognized feature, and the engineering blue-prints of our large machines for accelerating particles are based on Einstein's relativistic equations.

As more and more energy is needed to accelerate a projectile, which resists higher speeds by becoming heavier, it is clear that this additional energy is being transformed into mass. In fact, according to Einstein the law of conservation of energy has become invalid and must be replaced by a form which also takes account of the change in mass. In order to equate energy and mass, the latter must be multiplied by a factor of proportionality of the correct dimension and this turns out to be the square of the light velocity. This quantity happens to be very large and in our standard units of physical measurement is a number with twenty-one noughts. It explains at once why this transformation of energy into mass and *vice versa* had never been observed before Einstein predicted it from his theory of relativity. Owing to the large factor involved, the mass changes accompanying our conventional forms of energy production, like the combustion of coal or oil, are so small that they escape detection with even the most sensitive instruments. It was again the same thing as with the relativistic deviations from Newtonian mechanics which only became important at very high speeds. For the great majority of applications, the classical law of conservation of energy is quite good enough, its relativistic mass changes are only important at high energy concentrations.

Like the relativistic deviation at high speeds, the equivalence of mass and energy at first seemed to be of only theoretical interest. For once it was Planck and not Einstein who in 1908, almost with clairvoyance, commented on the immense energy which is locked up in the mass of the atom and which might possibly be liberated. He must have felt like a prophet of doom when, almost forty years later and two years before his death, he learned of the destruction of Hiroshima and Nagasaki. The first application of Einstein's equation was the solution of a problem that had worried chemists for a long time. They knew that the weights of many atoms are simple multiples of that of the hydrogen atom. Unfortunately this is not strictly true and much better agreement would have been obtained had the hydrogen atom been a little lighter. In fact, four hydrogen atoms weigh rather more than the next heavier one, that of

helium. This discrepancy can be avoided by assuming that when four
hydrogen atoms are fused into one helium atom, the excess weight is
transformed into energy. As we now know, this process does indeed occur
inside the sun and sunshine is, in fact, the relativistic energy production
arising from the 'mass defect' of hydrogen.

The relative nature of time, too, is quite a straightforward consequence
of the invariance of the velocity of light as can be illustrated by a simple
example. Let us think of two spaceships that are flying past the earth
on a parallel course and with the same speed. The first ship sends out a
light signal which is reflected from the surface of the second ship and
then recorded again when it returns to the first one. If the ships travel,
say, 150 000 km ($1 \cdot 5 \times 10^{10}$ cm) apart, the observer in the first ship will

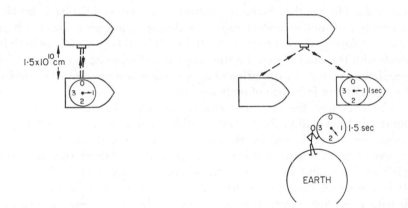

note that his signal comes back to him after one second since the speed
of light is 300 000 km per second. To an observer on Earth, however, the
path of the light signal will appear longer because, relative to him, the
ships, too, have travelled some distance while the signal was under way.
Now, according to Einstein, the speed of light is invariant and the
observer on Earth therefore finds that more than one second has elapsed,
since from his point of view the light had to travel more than 300 000 km.
Thus the time interval between the same two events, sending and receiving
the signal, varies according to the relative state of motion of the observers.
If for the observer on Earth the signal has covered a total distance of, say,
450 000 km, $1 \cdot 5$ seconds must have elapsed for him and he will conclude
that the clock on the spaceship is slow. Here again the relativistic prediction has since been verified by experiments. For instance, the time of
radioactive decay observed on a cosmic ray particle, arriving on Earth
with very high speed, was found to be many hundred times longer than
that measured when the particle is at rest.

Altogether, the time-honoured concept of simultaneity had lost its meaning. It became useless to say that two events took place at the same time unless the position and state of motion of the observer, too, was specified. Moreover, it is not much sense for an astronomer, who sees a flare appear on the sun, to say that the flare occurred eight minutes earlier because light takes eight minutes to travel this distance. Since no faster means exist to inform the observer sooner of this event, the latter only acquires physical reality for him at the moment when he sees it.

During the war Einstein had extended his theory of relativity from uniform to non-uniform motion. The basis of this 'general' theory is the equivalence of gravity and inertia which had already been considered by Newton. An observer inside a closed box sees a projectile passing through and, when plotting its path, notices that this is curved downward and a parabola. He has the choice of assuming that either his box is moving upwards with uniform acceleration or that it stands on a massive base, say the Earth, which attracts the bullet. The theory which essentially deals with the effect of mass on the properties of space leads to astonishing predictions such as the deviation of light passing by a massive astronomical body and to an influence of mass on time.

Unfortunately, the predicted effects are so small that they are at the limit of observability. Such confirmation as has been obtained might, moreover, be explained by theories of gravitation, different from that proposed by Einstein, although it is generally assumed that the road pioneered by Einstein's general theory of relativity is basically correct. It involves such concepts as the curvature of space and the variation of it with time. Space curvature was, incidentally, not a new concept and about a century before Einstein, Gauss had carried out a triangulation between distant mountain tops to see whether the sum of the angles was 180 degrees. It was, and today we know that any deviation from linearity in our part of the universe will make itself felt only at astronomical distances. The general theory further assumes that gravity, like electro-magnetic radiation, travels with the speed of light and attempts, so far unsuccessful, have been made to observe gravitational waves. Unlike the special theory, general relativity is far from being a completed chapter in physics. On the other hand, its cosmological significance is immense.

Even when we leave out the staggering prospects of Einstein's general theory of relativity, it is obvious that the results of special relativity were already bound to play havoc with many sacrosanct tenets of classical physics. Like any severe shock given to the human mind, the effect of relativity on physics was a delayed one. In the years before the war there had probably not been more than a dozen physicists in the whole world who fully understood the new theory in all its implications. To others it remained largely incomprehensible in its mathematical formulation and most had never even heard of it. The seeds of the scientific revolution were slow in germinating.

Then came the war and after the first few months of martial excitement came the long years of misery and tedium. Nernst was not the only one who tried to find solace in the escape provided by theoretical physics. Weary and dispirited, scientists everywhere turned to their subject, and one of the most important papers published by Einstein's pupil, Otto Stern, is dated from 'Lomscha, Poland' where his regiment was fighting. It was also a time for taking stock since in all countries experimental research had been stopped and no new results were coming in. This means that people were taking a second and closer look at the old results, and those who before the war had been too busy to read difficult theoretical papers now enjoyed doing so. These were the years when Einstein's theory was discovered by his colleagues.

Their reactions fell into two clearly divided groups—enthusiastic admirers and bitter enemies. The break with established concepts was too severe and the issue too important for physicists to stay neutral; you had to be either for or against. This division reflected the whole mental attitude of Germany after the war. There were the older people whose one wish was to return to conditions similar to those they had known before 1914, whereas the younger ones realized that an era had come to an end and that the clock could not be turned back. They sensed that the orderly and authoritarian pattern of the Prussian State had gone for ever and that there was a new world to come with intoxicating prospects of freedom, world peace and socialism. They felt no regrets at the prospect that physics would never be the same again either.

It has to be remembered that in those days there existed as yet no experimental proof whatever of Einstein's ideas, and their acceptance or rejection came close to articles of faith. The question which each physicist had to answer for himself was whether or not, at the state of existing knowledge, Einstein's theory was likely to be correct. There were only very few who, like Planck, saw that Einstein's hypothesis of the invariant speed of light removed at one stroke all the difficulties that the ether concept had created. Even fewer realized that, in spite of its revolutionary nature, relativity provided a purification of classical physics rather than its destruction.

As discussion on relativity flared up after the war, its supporters were in the minority. However, the majority had been driven into the hostile camp because their judgement was clouded by lack of understanding. Einstein had stated his theory in strict mathematical form which most physicists at the time found difficult to interpret in terms of everyday observation. This is not accidental since relativistic deviations from Newtonian mechanics only occur at speeds that are so high that they are beyond the usual range of experiment. In fact, phenomena such as relativistic mass change or time change are not part of our daily experience. In the past, mathematical description had been used as a concise form of shorthand to give an account of the physical laws discovered by experiment. Sometimes this mathematical framework had been extremely useful in predicting further phenomena but these, in the end, could be comprehended in ordinary non-mathematical language.

It was different with relativity. In addition to his superb powers of analysis and his deep insight into the meaning of physical laws, Einstein had a brilliant command of mathematics. The logic by which he proceeded in his work was purely mathematical and it was then a further task to discover the physical meaning of the results. Often there is no way at all to comprehend them in terms of daily experience. The space-time continuum is four-dimensional and while we can use certain mental subterfuges to help us, we simply cannot visualize four-dimensional space. Nevertheless, as the observational results show, four-dimensional space has as much reality as any of the descriptions on which we rely in ordinary life. Thus, in addition to his fundamental contributions to physical theory, Einstein laid the foundation of a new philosophical method which has completely revolutionized all physical science.

The method consists in relying only on the result of direct experimental observation, to express it in mathematical form, and then to correlate this with the mathematical interpretation of other observations. The final aim is to construct a consistent mathematical edifice on the basis of which further experiment can be designed. Two things have to be emphasized. First, the final proof of the usefulness of the mathematical structure rests with the experiment undertaken for its confirmation. Secondly, the choice of the mathematical method is not an automatic process. It is here that the genius of the outstanding theoretician must make the correct selection or even develop new mathematical techniques. It means that by his calling he has to be a physicist who knows a lot of mathematics and not a mathematician who knows physics.

Naturally, ingenious choice of mathematical methods or their creation goes back to Newton and Leibnitz. However, modern physics as initiated by Einstein goes a step further since it purposely divorces itself from visualizing the result. Here mathematical logic proceeds in its own right and its conclusions may lead to new physical properties to which we give names as the 'spin' or 'strangeness' of elementary particles which pass our comprehension but which nevertheless turn out to be relevant quantities, the usefulness of which can again be tested by experiment.

Many physicists who comprehended the results of special relativity also comprehended the radical change in physical thinking which its acceptance would involve. For those who abhorred this change the only way out was to hope that the theory might be wrong. This then would mean a return to models that could be visualized in concrete form. Among them was Lindemann. On his shelves I found a doctoral dissertation on relativistic problems which his friend and co-student Walter Schottky had sent him. It is dated 1912 and contains the handwritten dedication: 'To the esteemed enemy of the theory of relativity, with kindest regards'. Needless to say, Lindemann soon realized that the stand he had tried to take was quite untenable and he, too, became an ardent admirer of Einstein's. His case, that of a man of the highest intelligence but with a conservative trend of mind, is typical of most of his contemporaries. They instinctively disliked a radical change being forced on their subject but became ardent adherents when they discovered that it was a change for the better which offered new avenues of cognition.

However, there remained a few who unbendingly denied the value of relativity and who reinforced their statements by personal attacks on its author. Most of these were scientists who had failed to gain recognition for their own work—usually for good reasons—and therefore bore a grudge against anyone who had been successful. However, there were two notable exceptions. Philip Lenard and Johannes Stark, who both received Nobel prizes, but in later years turned into rabid anti-Semites. Lenard's case, in particular, was pathetic and ludicrous at the same time. He was a Hungarian, born in Bratislava, who became professor at Heidelberg and was forever keen on trotting out the Germanic heritage. Moreover, he had been a student of the great Jewish physicist Heinrich Hertz and was so proud of this connection that he wrote Hertz' biography. In his later years, this proved a constant source of irritation to Lenard and he and his Nazi friends were forever trying to explain it away. In the end he decided that Einstein and the Jews had succeeded in poisoning the whole of German physics and the door to his office bore the notice 'No entry to Jews and Members of the German Physical Society'.

This sort of thing could be passed over in silence if it had not found an echo in much wider circles. At the end of the war the theory of relativity was discovered not only by the scientists but also by the Press. The idea of a fourth dimension irresistibly attracted journalists, spiritualists and a lunatic fringe of philosophers. Einstein suddenly became a figure of public interest and scores of articles and books on relativity were published, mostly by people who had not the slightest notion of physics. Inevitably, the anti-Semitic attacks by men like Stark and Lenard were taken up in some of the papers, and soon enough there were anonymous threats to liquidate the 'relativity Jew' Einstein. Unfortunately, utterances of this kind had to be taken seriously since in the years after 1918 assassination had become commonplace in Germany. Einstein seriously considered again leaving his native country, to which he had returned rather reluctantly a few years earlier. However, Planck, Nernst and almost every scholar of standing acted promptly and with commendable vigour, with the result that the campaign in the gutter Press died down immediately. The anti-Semitic attacks ceased—at least for a time.

The wave of anti-Semitism that began to engulf Germany after the war was not an accidental phenomenon. The myth, created by the generals after the war, that they and their troops had never been defeated was, of course, unacceptable unless the blame could be attributed to somebody else. Ludendorff, who after himself admitting defeat on the 29th September, 1918, and then fleeing to Sweden, was particularly interested in establishing this legend firmly and he is credited with finding the solution. He was a rabid anti-Semite who had turned away from Christianity because it was founded by a Jew and he announced that at the moment of certain victory, the army had been 'stabbed in the back by the Jews'. How this was done, never became clear, but in due course his battle-cry was taken up by the Nazis. For the time being, the generals decided on the 'elimination' of prominent Jews and their sympathizers. Einstein, needless to say was on their list.

The special branch entrusted with this task operated under the code name *Organisation Consul* under a Captain Hermann Ehrhardt who, at the same time quite openly led a commando of toughs known as the Ehrhardt brigade. It was one of the *Freikorps* composed of ex-service men which were formed by former army officers after the war. The Ehrhardt brigade which soon became the most notorious of these organizations had its training in the Baltic provinces and they had chosen as their emblem the swastika painted on their steel helmets. Later, Hitler took it over for the flag of his Nazi Party.

The existence of the *Organisation Consul* was kept rather quieter, although it was clear to everybody that the assassinations were always well planned. The right-wing Press described them as *Feme*, an expression derived from the illegal secret courts in the Middle Ages. This term was meant to elevate these brutal and cowardly murders into heroic deeds of patriotism. After wholesale liquidation of left-wing political leaders, the most important targets were successful politicians of the republic. In 1921 Matthias Erzberger, a former Minister of Finance, was shot while on holiday. In 1917 he had agitated in the Reichstag for peace negotiations and later had introduced financial measures that were helping the republic to regain prosperity. One year later it was the turn of the Foreign Minister, Walther Rathenau. He was murdered in broad daylight in Berlin on the way to his office, when his car was machine-gunned and attacked with hand grenades. Owing to his high executive position during the war Rathenau had been a close witness of the General Staff's mismanagement and now he had become even more dangerous. His integrity had gained the respect of Germany's former enemies and he was on the way to consolidating European policy aimed at lasting peace. Usually the *Organisation Consul* succeeded in arranging for the escape of its assassins into safe countries. In the rare cases when the murderers were caught red-handed, they were given ridiculously light sentences by judges who knew what was healthy for them.

Walther Rathenau had been one of Nernst's close friends. The news of the assassination shattered him completely. Like so many German intellectuals, Nernst hoped that the Weimar Republic might develop into a new democratic Germany without too drastic a break with the past. He never engaged in party politics but frequently used his very considerable influence to condemn racial propaganda and extremist agitation. As his career shows, he was a pretty good diplomatist who knew how things could be done efficiently but he was at the same time completely fearless when speaking up for important causes. In 1917, when Ludendorff's power was at its zenith, Nernst openly advocated peace negotiations under conditions that went even farther than those favoured by the Reichstag opposition. Being convinced that the war had been lost a long time ago, he pointed out that to forgo annexations was just not good enough and that the return of Alsace Lorraine, taken away from France in 1871, would have to be offered. Discrimination on racial or religious grounds, such as anti-Semitism, was to Nernst quite inconceivable, and he regarded it as beyond the limits of elementary human decency. Rathenau had been just one of his many Jewish friends and Nernst's complete lack of prejudice was shown when in 1920 his eldest daughter Hilde married Dr Heinz Cahn, a Jewish pupil of Emil Fischer.

Nernst had sold the Rietz estate in 1917. Each visit had evoked memories of the happy days when he took his two boys there shooting and he could not bear it any more. Instead he bought Dargersdorf, north of Berlin, but before he could get accustomed to the place, he decided to sell it again. Early in 1920 a crisis had arisen. The Allies were preparing a list of persons who might be prosecuted as war criminals and it transpired that all scientists who had worked on weapon development were on it. Nernst was not so much perturbed as furious, pointing out that it was all the fault of Haber with his chemical warfare. In fact the German Ministry of Foreign Affairs had warned the scientists that they might be in serious trouble and issued them with false passports advising them to leave for 'safe' countries. So Nernst sold Dargersdorf in a hurry in order to provide the family with liquid assets which might be needed in this emergency. He went first to Sweden and then to Switzerland but soon the scientists were taken off the list and Nernst and his colleagues returned to their posts.

In fact, in the same year Nernst received the Nobel prize for the third law of thermodynamics. Einstein was to follow in 1921. Altogether the Germans were harvesting at this time a rich crop of these outstanding awards. In 1918 Haber had received the chemistry prize and Planck the physics one. Other prizes had gone to Willstaetter in 1915 and to Stark in 1919. Wien, on whose radiation formula Planck had based his work, had been honoured in 1911 and one of Planck's pupils, Max von Laue, had been given the physics prize in 1914.

Laue was the unique case of a member of the Junker class to become an outstanding scientist. Even so, throughout his life he looked and spoke like a Prussian general. His lectures and his discussion remarks consisted of a series of short barks, which issued not very distinctly from underneath a moustache. He himself was acutely aware of this failing and went so far as to undergo a course of speech therapy which, however, proved quite worthless. His writings, on the other hand were most concise and elegant. Training as a Prussian officer had made Max von Laue a very courageous man and it is perhaps significant that he alone stood up against Nazi persecution of his colleagues. The fact that he belonged by birth and upbringing to the inner circle of the Officers' Corps may possibly have saved him from punishment. If so, he himself was unaware of it since, even after the Second World War he used to say 'the generals' were after his skin. Nernst was a close friend of Laue's, though on occasion he found his extreme correctness amusing. There was a prize awarded by the university which, by silent agreement, went in rotation to different faculties. One year it was the turn of physics and one of Laue's pupils was the only applicant, so Nernst congratulated Laue before the event. Laue was taken aback, pointing out that the prize was open to all subjects. Nernst was deeply shocked. 'Just imagine,' he said to me, 'colleague von Laue did not even know that the whole thing is fixed.' At one of the university festivities Nernst met a retired general whom somebody had brought along as a guest. Learning that Nernst was a physicist, the old man recalled that many years ago at the famous officers' training school at Lichterfelde they had had a cadet who had proved utterly useless at military life. This was particularly sad since he had come from a good old Prussian family, and the fellow had then decided to study physics. However, the general felt that Nernst probably would never have heard of him, a certain Herr von Laue. Nernst told the general that not only did he know Laue but that Laue had received the Nobel prize. At this the old man's eyes lit up and he said how glad he was for the family that the cadet whom they had to send away had after all proved not completely useless.

The first visitor from abroad after the war was Lindemann, who turned up in Berlin unannounced, and straightaway went to Nernst's house, Am

Karlsbad. The only member of the family there was Edith, who was surprised and delighted, having had a girlish crush on the tall, good-looking tennis champion in the days before the war. She rang up her parents at their estate of Zibelle and immediately took Lindemann out to see them. Their meeting turned out to be completely unaffected by what had happened in the intervening years. No shadow had fallen on the old friendship between teacher and pupil which had been forged in years of common interest and work. Fortunately, science tends to be thicker than politics, and Lindemann was happy during his stay with the Nernst family. He was delighted when Emma immediately prepared for him the special vegetarian dishes of which, she knew, he was fond. Lindemann tended to be a shy, lonely man and this isolation increased with time. Probably the years of his doctorate work in Nernst's laboratory were the happiest in Lindemann's life and also the most formative. In spite of the difference in character and appearance between the two men, many of Lindemann's attitudes in later life were a clear legacy of his apprenticeship with Nernst. Above all, the certainty that his judgement was right and the tenacity with which he stuck to it were the results of Nernst's influence.

Lindemann had exhibited this supreme confidence in his own powers during the war in a truly spectacular manner. One of the main problems confronting scientists at the aircraft research establishment in Farnborough, where Lindemann worked, was the phenomenon of 'tail spin'. A 'plane whose engine failed would often go into a steep nose-dive, slowly rotating about its own axis and many pilots crashed in this way. Lindemann worked out on paper that, provided the failure occurred at sufficient height, the kinetic energy gained by the plane in its fall should be large enough to provide a subsequent glide to a safe landing. Although his own flying experience was very limited, Lindemann took up a 'plane, cut out the engine and then, fairly close to the ground, he pulled the 'plane out of the nose-dive and landed it safely.

Immediately after the war Lindemann had been elected to the professorship of physics at Oxford and he was now hoping to continue there the kind of work in which he had been engaged with Nernst in Berlin. However, Nernst himself was beginning to lose interest in physical chemistry. The monograph on the third law, written in the dark days of 1917, was more or less his farewell to the subject. He had no doubt that a number of awkward cases which still seemed to contradict the third law would be cleared up to satisfaction, though this opinion was not necessarily shared by all his colleagues. However, he was fortunate to gain just then a very gifted research student, F. E. Simon, who was to make the firm foundation of the third law his life's work. Nernst now turned his mind to those problems which he himself considered still unsolved. Foremost among these was the phenomenon of 'gas degeneracy' which he had predicted. However, before it could be solved, physics still had a long way to go.

After his return from the escape to Sweden and Switzerland, Nernst looked for another estate to buy and finally succeeded in acquiring Zibelle, near Muskau in Silesia, a little over a hundred miles south-east of Berlin. The purchase had been difficult since hardly anyone was willing to sell land. The reason for this reluctance was a further calamity which had befallen Germany after the war. With the demand for enormous reparations and the exhaustion of resources during the war, economic difficulties were piling up. In an attempt to overcome these, the Government had begun to print more and more money without proper security. The lack of cover by assets produced devaluation of the currency which prompted the printing of still more money and the country was plunged into an ever deepening vortex of inflation. Unfortunately this was not sheer incompetence and stupidity and there was method in this madness. Debts, particularly those owed by industry, were wiped out because they could could now be repaid in money that had become essentially valueless. It was not a painless process. People with fixed incomes, pensioners and those who had saved for retirement became paupers in the course of a few months.

The backbone of stable German society, the large middle class which had suffered badly during the war, now ceased to exist. Instead a new type appeared, the *Schieber* which literally means 'shifter', operators on a small scale who knew where to find all kinds of supplies, often from forgotten or unguarded army stores. They traded in any commodity from butter to drugs and especially in smuggled foreign currency. Even one single dollar note was worth having at a time when its value amounted to 4 000 000 000 000 marks. Prices, too, rose in truly astronomical proportions and there was a time when a newspaper had to be bought at the tobacconists' for more than a hundred-thousand million. These were figures to which nobody's savings could stand up and selling any valuables that they possessed was the only means by which many elderly people could secure a meal. Their fur coats and jewellery promptly reappeared on the pretty, if vulgar, young escorts whom the *Schieber* paraded around.

Schoolboys suddenly became aware of the fantastic value of their stamp collections, and, being young and alert, they quickly learned to operate their wealth to advantage. Berlin's sixth formers took to speculation like ducks to water and the possession of a few industrial shares, bought with their stamps, turned them within a few weeks into the wealthiest members of their otherwise respectable families. These worldly-wise young scholars had no difficulty in dealing with the ordinary *Schieber* on his own terms and, being more intelligent, younger and having a better education, they outsmarted him as often as not. Their penniless parents whom they could now invite to an expensive meal, the opera or a week-end at the lakes, were hardly in a position to preach morals to these inventors of the permissive society. By the time these young lions were ready to enter university, life held few secrets for them. Strange as it may seem, their inflationary adolescence did not prove a bad education. The opposite sex had found a reasonable place in their life at an early date and they had become cognizant of all human aberrations, peculiarities and perversions long before they themselves were old enough to practise them. Justifiably, they were unimpressed with 'eternal values', including those of classical physics.

7. The New Babylon

Like any proper tragedy, the German drama, too, had its peripeteia, the moment in the fourth act when the action, all set for a final catastrophe, is given the chance of a happy ending. The inflation had now served its purpose and the State and industry could pay off their debts in worthless currency and the time had come to think of stability, production and profits. Hjalmar Schacht, a capable financier on the board of one of the big private banks, was made President of the Reichsbank and established a new currency, provisionally called *Rentenmark*. Its value was based on a mortgage of industrial and agricultural assets and it proved perfectly stable, right from the day of issue.

The decade following the stabilization of the mark has now become a fabled age of achievement and debauch in which the latter aspect has secured the limelight in novels and pseudo-historical accounts. Its distinctive feature was the growth of a social pattern that arose out of a unique set of circumstances. Its basis was still the solid achievement of the Hohenzollern empire which contained the germs of a multitude of new ideas that had been lying dormant during the war. There was now no restraint to revolutionary thought. War and inflation had played havoc with what used to be accepted ideas and the new generation started out on a path of ruthless experimentation in all aspects of life, ranging from morality to scholarship. The result was the growth of a permissive society which, however, unlike its successor in the late 'sixties, was not an affluent one. Permissiveness in Berlin in the 'twenties was not the result of social security. On the contrary, it was practised by young people who never in their lives had known security and who had passed through an adolescence of collapsing social values. They had learned, when they were still almost children, that they themselves had to make sure of their own survival.

However, permissiveness did not mean recklessness. Your right to live your own life depended entirely on your ability to pay for it. Securing a job and holding it was the one moral principle that had to be obeyed in a world where, even at the best of times, unemployment was a constant threat. Men and women were free to shape their own destiny and there was nobody to relieve them of their irresponsibility. On the whole the system worked remarkably well and people enjoyed the exercise of personal responsibility since it gave them the sense of individual achievement.

The post-war years brought Nernst honours which come to a senior scientist of his distinction. Already some time before receiving the Nobel prize he had been given the title of 'Geheimrat', a civil honour roughly corresponding to the British C.B.E., bestowed on outstanding scholars of suitable age and status. More important, he was elected Rector of Berlin University for the academic year 1921–2. His tenure of the rectorate took place in a difficult time of political unrest in which, only too often, students of the university were involved. Nernst was always too free from prejudice to identify himself with any of the political parties and he preferred to follow his own personal opinion, which could hardly be combined with party loyalty. Generally speaking, he was strongly influenced by the standard of the years before the war and to the end of his life he remained proud of the confidence which the Kaiser had shown in him. His accounts of lunches and other appointments at Court emphasized the lack of formality with which he could move in this exalted circle. As he once told me, he turned round abruptly and hit the man behind him with his elbow. 'You see', he said, 'I pushed the Kaiser in the stomach; it did not matter in the least.'

However, his regard for the Hohenzollern age never blinded him to its faults. He disliked the privileged position of the army and the narrow-minded attitude of a powerful officer corps. In fact, he was very upset when his younger son wanted to make the army his career and insisted that the boy first had to take a university degree before applying for a commission. His distrust of the generals' ability was justified by their failure to carry through the Schlieffen plan and already by the end of 1914 he was, as we have seen, thoroughly disillusioned. After the war Nernst was, like most people of his age, convinced that the political extremists had to be put down by force but he never advocated a return of 'the good old times'. His personal friendship was with men like Walther Rathenau who believed in a German renaissance as a democratic republic. When, as sometimes happened, he criticized the brash younger generation, it was because of what he considered, their lack of manners and not for their ethics. In fact, he made great efforts, especially when he was Rector, to ease the economic plight of the students and to create conditions favourable for scientific research. He was largely instrumental in the setting up of an agency, the *Notgemeinschaft der Deutschen Wissenschaft*, Emergency Syndicate for German Science, which administered a large fund, contributed to by the German States and by industry. It proved to be of immense value in providing means to pay young research workers and also in financing projects beyond the means of individual universities. Altogether, as time went on, the *Notgemeinschaft* became the mainstay of scientific development in Germany.

Nernst was not insensitive to the value of honours and titles and one has every reason to believe that he would not have turned one down lightly. Nevertheless, this happened when he was offered the German Embassy at Washington. The offer was clearly a great tribute to Nernst's common sense and to his ability for analysing situations accurately. These qualities and his friendship with Rathenau, as well as his close acquaintance with Reichspresident Ebert, made Nernst an ideal candidate for the office. In addition, his close relations with industry would be a definite asset in a man who was to represent Germany in the United States. It took Nernst only twenty-four hours to decline this impressive offer and while the reason given by him was correct, it was hardly the cogent one. Nernst said that his command of English was inadequate for the post and while it was true that he did not speak English perfectly, it is most unlikely that this shortcoming would have stopped Nernst from becoming 'His Excellency' if he had wanted the job. It is more probable that he neither wanted to leave science nor did he cherish the prospect of having to follow Government directives. His refusal was probably a wise one since the near future was to demonstrate his inability and unwillingness to get on with officialdom.

How much Nernst had become attuned to the post-war period is shown by the fact that his dignified status did not prevent him from becoming a regular of the casinos that were springing up all over Berlin. Gambling had always attracted him, probably as much for the entertainment and thrill as for his idea that limited prediction of luck was possible through mathematical operations. At the centenary celebration of his birth, his daughter livened up the solemnity of the occasion by relating how, at the age of eight, she had received from her father, intensive coaching in playing baccarat. It appears that Emma was as keen on trying her luck at the gambling tables as her husband since she always accompanied him on his exploits. The daughters recall that there would usually be presents after the parents had been in luck.

A 'Geheimrat' frequenting gambling dens was not at all incongruous in post-war Berlin and one of Nernst's colleagues, a famous mathematician who used to spend many hours in his bath, had a telephone installed there, so as to keep in close touch with his broker at the Stock Exchange. The only invasion of Berlin's underworld into the world of physics concerns a man, whom we shall call Schmidt, and who did research in Nernst's laboratory. He did not get on all that well with his colleagues because his personal, as well as his scientific, conduct was somewhat out of keeping with that of the rest of them. There was some sort of a row after which Schmidt faded out and it was only many years after Nernst's death that the relevant details of the story were told.

Nernst had met Schmidt originally in one of the gambling places and had learned from the good-looking young man that his greatest wish was to become a physicist. This, strangely enough, was probably true, but if Nernst had been a sound judge of personality, he would have left it at that. Unfortunately, his brilliant assessment of situations did not extend to people and he was so taken with Schmidt's laudable ambition that he offered to give him a chance in his department. Schmidt was not without means which were acquired periodically in a very simple manner by first getting closely acquainted with wealthy married women in middle age and then threatening them with disclosure of the affair to their husbands. However, it was part of his ambition to do things the hard way and so he asked Nernst to get him a *Notgemeinschaft* grant. This led to an amusing incident which only came to light a few years ago when one of my colleagues in East Berlin went through the long forgotten files. There was a terse letter from the *Notgemeinschaft* to Nernst, saying that they had reason to believe the grant-aided Mr Schmidt to be in possession not only of his own motorcar but even of a private 'plane, and would Nernst please comment. This ghastly revelation might have floored any professor, but not Nernst. His reply, also on the file, was concise and to the point. His enquiries showed, so it said, that the grant-receiving research worker indeed had a private car as well as a 'plane and when questioned had stated that: 'He had his reasons'.

Nernst still did some work on the mechanism of chemical reactions but eventually left these to his pupil Bodenstein who, in 1922, was to become his successor at the Physicochemical Institute. Instead his mind turned to problems of astrophysics and to the unsatisfactory prospect held out for the future of the universe by the second law of thermodynamics. This law requires that in all spontaneously occurring processes the entropy, which means the degree of statistical disorder, must continually increase. It suggests, with the sun and stars constantly pouring out energy in the form of high entropy radiation, that the universe must be running down all the time and ending up in some form of lukewarm broth in which any further change would be impossible. While Nernst saw no clear escape from this unsatisfactory end, he tried to show that the 'entropy death' was much further off than was generally believed. Here again he found the essentially correct solution, even if the detailed mechanism had to elude him. He postulated the liberation of nuclear energy as the source of sunshine but had to look for some way in which it could be explained in terms of radioactivity as far as it was known in his day. The plausible process, the nuclear fusion of hydrogen into helium, was only suggested three years before Nernst's death by Hans Bethe when more data on nuclear reactions had become available.

Nernst's interest in unknown processes of energy production in the universe led him to sponsor a line of research which eventually, again many years after his death, was to yield a rich harvest in fundamental research. In 1911 Victor Hess had made a number of balloon ascents in order to see up to what height the radioactive gamma radiation could be traced which was emitted from minerals in the Earth. His results showed that far from decreasing, the radiation became stronger the higher the balloon rose, and Hess concluded that the *Höhenstrahlung* must originate in some extra-terrestrial source. While Hess himself continued his work, not much notice was otherwise taken of this discovery until it attracted Nernst's attention. He immediately realized its potentially great importance and the need for systematic investigation which, at his suggestion, was done by setting up a permanent research station under Werner Kohlhörster at the Jungfraujoch. Its results paved the way for the discoveries of new elementary particles in this 'cosmic radiation'. Nernst only saw the first results of this exciting research but they were promising enough to encourage him in postulating a process of constant mass and energy production in the universe, a 'steady state' that might avoid the entropy death.

While his interest was shifting from other aspects of his earlier work in low temperatures, there remained the unsolved problem of gas degeneracy. Nernst, as we have seen, postulated the existence of this strange phenomenon purely on the grounds that it must exist because he expected his theorem to be a general law of nature. He scorned the explanation that the failure to observe gas degeneracy might be due to the fact that no real gas could ever be brought into a state where it would be apparent. Even an ideal gas, he maintained had to obey his law. The nature of the problem, on the other hand, had become quite important and it was equally clear that nobody could see a way to its solution. The quantum theory demands that energy is always emitted or taken up in definite amounts, the quanta, whose size is determined by the frequency of an oscillation, which comes to the same as saying that it must correspond to a definite wavelength. In Einstein's theory of the specific heat of a crystal there was no difficulty since the atoms are vibrating in the regular array of the crystal lattice. This vibration then provides the frequency that determines the size of the quanta. On the other hand, the atom or molecule of a gas, moving in a straight line and at constant velocity through space, could not be associated with an oscillation, and the required frequency for quantizing its energy was clearly missing. It was this missing frequency belonging to the free motion of an atom that was needed to understand the predicted phenomenon of gas degeneracy. When eventually the riddle was solved, physics had been changed out of all recognition by the most profound revolution through which any field of science has ever passed. The major part of this revolution was the work of the Berlin Physics School and the most exciting phase of it fell into that short scintillating period of the 'twenties.

While the limelight of popular interest in the post-war years was focused on relativity, the quantum theory remained a domain strictly reserved for physicists. The main reason was its obviously incomplete character, which made the most important aspects of it incomprehensible even to its author. Relativity was revolutionary but it was a revolution built upon the structure of classical physics which retained its place, albeit with far-reaching modifications and with consequences that left little of it unchanged. Even so, there was no irreconcilable break with Newton's world. It soon became clear that things were different with the quantum theory. This was a revolution which did not just rock the edifice of classical physics, but shattered it. Its progress turned out to be inflexible and ruthless, admitting of no compromise with accepted ideas.

The origin of the quantum theory was an exercise in extreme intellectual honesty. Its creator, Max Planck, was a deeply religious man who saw divine revelation in the absolute nature of the laws of physics. Accordingly he was profoundly impressed with the generally applicable formalism of thermodynamics—the thermodynamics of Clausius that was based on measurable macroscopic quantities such as pressure, volume and temperature. He disliked Boltzmann's statistical approach to this subject because it introduced into physics two aspects which to Planck's mind bordered on heresy.

In the first place Boltzmann's statistics were based on the behaviour of individual atoms and while Planck did not doubt their existence, atoms were beyond the limit of physical measurement and he regarded them as an unnecessary complication. In the second place, and this was far more serious, statistical computation involves the concept of probability and this Planck regarded as anathema to his own concept of absolute laws. Planck himself never attacked Boltzmann but he probably encouraged one of his pupils, Zermelo, to publish a paper criticizing the statistical approach. It is clear that Boltzmann was right and that Zermelo as well as Planck had failed to appreciate the importance of the new method. In his brilliant reply Boltzmann permitted himself the mild sarcasm of saying that Zermelo would probably suspect the dice to be loaded because he had failed to roll a six a thousand times running, since the probability of such an event was not completely zero.

In order to trace the origins of quantum physics we have to go back to the turn of the century. The problem to which Planck had turned his mind has been mentioned earlier on. It was to find a law describing the all-embracing phenomenon of electromagnetic radiation, involving light, heat, X-rays and radio waves. Such a law had clearly to be of very fundamental character, expressing a relation between radiant energy, temperature and wavelength. Partial solutions had been obtained earlier but, in spite of many efforts, the complete description containing all three quantities in the same equation had eluded them. Planck, with his superb command of thermodynamics, was better fitted than anyone else to attack the problem and he soon found out where his predecessors had gone wrong. Instead of looking for a relation between the temperature and the energy of radiation, Planck used the entropy, that quantity which denotes disorder and the irretrievable loss of energy in spontaneously occurring processes. Radiation, he argued, is poured out from its source, never to return.

Planck's approach yielded immediate success and he found that by using the entropy he could write down an empirical formula which perfectly fitted the observed data. He had clearly made an inspired guess and all that now remained was to explain the pretty rabbit which he had conjured out of the hat. In other words, he had to derive his successful equation from first principles of physics. With so much to go by now, this last step promised to be easy but, strangely enough, this was not the case.

After vainly trying numerous approaches, Planck finally had to venture on the path that he detested and distrusted—Boltzmann's statistical method. It worked at once and Planck now had to concede that the objectionable introduction of probability had succeeded where his own 'absolute' approach had failed. Being Planck, he not only wrote immediately to Boltzmann, with whom relations had been strained, but he was at pains to stress in his writings his own failure to appreciate the importance of the latter's work.

Having overcome his dislike for Boltzmann's kind of physics, Planck now had soundly established what many had been trying to find—the fundamental radiation law. His formula, which perfectly fitted the latest experimental results obtained by his colleagues Hagen and Rubens in Berlin, only contained, what Planck then considered, a mathematical blemish. The radiated energy appeared as a direct function not of its frequency but of the frequency multiplied by a constant. He felt confident that by suitable mathematical manipulation this blemish could be removed, but then, to his irritation, he realized that he was quite unable to do this. Whenever he got rid of the constant, the agreement with observation also vanished. In the end, he had to give up and to admit that this was a new fundamental constant of physics and he calculated its value. It turned out to be a very small number, far below the magnitude of ordinary human measures, and like another basic constant found earlier by Boltzmann, it was of atomic dimensions. Boltzmann had introduced his constant as a bridge between the large-scale thermodynamic measures and the atoms on which his statistics were based. Now Planck's constant indicated the existence of another such bridge for the energy.

The 14th December, 1900, the day on which Planck read his paper before the Berlin Physical Society, was destined to become the starting-point of a tremendous revolution in science. For many years to come, but without avail, Planck tried to reconcile his discovery with classical physics and this gave rise to the opinion that Planck himself never fully realized the magnitude of his achievement. This interpretation of events is patently untrue. In fact, in the preface to this first paper, he said that the result he was about to present was likely to have a profound effect not only on physics but also on chemistry. Although he disliked what he had discovered, he realized immediately that energy had now ceased to be a structureless fluid which could be divided up arbitrarily and *ad infinitum*. Instead, radiation turned out to be corpuscular, made up of 'energy atoms' each of a size determined by the radiation frequency, multiplied by Planck's constant.

The sequel to Planck's great discovery was a complete anticlimax. Nothing at all happened and nobody took note of his important result. It often occurs with outstandingly new discoveries that their sheer enormity prevents them from being recognized. In this case the failure was helped by the fact that Planck, the originator of the new idea, himself remained silent. His reticence is easily explained by his search for the link with classical physics. Five years passed and then, where Planck feared to tread, the revolutionary young clerk at the Berne Patent Office rushed in with a truly iconoclastic paper.

Einstein had for some time been looking for an explanation of the Michelson experiment and his first paper on relativity was to appear in a few months. He already knew that he was going to do away with the hypothetical ether for good and ever but there remained the awkward question as to what else was carrying the light waves. Then, coming across Planck's forgotten paper, he saw the solution in a flash; light waves were not required. In this paper, he starts by paying lip service to the wave theory of light and its undoubted success but, he continues, these are all large-scale phenomena that lead to awkward problems when one has to consider the generation of light on the atomic scale. He then quotes Planck's formula and the quantized structure of radiation. Mass and electricity, Einstein argues, have been found to be of particulate structure, why not light as well. He winds up by citing experimental support for his ideas, in particular the fact that a minimum frequency, that is a minimum quantum of energy, is always needed to liberate electrons from a metal surface.

Nowadays Einstein's paper is usually quoted for providing an explanation of this 'photo-effect' on a quantum basis but this success was merely a side issue. What really mattered to him was the nature of the energy quanta to which he was now ascribing physical reality, going so far as to describe them as individual *Lichtpfeile*, darts of light. Planck was deeply shocked by this audacity in paving a road he wished to avoid, and he passed over Einstein's paper in silence.

To the Berlin physics students of the 'twenties, like myself, who listened to Planck's course on theoretical physics and who watched him at the weekly colloquia, it seemed inconceivable that this was the man who had ushered in the revolution. The spare figure in the dark suit, starched white shirt and black bow tie looked like the typical Prussian civil servant but for the penetrating eyes under the huge dome of his bald head. The outward appearance was underlined by a precise, if somewhat dry, style of lecturing and his reluctance to take part in the scientific discussions that were raging all round him at the weekly meetings. One of his pupils, Lise Meitner, has commented on Planck's extreme caution before committing himself to an opinion. His reply to her questions was invariably 'I will give you my answer tomorrow'. Planck, the descendant of a long line of legal lights who had taken a prominent part in fashioning the Prussian civil code, had infinite regard for the laws of both God and man. To him the revelation of Divine perfection in the laws of nature had to be clear and without blemish and he was deeply concerned that his own great work seemed to offend against these concepts.

For most of his long life he was looking for a way in which the quantum concept could be reconciled with classical physics. However, each new hope turned out to be a mirage and in the end he had to admit that he himself had dealt the death-blow to classical physics. When Planck died in 1949, shortly before his eightieth birthday, not only his world of physics had collapsed but Germany, too. With philosophical fortitude, sustained by a trusting belief in the wisdom of God, he endured a terrible series of personal losses without complaint, and remained unchanged. Both his daughters died in childbirth and his son was done to death in a horrible manner as accomplice in the plot against Hitler. His house and his beloved library were destroyed in the air raids on Berlin and the old man became a refugee finding shelter at a house in the combat zone from which the advancing Allied Forces saved him.

There was a high mutual regard between Nernst and Planck as far as their scientific achievements were concerned but never a close friendship. Planck's almost pedantic method of approach to physical problems and his cautious conformism did not appeal to a man like Nernst who was always deeply involved in the affairs of life. In his detachment Planck seemed to be far removed from the pulsating life of the turbulent city in which he was professor of theoretical physics. However, one evening in the late 'twenties when I was enjoying a typical mixture of political and *risqué* entertainment in an intellectual Berlin cabaret I was astonished to see Planck come in. He was accompanied by his wife and a friend, and good-naturedly laughed off the reference made from the stage to the late-comer's impressive egg-head. Apparently, even Planck could not escape completely from the vortex of the new Babylon.

No two people could have been more different in heritage, outlook and habits than Planck and Einstein but a strange friendship sprang up between them. The basis was physics, on which they so often disagreed, and music, which they both loved and in which their tastes completely coincided. Removed from the world, they would spend hours together, Einstein with his violin and Planck at the piano, playing chamber music.

As we have seen, it was Einstein rather than Planck who championed the quantum concept. Einstein was unimpressed by the magnificence of nineteenth-century physics; he found the atmosphere in the proud classical edifice both musty and sterile. His feelings were expressed when he said that 'In the beginning God created Newtonian mechanics with all the necessary forces and masses'. To his mind it was just as well to start again from the beginning without being too much encumbered with all the notions that had been accumulated since, many of which he regarded as unfounded prejudices. His own theory of relativity was breaking free of them and now he found that another set of fresh vistas was provided by the quantum concept.

In his paper of 1905 he set in train the two lines of thought that were to dominate twentieth-century physics. The first was his suggestion to treat the quantum of radiation as a particle rather than a wave. Newton, of course, had originally thought on the same lines but soon the experiments began to favour the wave concept proposed by his contemporary Huygens. The most convincing evidence was provided by the phenomenon of diffraction, investigated in the nineteenth century by Young and Fresnel. We often come across it when looking at a star or a distant streetlamp through the fabric of an umbrella or a gauze curtain. Instead of a single spot of light we see a number of them, grouped in a regular pattern. This is caused by 'diffraction' of the light waves on the threads and the light spots are the places where the crest of one wave reinforces that of another. Similarly, when a crest meets a trough, the wave is evened out and we have regions of darkness. Material particles, on the other hand, say a stream of sand falling on to a sieve, do not produce such a pattern. Hence diffraction had come to be regarded as the direct proof of the wave nature of light, and it is clear why Einstein was anxious to call diffraction a large-scale phenomenon when drawing attention to the particle aspect of the light quanta.

Here again, Einstein had found the correct explanation by making the distinction between large-scale phenomena and those occurring on the atomic scale, but two decades of searching and confusion had to pass before its significance was realized. As things stood, the strange dualism of wave and particle remained unsolved. The latter was clearly apparent in the photo-electric effect that Einstein had chosen as an example. In order to explain the liberation of a single electron out of a metal surface, the impinging energy clearly has to be concentrated on a spot, like a bullet hitting it, and not a wave that expands and thins out in all directions. Before this dualism was eventually resolved, it got, as we shall see, much worse. In the early 'twenties the Nobel Laureate, Sir William Bragg, exclaimed in despair that he was teaching the wave theory of light on Mondays, Wednesdays and Fridays, and the particle theory on Tuesdays, Thursdays and Saturdays.

While the wave–particle dilemma continued to bedevil physics for a long time, the other line of thought raised in Einstein's paper brought more immediate results. Unlike Planck's generalized concepts about the creation of light, Einstein's approach focused attention on the individual atom or molecule as the place where the light quanta are created. In his usual iconoclastic manner he swept away the time-honoured classical concept of the indivisible and immutable atom without even apologizing for his heresy. He tacitly assumed that the atom must undergo a change when it emits light and it must therefore have structure. Going even further, he saw that this would not be a classical but a quantum structure and thereby he firmly fixed quantum physics as the fundamental law of events on the atomic scale. Finally, he postulated that an atom will not only emit radiation in discrete quantized steps but that it should be able to accept energy only in the form of definite single quanta.

For a few years nothing happened since there was nobody to take up or even understand these revolutionary concepts. However, things changed when in 1914 Einstein moved to Berlin. In the following year two young physicists at the laboratory there, James Franck and Gustav Hertz, performed the famous experiment for which they were to receive the Nobel prize. They showed that individual mercury atoms will take up or radiate energy only in definite quantized steps. Direct experimental proof had now been obtained that the atoms of matter were quantum structures. Moreover, the experiment left no doubt that the spectrum lines which Kirchhoff and Bunsen had used to identify the chemical elements indicated the quantized energy steps characteristic of their atoms.

The suspicion that atoms might be composite structures had been growing for some time. Electric discharges through rarified gases had revealed the existence of the electron, a particle two thousand times lighter than the lightest atom. It seemed probable that this 'corpuscle', as its discoverer J. J. Thomson called it, as well as the particles emitted in radioactive decay were constituent parts of atoms. Moreover, direct evidence of the existence of atoms had been obtained in 1912 by the ex-cadet, Max von Laue. He had carried out a diffraction experiment in which he used instead of light the X-rays discovered by Roentgen and instead of the threads in the fabric a crystal. The 'light spots' recorded on the photographic plate then showed that the atoms in the crystal were arranged in a regular array, like a lattice of fabric.

It was left to the genius of Ernest Rutherford to find the way of probing directly into the atomic structure. He bombarded thin metal foils with radioactive alpha-particles, that is, positively charged helium atoms. From the way in which his minute projectiles were deflected, he deduced that the atoms constituting the foil were surprisingly open structures. Each consisted of a tiny nucleus containing practically all the mass surrounded by a very loose assembly of electrons. In view of his discovery that most of the atom's volume was just empty space, Rutherford was struck by its similarity to the solar system. There, too, nearly all the mass resides in the sun with the planets circling through empty space in wide orbits. The forces acting within the atomic structure, were not, however, those of gravity but the electric attraction between the positive nucleus and the negative electrons. Even with this difference, the Rutherford model of an atom was a perfectly classical structure.

Rutherford had published his idea in 1911 and in the following year a young Danish theoretician joined his laboratory in Manchester. His name was Niels Bohr. He was then a man of twenty-five, young enough to accept new and unconventional ideas and fully conversant with the work of Planck and Einstein. The freshness of his approach was shown by asking a new and relevant question. Why are atoms of the size they are and not larger or smaller? To this the Rutherford model gave no answer because the mass and charge of the electron permit any size. Since Einstein had postulated the quantum nature of the atom, Bohr invoked Planck's constant h to provide the missing dimension. This met with instant success; the atomic size came out correctly. The next step followed automatically. In the new model the electrons could not take up any arbitrary orbit but had to be confined to those whose energy corresponded to whole multiples of h, such as h, $2h$, $3h$ and so on. Finally, and this was Bohr's most audacious postulate, the energy radiated or accepted by the atom was to correspond to a 'jump' of an electron from one into another of the quantized planetary orbits. Using his model, Bohr could now give a satisfactory account of the spectral lines of the simplest atom, that of hydrogen.

Unlike the papers by Planck and Einstein, Bohr's theory found immediate response. The relation between the atomic model and the spectral lines was comprehensible to any physicist and the floodgates of research were opened. In spite of the impact of war, work correlating the theory and the multitude of existing spectroscopic data proceeded at an astonishing pace. The main centre of it became Munich where Arnold Sommerfeld and his school attacked these problems by a massive research effort. Some of the calculations were, in fact, carried out between battles in the trenches. By the end of the war a tremendous amount of theoretical work had been done and in 1919 there appeared the first edition of Sommerfeld's *magnum opus*, *Spectral Lines and Atomic Structure*, a compendious volume that grew with each new printing and which served a whole generation of physicists as their most important text in the new world of quanta.

However, in spite of its great success, it soon became clear that the Bohr model raised even more questions than it answered. Some of these looked as if more careful work might resolve them but others were so baffling that people were inclined to look away. After all, they argued, first things first, let us deal with those problems that we can tackle, maybe the rest will follow. Instead, far from solving the outstanding questions, they were confronted with even more awkward ones.

First of all, there were many more spectral lines than those expected according to Bohr. Sommerfeld scored an impressive success by pointing out that the electrons need not run in circles but might describe ellipses around the nucleus. Again not all ellipses were permitted but only those corresponding to quantum conditions. Moreover, the speed of an electron running in an ellipse must vary from point to point and the calculations had to take into account relativistic corrections. All this Sommerfeld did, but while he achieved a good deal of success it was clearly not the last word. It had been simple to number the orbits in the Bohr model but now Sommerfeld's work required a second 'quantum number' to characterize each energy state. However, when the data were compared with Sommerfeld's computations there appeared the need for a third quantum number. Its meaning, which has no counterpart at all in classical physics, was given by a twenty-one year old physicist, Wolfgang Pauli, who called it 'space quantization'.

Even including Sommerfeld's refinements, the Bohr atomic model was basically a classical structure. It was a planetary system to which had been applied rules involving the quantum principle, but these rules remained quite arbitrary and no reason could be given as to why they worked. First of all, classical physics would never have permitted an electron to orbit round the nucleus without losing energy by radiation. Bohr's model required nonradiative orbits but no better reason could be given for this nonclassical postulate than to say that in this way the model produced the correct result. Equally, no reason could be given for the 'quantum jumps' from orbit to orbit, except that they provided the right energy for the observed spectrum lines. Physicists uncomfortably began to realize that they were playing a game the rules of which they had to discover as they went along but they had no idea what these rules signified. Sommerfeld's second quantum number could still be fitted into these rules but the meaning of the third number seemed to be divorced from all physical experience. Bohr and Sommerfeld had postulated quantization of the size and shape of the electron orbit and now Pauli suggested that its position in space, too, was only permitted in certain quantized directions. This new postulate was far removed from any classical concept. Only a new generation to whom even Einstein's ideas appeared tainted by classical lore could contemplate such a step.

Nevertheless, a year after it had been suggested by Pauli, space quantization was shown to exist by a direct experiment. This brilliant feat was performed by Otto Stern, Einstein's pupil in his Prague days who later, on the Eastern Front, had written the paper on statistical mechanics which was edging closer to an interpretation of gas degeneracy. After the war, Stern took the unusual step of trying to match his theoretical ability by experimental skill and in this he was completely successful. Together with his co-worker, Walter Gerlach, he designed an apparatus that would emit a narrow beam of single atoms of silver. Passing this stream through a magnetic field, they showed that the metal was deposited on a screen in distinct spots which corresponded to the quantized directions in space that the atoms had taken up. The physical reality of the third 'magnetic' quantum number had been demonstrated.

This work and the direct determination of the magnetic moment of the proton carried out later by the same method earned Stern the Nobel prize in 1943. Ten years earlier he had been driven from his professorship at Hamburg by the Nazis. Like so many Jewish scientists he had found refuge abroad, holding a research professorship at the Carnegie Institute at Pittsburgh. Two years after receiving the Nobel prize he retired to live in California, a place that suited him both climatically and temperamentally. Otto Stern was a genial person with a bald head framed by short curly hair. He was a bachelor whose constant companion was a cigar between his lips and he was blessed with perpetual good humour. Contentious scientific arguments would be brushed aside in the most affable manner since he knew beforehand that he would be right. Later in life he became completely addicted to the products of the motion picture industry to which he exposed himself often twice every twenty-four hours. He died in California at the age of eighty and, true to form, in the cinema.

During his time in Hamburg, Stern established a flourishing school of physics that was distinguished by his own type of approach, combining experimental ingenuity with profound theoretical understanding. Among his many pupils was Isidor Rabi, who himself earned the Nobel prize for work based on Stern's original researches. Another was Otto Frisch who, together with Lise Meitner, conceived the idea of nuclear fission and whose calculations led to the fast neutron reaction that became the key in developing the first atomic bomb. It was only natural that, in building up the Hamburg Physics School, Stern should have his eye on the brilliant young pupil of Sommerfeld's who, more clearly than any-one else, had understood the concept of space quantization. Pauli had just spent a year with Bohr at Copenhagen when Stern invited him to take up the position of *Dozent* for theoretical physics at Hamburg. Typi-cally, Pauli's inaugural lecture did not deal with his achievements but with the aspects that he failed to understand. The three quantum numbers worked well for light atoms but a new difficulty arose when the spectra of heavy atoms in a magnetic field were analysed. Sommerfeld himself had darkly hinted at the possible existence of a fourth quantum number but its meaning was obscure.

Pauli, who was to become one of the greatest figures in shaping quantum physics, was probably the first physicist to realize that the usefulness of the Bohr atomic model had been exhausted. It was, as we have seen, a classical structure to which quantum conditions had been applied in an *ad hoc* manner. Bohr had tried to bridge the gap between the old and the new physics by his 'correspondence principle' which tried to correlate the observed quantum effects with appropriate classical phenomena. This worked reasonably well for the first two quantum numbers but space quantization was difficult to fit into this scheme. Einstein had made a distinction between large-scale physical phenomena and those taking place on the atomic scale. Pauli now pursued this idea further, suggesting that the atom was a physical world, subject to laws completely outside our large-scale observation. This was the most crucial turning-point in the transition from the old to the new physics. He pronounced the enig-matic fourth quantum number as 'classically nondescribable'. From now on, he argued, mathematical description alone had to take over as the sole means of interpreting events on the atomic scale.

Pauli's command of mathematical methods was superb but it would be entirely wrong to describe him as a mathematician. On the contrary, of all the outstanding scientists of his age, he may have had the most profound understanding of physics. Coupled with this deep insight there was penetrating and merciless criticism which he applied both to his own work and to that of others. His own great discoveries may have been obtained in a flash of intuition but they never saw the light of day, except after the most searching scrutiny and, even then, Pauli was usually anxious to point out all the uncertainties that still beset him. He soon became not only admired but even more feared for the devastating criticism which he was always prepared to apply to anyone, irrespective of their standing. I remember Pauli in the chair when another outstanding physicist gave a paper on some new development. As the talk proceeded Pauli's nervous habit of rocking his body to and fro assumed proportions that were well known to be a danger sign and the speaker had hardly finished when Pauli got to his feet to pronounce the lecture 'worth exactly nothing, and', he added with conviction, 'if the speaker had been in the chair he would have been the first to pass this judgement'. The speaker grew red in the face but kept his composure and replied smiling 'That may be so, but I would have done it in a more polite fashion'.

On the other hand, Pauli never delivered his criticism except when it was justified and his caustic remarks usually had a salutary and restraining effect on the headlong manner in which physics tended to proceed in the 'twenties. The theoretician Ehrenfest once called Pauli 'the scourge of the Lord'. Shortly before his death Pauli was handed the paper of a young American physicist whom his colleagues suspected of being a budding genius. After studying it carefully, Pauli, rocking sadly, gave it back with the acid comment: 'It is not even wrong', meaning that there was not a spark of imagination in it.

He never forgave one of his most gifted pupils, H. Casimir, that instead of accepting a chair of theoretical physics, he had chosen to become the scientific director of the Philips Company. When one of his students told Pauli that he wanted to meet Casimir, Pauli gave him a letter of introduction, saying that Casimir was a very busy man but, being an old pupil of his, he would find time for the student. 'Be careful', said Pauli, 'always to address Casimir as "Herr Direktor"— because that annoys him'. When Casimir visited Pauli in Zürich one day, to his astonishment he found Pauli waiting for him at the station with his own car. Pauli's lack of dexterity was proverbial and by the time they arrived at his house above the lake, Casimir was a nervous wreck. He told Pauli that never again would he sit down in a car driven by the latter. 'All right', said Pauli soothingly, 'let's come to an agreement. You will not comment on my driving and I will not comment on your physics'.

Pauli had one further mark of distinction. Of all the physics professors in creation, he looked least like one. Short and fairly corpulent, of sallow complexion and with heavy, hooded eyes, he looked like an inscrutable Levantine businessman. It seemed strange that in this unscholarly frame there lived an acute mind of beautiful clarity and unique perception. Sitting opposite him at lunch could be an unnerving experience. Conversation that had been flowing effortlessly would stop abruptly and Pauli's eyes would lose all expression. Only the gentle rocking of the body was evidence that he was alive—and thinking. Pauli's father was professor of chemistry in Vienna and he had grown up in an academic atmosphere which may have contributed to his early development. When Einstein saw an article written by Pauli on his own field of relativity he commented 'Whoever studies this mature, and grandly conceived work, can hardly believe that the author is only twenty-one years old'.

Pauli had been over-cautious about the impossibility of a model for the fourth quantum number. While he was still working on the subject, a startling discovery was made by two young Dutch scientists, Samuel Goudsmit and George Uhlenbeck. The third quantum number, determining the position of the electron orbit in space, is connected with the magnetic effect produced by the circling motion of the electron's negative charge. Uhlenbeck and Goudsmit now showed that in addition to its orbital motion the electron was also turning round its axis. At first, Pauli was very doubtful about the existence of this 'electron spin' because, unlike most of his colleagues, he realized that it must be classically impossible. However, when he became convinced of the correct interpretation of the experiment, he accepted spin as the physical basis for the fourth quantum number.

While his contemporaries tended to regard the electron spin as an angular momentum like the spin of the Earth about its axis or the rotation of a flywheel, Pauli saw that spin on the atomic scale had a far more fundamental significance. Unlike the flywheel, which may or may not rotate, the spin of the electron is an intrinsic property of this particle, equally important for its description as its mass or charge. There exists no counterpart in our large-scale world for the significance of this property as Pauli was now going to show by his great discovery.

Classically, it should be possible for two planets or two electrons to rotate in the same orbit. Pauli now postulated that in one atom no more than two electrons can be in the same energy state, and these two electrons must have opposite spin. This new law of physics, which has become known as Pauli's 'exclusion principle', has a profound influence on the constitution of all matter. However, to this day, it remains a purely empirical law which we must accept but which we cannot 'explain' by deriving a connection with other physical phenomena. In its mathematical form, the exclusion principle is closely connected with the concept of symmetry which is of no essential relevance in large-scale physics but which appears to be of paramount importance in sub-atomic events.

The immediate result of Pauli's discovery was an understanding of the chemical properties of the elements. A century ago, the Russian scientist, Dimitri Mendeleyev had drawn attention to certain chemical similarities among the elements and he had arranged them according to increasing weight in a tabular form. This 'Periodic Table' shows that certain properties recur in the list of elements and Mendeleyev's pattern turned out to be accurate enough to predict and find elements, still unknown, on the basis of the properties postulated by the table. No further progress was possible until some knowledge of atomic structure had been obtained, but then, as early as 1916, Walther Kossel was able to correlate some features of this periodicity with the Bohr–Sommerfeld model of the atom. The more fundamental question concerning the origin of this periodicity had remained unanswered. Now the exclusion principle showed clearly that only a certain number of electronic energy states were permitted and these then accounted beautifully for the structure of the known atoms. Even more important, Pauli's law showed why just these and no other species of atoms can exist in nature.

It soon became clear that Pauli's principle extended far beyond the confines of the individual atom, leading in the end to the solution of Nernst's gas degeneracy problem. Its range of action seemed to be endless and innumerable questions that had remained unsolved for many years suddenly yielded to its application. Among them was a discrepancy in the entropy of hydrogen calculated in different ways by means of the Nernst theorem. Eucken and Simon, two of Nernst's co-workers, were quarrelling bitterly and with much acrimony as to its existence, Eucken denying it and Simon regarding it as a still unsolved problem. Now the exclusion principle seemed to suggest a small energy difference, just big enough to account for the value postulated by Simon. It should be detectable by measurements of the specific heat of solid hydrogen close to absolute zero.

It promised to be an uphill job and, like a fool or a saint craving for penance, I asked for it to be given to me for my doctorate research under Simon's supervision. I had little idea of what I had let myself in for but soon realized my rash zeal as the required apparatus grew more complicated and elaborate month by month. Nernst, whom I had known so far only in the lecture room, came personally to inspect it and his comment was not exactly encouraging. 'My dear young man', he said, 'the problems of my day were solved with much simpler means. If I had been in your shoes, I would have taken to the study of law or something else a bit easier'. Unfortunately, his forecast was, as usual, correct and I had to spend a year longer than the other research students. However, in the end the results were coming out and, at the very lowest temperatures that I could reach, the predicted rise in the specific heat became apparent. It was a moment of extreme elation when, plotting the first graph, I saw this new evidence for the mysterious exclusion principle. Suddenly the strain of innumerable nights spent in the laboratory had vanished into nothing.

The year 1925, in which Pauli enunciated his principle, saw another important step towards the new quantum physics. From Bohr's semi-classical model to the exclusion principle we have travelled along one of the lines of thought suggested by Einstein's 1905 paper: the structure of the atom. The other problem, that of dualism of wave and particle, remained completely unsolved. Again it was a young and unprejudiced mind that opened the door to a new world. Prince Louis de Broglie was a history student whose knowledge of physics came to him second-hand from an elder brother who was a physicist. His argument was of extreme simplicity and straightforward, but of a nature that no professional physicist would have cared to prejudice his career with. De Broglie simply suggested that, as light waves seemed to show properties of material particles, particles might equally well exhibit wave properties.

This proposal could have been made in 1905 after Einstein's famous paper and it would then have been completely disregarded as a crank suggestion. Now, in the mid-twenties, the scientific temper had changed and the young generation of physicists felt that anything was possible. Significantly, it was in the reckless intellectual atmosphere of the Weimar Republic that de Broglie's outrageous idea found the greatest response. Only one year after de Broglie's suggestion there appeared a paper by Erwin Schrödinger, which did away once and for all with the classical aspect of the Bohr atom, substituting for it a wave picture, which has since become the introductory chapter to any book on quantum physics.

Schrödinger was born in Vienna in 1887. His mother was the daughter of a chemistry professor and his father was a chemist who had turned to painting. The wide range of interests in his home left a strong imprint on a boy with a naturally artistic temperament. His teacher at Vienna University, Hasenöhrl, guided Schrödinger into the classical theory of vibrations in continuous media such as the distinct modes of oscillation of which a violin string or the air in an organ pipe is capable. Only after serving in the First World War, when Schrödinger accepted a lecturership in Jena and then professorships in Breslau, Stuttgart and finally in Zürich, did he become interested in the topical problems of the time. With his heritage of classical physics, Schrödinger, like Planck, disliked the discontinuity of the quantum concepts and the idea of electrons jumping from one orbit to another in the Bohr model. There was nobody better equipped to operate wave equations than Schrödinger and when he read de Broglie's paper, he suddenly saw a way in which the unsatisfactory old Bohr model could be expressed in terms of continuous matter waves. The experimental data which had frustrated so many attempts now yielded like magic to the Schrödinger treatment and within a few months an entirely new and remarkably flawless edifice had arisen in physics: wave mechanics.

At first the physicists just could not believe that in a flash and in an almost effortless manner a perfect and nonclassical model of the atom should have been created. The whole operation looked too much like a conjuring trick. However, it soon became clear that the Schrödinger wave equation always provided the correct answer and it became the basis of all future work. Planck, of course, was delighted with the prospect that the continuous nature of the wave might reconcile his revolutionary idea with the tenets of classical physics. As his own retirement from the chair of theoretical physics in Berlin drew near, he exerted his great influence to have Schrödinger as his successor, an appointment that was enthusiastically received by the Berlin Physics School.

For the moment the success and wide applicability of wave mechanics overshadowed the problem of its true meaning and those who tried to understand the nature of the matter wave held completely different opinions. The basic aspect of the problem was not in doubt. De Broglie's postulate associated with any material particle a wave whose length was given simply by its mass and speed, with Planck's constant h providing the order of magnitude. According to Schrödinger the orbits of the Bohr model now became the diffraction pattern that the waves belonging to the electrons form around the atomic nucleus. Instead of the well-defined planetary orbits wave mechanics provides a diffuse pattern of standing waves, gradually thinning out into space and without clear demarcation.

Where, some people asked, was the electron in this tenuous smoke-ring? Others treated this as an inadmissable question because, they maintained, the electron itself *is* a wave. Nonsense, decided a third opinion, how can the electron's mass and charge be smeared out over a large space? While the physicists still argued wildly and inconclusively over the physical reality of matter waves, a bombshell fell into these metaphysical discussions. In the spring of 1927 the journal *Nature* published the reproduction of a photographic plate on which the diffraction pattern of electron waves was clearly recorded.

The story behind this startling discovery is both amusing and significant. In the early 'twenties Clinton Davisson, a man of about forty, and his colleague Germer, were working on electron problems at the Bell Telephone Laboratories in New Jersey. There was nothing of fundamental import in their research which consisted of measuring the scattering of electrons directed on to a nickel surface. Spectacular results were neither expected nor obtained until, in the spring of 1925, they had a mishap to their apparatus in which the nickel plate was temporarily heated up. This accident evidently caused the metal surface to change into one single crystal of nickel and from now on the data obtained were different. The electrons, instead of being scattered in all directions, bounced back only at certain angles. Davisson was mystified by these results and wrote to Max Born in Goettingen, a noted authority on crystal dynamics, hoping that the latter might be able to furnish an explanation.

Born was one of the outstanding theoreticians of that time who eventually was to solve the mystery of the matter waves. After work at Breslau, Cambridge and Berlin he had been appointed professor at Goettingen where he founded a flourishing school of theoretical physics. James Franck had also come to Goettingen from Berlin and together with Born he

E

immediately connected the strange results with de Broglie's postulate of which the American workers were completely unaware. Born and Franck gave the problem to an outstanding young research worker, Walter Elsasser whose calculation then suggested that the angles noted by Davisson were indeed the diffraction pattern of the electron waves. They corresponded to the similar pattern which Max von Laue had obtained by shining X-rays on a crystal. Born and Franck now wrote to Davisson, telling him of the great discovery that he had inadvertently made and suggesting modifications to the apparatus which would clinch the matter. These were carried out by Davisson and Germer who early in 1927 communicated the full account of their work.

It looked as if, but for the timely accident to Davisson's apparatus, the matter waves might have escaped discovery. However, science does not work like that. When a discovery is due, it will be made, if not in one way then in another. Two months after the Davisson and Germer paper, the photograph of an electron diffraction pattern was published by G. P. Thomson in England. He and Davisson shared the Nobel prize for this work. Now the reality of matter waves had been established and this made things worse rather than easier. Patterns on a photographic plate clearly cannot be treated as a mere mathematical figment. Far from being resolved, the particle–wave dualism had only become more firmly established.

Writing in retrospect about the development of physics in the 'twenties, it is inevitable that one imparts to the story an aspect of clear purpose and consistency. It looked very different at the time. After an interval of almost half a century, only the relevant steps are remembered, the useless theories and the bogus results have been forgotten. However, at the time nobody had the slightest idea as to the direction in which the correct path would lead and finding it was not made easier by the innumerable red herrings that were drawn across it. Quite apart from all the ingenious mathematical schemes which in the end led nowhere, the experimentalists were busy, and sometimes too busy. The search for a way out of the maze of unconnected facts and ideas was becoming hectic and it was clearly a 'free for all' as far as guesses were concerned. It was tempting to assume that any guess was inspired and occasionally somebody stuck out his neck a little too far in trusting his luck. There was a group that got electron wave pictures that were nice but, as the authors thought, with some of the detail a bit too faint to be convincing. It seemed justified to retouch the plates just a bit and, getting into the habit, their products eventually became out-and-out fakes, showing clearly the spots which they thought ought to be there. The small energy difference in hydrogen which was mentioned earlier encouraged an enthusiast to look for the same effect in nitrogen. He promptly found it but, unfortunately for him, the experimental result, rushed out at great speed, preceded the theoretical calculation showing clearly that the effect could not exist.

The imprudent overconfidence of some experimentalists was more than matched by the reckless irresponsibility of many of their theoretical colleagues. After all, they felt, if de Broglie got away with his outrageous suggestion of matter waves, anything might be possible and there was no harm in trying. Admittedly, nobody took these new theories as seriously as a new and staggering experimental result but these theories, often couched in unhelpfully general terms, were more difficult to disprove. Even worse, valuable theories were often treated with the same distrust as the useless ones. It was here that 'the terrible Pauli, the scourge of the Lord' came into his own. His discerning eye unfailingly spotted the evil-doers and he stung them with the lash of his tongue. Even the mighty were sometimes made to feel his irony. When later in life Einstein hoped to express all the physical phenomena in one universal field equation, Pauli sounded the gentle warning: 'Man shall not join what God has put asunder'. When confronted with a similar effort by one of his most famous contemporaries Pauli took a piece of paper and drew on it a picture frame. 'You see', he said, 'I, too, can paint as beautifully as Rembrandt, only the little details are missing'.

In the new Babylon, experimentation that broke with all tradition and convention was not limited to science. In the theatre, art and architecture, too, there was a similar revolution, looking for new and untrodden paths. Again, many of these paths never became roads but petered out; now long-forgotten back alleys. Others, however, broke through successfully and came to stay as permanent features that have moulded the image of our century. Skyscrapers in steel and glass, and the daring use of reinforced concrete originated from the 'Bauhaus' under its originator Gropius and his successor Mies van der Rohe. The main idea of this institution was to combine art, craftsmanship and functional design as integral features of any product. The Bauhaus concept not only replaced *art nouveau* which had aimed at adorning technological design but formed a strong and vigorous opposition to expressionism in art which had become sterile. The Bauhaus attracted and sponsored outstanding young men from all over the world, among them Paul Klee, Kandinsky and Moholy-Nagy.

Another field in which the Berlin 'twenties set a new and lasting trend was the theatre and the cinema. Stage design and acting had remained essentially unchanged for a century. Now a host of new ideas burst upon production and direction. Its first pioneer was Leopold Jessner, the director of the Berlin State Theatre who produced 'classical' plays in modern, and often eccentric, form against the fierce opposition of the conservative section of Press and public. The most outstanding figure in the theatre became Max Reinhardt, first an actor who later, as producer, achieved world-wide fame. He bought one of the two permanent circus buildings in the centre of Berlin and had it transformed into a theatre. Its redesigned interior served as model for much of modern theatre building. The action of a play would move for its most dramatic moment from a conventional stage into the centre of the auditorium, establishing close contact with the spectators. The audience became the Roman Senators before whose eyes Caesar was murdered and the crowd whom Mark Antony addressed.

Under the influence of Ernst Lubitsch and Fritz Lang the film, which had been a stage play put upon the screen, became a performing art in its own right. Drama, which at first was still the conventional type in a new guise, also gained an entirely new dimension towards the end of this era in the work of Bertolt Brecht and Kurt Weill.

Arthur Schnitzler's notorious play *Reigen* was written in 1900, but then considered so scandalous that nobody dared put it on stage, until Berlin in the 'twenties provided this opportunity. Again the Public Prosecutor helped the production along with a protracted trial that filled the theatre every night for many weeks because each night might be the last one. Schnitzler himself was so disgusted with the affair that in his will he prohibited any future stage production of the play. However, he had overlooked the cinema and thirty years later the film version achieved world success under the title *La Ronde*.

Commercialization of the newly discovered libido was good for the tourist trade and brought in much-desired hard currency, preferably at black market prices. Sometimes these efforts to shock and debauch foreign visitors overreached themselves. An enterprising café proprietor ingeniously went back to the Roman idea of providing patrons with couches instead of chairs. At first the place was packed out but then had to shut its gates. Not that the police closed it down, but the customers soon found out that the novelty of sipping coffee with one's companion horizontally was too expensive since it involved the cost of having a suit pressed.

As for us, the lakes and forests around the city provided ample scope for cheap outings and enjoyment of life all the year round. In between lectures and research there was the Café Heyl close to the laboratories where over a cup of coffee our problems were discussed. For those whose thesis was approaching the final stages, the subject of philosophy became of burning interest. When the University of Berlin was awarding a D.Phil. degree, they meant what they said and any candidate, be he a physicist or a biologist, also had to pass an examination in philosophy. The only concession was the tacit understanding that the examiner's first question would be as to the particular branch of the subject in which the candidate was mainly interested. The conservative element among us would plump for Greek philosophy which was well documented and could be swotted up for the occasion. The more adventurous spirits would choose psychology, a subject that had acquired burning interest with the recent development of Freud's psychoanalysis. There was an enthusiastic young lecturer who discoursed on this subject and who also asked his students to report any unusual dreams or desires, for analysis in class. He provided a letter-box into which these secrets of our life could be deposited anonymously. Thus the tedium of learning philosophy was broken by two afternoons a week at Heyl's, when we would invent and concoct aberrations beyond the analyst's wildest dreams. It should be said in his favour that he was able to explain all of them.

Most of the time at Heyl's was, of course, devoted to the progress of physics, or rather to our frantic efforts to understand it. On the whole it was a good and testing exercise. In any case, the subject had now reached such a state of confusion that one could ask the silliest question without being branded a fool. Schrödinger's wave mechanics and its brilliant success would have opened a clear view of future development to us, but for the fact that it did not stand alone. While Schrödinger was still working on his wave theory, there appeared a paper from the Goettingen Theoretical Physics School by Born, Heisenberg and Jordan proposing a completely different method of interpreting the atom. It made use of the mathematical scheme of 'matrices' and did not offer any chance of describing an atom in any other than this purely mathematical form. The lack of any physical interpretation baffled the physicists and the work might have been classed with the host of other mathematical schemes suggested at the time but for two reasons. The first was the eminent standing of Max Born who, one felt, would not have published this paper unless he himself had been fully satisfied that it represented the correct approach to the problem. The second reason was that Pauli had immediately applied the new 'matrix mechanics' to the hydrogen atom and obtained the correct result. When Born heard this, he exclaimed: 'As usual, mathematics has been wiser than visual imagination'.

With Pauli's matrix calculation and the success of Schrödinger's wave equation, a baffling situation had arisen. After years of searching and trying, physicists had now been rewarded not with one but with two quantum mechanical descriptions of the atom. Unfortunately, they were completely different and, embarrassingly, they were both obviously correct. It took Schrödinger more than a year to be able to prove that, although mathematically quite different, matrix and wave mechanics were physically completely equivalent. Paraphrasing Born's remark it might be said that mathematics had been too clever.

The basis of matrix mechanics was a philosophical postulate that Heisenberg had formulated during a hayfever cure at Heligoland. It states that only those quantities which, in principle, can be observed are allowed to be used in calculations. Like Pauli's idea of 'classically non-describable' properties of the atom, Heisenberg's postulate did away once and for all with regarding atomic particles as billiard balls, only very small ones. It had now become abundantly clear that the properties of particles or events on the atomic scale could never be described by the familiar models of large-scale physics such as the solar system or collisions on the billiard-table. It was only natural that no effort was being made to introduce model concepts into the mathematical formalism of matrix mechanics.

Into this atmosphere of pure mathematical abstraction there burst like bombshells the concrete physical picture of Schrödinger's wave model of the atom and then the physical reality of the matter waves. For a moment it appeared that not only could the atom again be visualized but that the wave pattern had restored classical continuity which the quantum jumps of the Bohr orbits had destroyed. However, as Heisenberg was shortly to show, the clock could not be turned back and classical physics did not return triumphantly carrying the quantum principle in her arms, as Planck had hoped.

Starting from his postulate, that only observable quantities may be used in calculations, and using the mathematical apparatus of matrix mechanics, Heisenberg arrived at a most startling conclusion. His theoretical investigation concerned the accuracy with which the position and speed of a particle, say an electron, can in principle be determined. In order to locate it, an experimental probe, such as another electron or a light quantum has to be used. In order to locate the particle precisely, the wavelength of the probing quantum must be short. However, then it carries much energy and, when colliding with the electron, it must change its speed in an unpredictable manner. Going to the other extreme of a long wave, the electron's speed will not be affected appreciably but now the long wave cannot locate it very precisely. Heisenberg could show conclusively that there exists a certain limit below which we must forever be in ignorance of the particle's speed and position, and that this limit is given by the size of Planck's quantum constant.

The physicists who, in the past decade, had been quite accustomed to the most unconventional ideas, were deeply shocked when in 1927 Heisenberg's paper was published. Determinism, the very foundation of their science, had been abolished. Until then it had been taken for granted that, given sufficiently precise measurements, a physical event could be predicted to any degree of accuracy. Physicists had assumed that, knowing the state of an atom at any particular moment, they would be able to predict all its future states just as they could calculate the position of the planets ten, a hundred or a thousand years ahead. Now Heisenberg's 'principle of indeterminacy' showed that they would never be able to know the precise state of the atom in the first place. The hallowed concept of causality seemed to have lost its meaning.

It is therefore not surprising that at first most physicists were reluctant to accept this dire prospect; but soon it became clear that Heisenberg's argument was unassailable. Although unwillingly, they had to admit that describing physical events below the limit of the quantum constant had ceased to be reality. Today, indeterminacy forms part of any course of modern physics and only the philosophers of science keep on disputing its existence. Far from destroying the meaning of physics, the uncertainty principle immediately solved the enigma that had plagued physics since 1900: the meaning of the quantum constant. Heisenberg had now shown that this mysterious number which had appeared in Planck's original calculations signifies the lower limit of physical reality.

The first phase of that revolution which Planck had initiated in his address to the Berlin Physical Society more than a quarter of a century earlier was drawing to its close, but the problem posed by Einstein in 1905 remained: the dualism of the wave and particle aspect of light. For two years now it had been aggravated by the further dualism of the particle and wave aspect of matter. Its solution was proposed by Max Born, and, while it is generally accepted, some of the outstanding leaders of quantum physics, such as Einstein, Schrödinger and de Broglie, remained unconvinced.

The problem to be solved was the explanation of the diffraction spots on a photographic plate when a beam of electrons is directed on a crystal. What was the nature of these electron waves? Schrödinger and de Broglie firmly believed that in some as yet undiscovered manner the particle itself must be endowed with some wave properties which caused the diffraction pattern observed on the plate. However, taking as example an electron, this concept immediately leads to a strange dilemma. Each electron carries unit negative charge and, in spite of many attempts, no smaller electric charge has ever been found. As the electron wave undergoes diffraction it evidently gives rise to locally separated spots, but where does its charge go if it cannot be divided into smaller quanta of electricity?

Born's ingenious solution of this puzzle went back to Einstein's 1905 paper in which with prophetic vision, when postulating the existence of individual light quanta, he had dismissed diffraction as a 'large-scale effect'. Born correctly interpreted this term as indicating an effect in which not only one but many particles play a part. Indeed, in the electron diffraction experiments a beam consisting of many electrons is directed on to the crystal. Born now argued that a single electron could never produce a whole diffraction pattern but that it would simply settle on the photographic plate in a region which corresponded to one of the photographically recorded spots. The process would then be the same for any of the individual electrons in the beam, each being diffracted into the same or another spot, the beam as a whole causing in this way the complete pattern. In this explanation, each electron remains localized instead of tearing itself apart to form the pattern and the difficulty concerning its charge is, of course, avoided. The charge can remain safely and undivided with the localized electron.

According to Born then, the diffraction pattern of the matter wave simply represents the statistical chance of any electron hitting the photographic plate somewhere after being deflected by the crystal. Some angles of deflection are statistically more favoured than others and these are therefore the directions in space followed by most electrons. Accordingly, the dark spots on the photographic plate correspond to these most likely directions while the white areas separating them indicate regions where it is less probable for an electron to arrive.

While this concept was being formulated in Born's mind, it was given a more concrete form by Heisenberg's discovery of indeterminacy. Combining this with Schrödinger's wave picture Born concluded that the particle wave is nothing else but a measure of the probability of finding the particle in a particular region of space. Heisenberg had shown that it must forever remain impossible to locate an individual electron with greater accuracy than that given by the quantum constant. Born now pointed out that, although it was impossible to state where the electron is within this space, it would be more likely to be in its centre than at its margin. In fact, one can draw the picture of a wave to cover the distance within which the electron might be found, with its crest at the centre and tailing off into nothing at the ends. Thus, according to Born the height of the wave at any point indicates the probability of finding the electron. As the crest of the wave suggests, the electron is most likely to be found at the centre and its chance of being located near the ends of this stretch diminishes as the height of the wave diminishes.

Now, the diffuse diffraction rings of Schrödinger's theory that had replaced the planetary orbits of the Bohr atom acquired physical meaning. They simply tell us that the electron is most likely to be in those regions where the rings are densest but there is always a small chance of its being elsewhere where the wave pattern is less dense. On the other hand, indeterminacy sees to it that, although we can accurately calculate the likelihood of the electron being in a particular place, we must forever be uncertain about the actual event. With Born's statistical interpretation of quantum mechanics the laws of physics had acquired a new aspect. While condemned to remain forever unable to predict an individual event on the atomic scale, sanity and the laws of nature are saved by statistics. Although one can never say with certainty to which spot of the diffraction pattern an individual electron will be deflected, the whole pattern can be predicted with certainty. All that is required is the use of a large enough number of individual events and then our laws of physics can again be stated to any arbitrary degree of accuracy. It was a strange surprise for Planck to see that the absolute nature of physical laws for which he had fought against Boltzmann now had to be saved by the despised concept of probability. Truth, it turned out, is always statistical.

Werner Heisenberg received the Nobel prize in 1934 for his momentous discovery of indeterminacy. It had completely changed physics, almost from one day to the next. It took much longer for Born's equally momentous discovery of the statistical nature of quantum physics to be recognized. It was a strange thing that the man who had set himself against non-mathematical concepts in quantum physics should have furnished an interpretation of the enigmatic matter wave that any first-year physics student can understand. When at last in 1954 Born was honoured with the Nobel prize, he, too, had been driven out of Germany by Hitler. Becoming a refugee at the age of fifty, he had to start again, first with a special lecturership in Cambridge, then at Bangalore; and in 1936 he was appointed to a professorship at Edinburgh. A kindly, even-tempered man with a large family of spirited and sometimes turbulent children and grandchildren, he could become surprisingly inflexible in matters of scientific controversy. Nevertheless, he never failed to draw attention to the opinion of others who might not agree with his own. His friends worried that he might not recover from a severe illness in his late sixties but, in fact, he lived on long after his retirement, dying early in 1970 at the age of almost ninety.

While Nernst did not make any outstanding contribution to the dramatic development of physics in the 'twenties, he certainly did not remain a silent spectator. He was a faithful attendant at the weekly Berlin physics colloquium where his outspoken intervention in debate used to strike terror into the hearts of the young scientists who had been briefed to report on recent work. If their exposition was not clear, Nernst would certainly demand to have it explained to his satisfaction. On one occasion, when an optical experiment was described, he irritably asked for clarification three times over until another Nobel Laureate went up to the blackboard, making it clear to Nernst that everybody else had understood. At last Nernst retreated, grumbling: 'Oh, now I understand, but with me the light always comes from the left'.

In 1922 he was offered the Presidency of the National Physical Laboratory, the 'Reichsanstalt', that had originally been founded for Helmholtz. Nernst could not resist the temptation of this exalted position which also carried with it the splendid mansion, built according to the demanding taste of Frau von Helmholtz. Life in the house Am Karlsbad ended for the Nernsts with the marriage of their second daughter, Edith, to Herr von Zanthier, a higher civil servant. However, Nernst's acceptance of the Presidency proved a disastrous mistake. Most of the large staff of scientific civil servants were meticulous and somewhat pedantic specialists who could not be hurried. Unlike his old band of enthusiastic research workers, they did physics in office hours only, countering Nernst's demands for a more enterprising spirit with irrefutable civil service regulations. The mixture of mediocrity and red tape was for Nernst intolerable and he lost his temper on more than one occasion. Faced with such an outburst, one of his division heads said censoriously: 'Mr President, you behave like a prima donna'. The poor man was clearly unprepared for Nernst's reply, 'I am a prima donna'.

After two years a state of affairs had been reached where Nernst gladly gave up the Presidency for a return to academic life. Rubens, the head of the university's physics department, had died and the chair was offered to Nernst. This was the large laboratory that had also been built for Helmholtz, with an official residence again designed according to Frau von Helmholtz' wishes. The department was an inspiring building, facing the river Spree to which Nernst's old laboratory had been a mere annex in the Bunsenstrasse. The professor's accommodation was in a wing at the opposite side, opening out into the Neue Wilhelmstrasse, a very select street with the residence of the Reichspraesident, the Prime Minister and the Foreign Office further down. In it were also situated two of Berlin's most exclusive restaurants and Nernst soon became a regular patron of one of them.

Like Nernst, the Reichsanstalt too, had learned a lesson, and the next President was the spectroscopist Paschen, a notoriously mild-mannered person. When a year later Nernst met one of the civil servants, he enquired solicitously into conditions at the Reichsanstalt and, on being told that they were now excellent, asked with his usual mask of astonished sincerity, 'And does my colleague Paschen still go near the place sometimes?'. He recompensed himself for the time lost at the Reichsanstalt by continuing to use the title of President. The chief attraction was its uniqueness. The titles of professor and Geheimrat he shared with others and he permitted these to be used by close associates, but to the research students he was definitely 'Herr Praesident'. He had a tactful and simple method of correcting a caller who was unaware of this by suddenly picking up the telephone and ringing through to his residence. He would then tell the maid that this was Herr Praesident speaking, and ask her to inform Frau Praesident that the Herr Praesident might be a few minutes late for lunch. This usually helped the students to guess how Nernst liked to be addressed, although there was the sad case of one who persisted in his abominable heresy; but, according to Nernst, 'he wasn't altogether very bright'.

The year 1922 ushered in another failure for Nernst. Forever with an eye to technical innovations which might prove profitable, he had become interested in the electronic production of music. Again it was a step ahead of his time that might have met with more response a decade or so later. The invention consisted of an instrument which by electronic means could produce the full scale of a grand piano. It was developed in conjunction with Siemens and the famous piano manufacturer Bechstein, and was marketed under the name Neo-Bechstein Flügel. The Press release was enthusiastic about the technological advance and emphasized that 'the great scientist himself is completely unmusical'. Perhaps it was this circumstance that made the success of the invention a very limited one. Nernst voiced his disappointment many years later to my wife at a dinner. He compared the musical venture with his invention of the lamp for which 'in the good old times' he had received a cash sum, whereas in the case of the piano he had been offended by being offered nothing better than royalties. One wonders whether he were really innocent enough to believe he could do it a second time.

It was after Nernst's return to academic life that the mystery of gas degeneracy was eventually solved. As mentioned earlier, Nernst had been able to derive the third law of thermodynamics only for liquids and solids and he had rejected the suggestion that this was, after all, sufficient since, near enough to the absolute zero, any real gas would liquefy or freeze in any case. He insisted that his theorem was a basic law of science and that even the specific heat of an ideal gas had to vanish, irrespective of whether such a gas could exist or not. Planck, Einstein and Schrödinger fully concurred in this postulate but nobody could see a solution of the problem. Einstein had been able to explain the vanishing specific heat of solid substances by applying the quantum theory to the vibration of atoms in the crystal. However, there was no oscillation that could be associated with a straight path of a gas atom through space. Then, suddenly, the whole problem was solved by de Broglie's matter waves, since the frequency of this wave is the vibration that was needed for applying the quantum theory.

To be historically correct, it has to be stated that this straightforward explanation had been anticipated a year earlier in a very curious manner. In the summer of 1924 Einstein had received for translation into German a paper by a young Indian scholar in Dacca, S. N. Bose. Bose felt that Planck's original derivation of the radiation formula, based on classical principles, should be replaced by one that only made use of statistics and the quantum principle. In order to achieve this he had to make an assumption and Einstein immediately saw that this assumption contained the key to the quantization of an ideal gas. The subsequent events are too involved to permit a simple account but three years later it had become possible to estimate the magnitude of Nernst's postulated effect. The formula demands that degeneracy will make itself felt most for a dense gas of small atomic weight. A computation for the most suitable gas, helium, showed unmistakably that the effect would be far too small to be observable. Gas degeneracy had now been elevated from the status of a vague hypothesis to a calculable physical phenomenon but it appeared that its existence could never be proved by direct experiment.

However, at this stage, Pauli again entered the scene. In a paper published in 1927 he revived the old concept of regarding the electrons in a metal as behaving like a gas but with a significant difference. The old theory had to be discarded because the specific heat of a metal shows no contribution that can be ascribed to an ideal electron gas. Pauli now suggested that the electrons, because of their small weight and high density, form a highly degenerate gas and he applied his exclusion principle, which so far had been limited to a single atom, to the whole of the metal. It was typical of Pauli that with extreme self-criticism he emphasized the tentative nature of his suggestion and refrained from calculating the specific heat. This was finally done in the following year by Arnold Sommerfeld, using a statistical method that had been developed by Fermi and Dirac on the basis of Pauli's exclusion principle. Sommerfeld's paper contained the explicit equation for the specific heat of a degenerate electron gas. It was very small but, being proportional to the temperature, it should be detectable near absolute zero where the specific heat of the metal crystal became vanishingly small. All that now remained was the experimental verification.

When the Sommerfeld paper came out, I was in the final stages of perfecting my apparatus for measuring specific heats at very low temperatures. The temptation was great to shelve the hydrogen project for a few weeks and try my hand at the much simpler determination of the specific heat of a metal, and I promptly succumbed to it. The purest metal sample I could lay hands on was an ingot of electrolytic iron and to my immense delight the whole thing went without a hitch. As I plotted the data on graph paper they showed exactly the predicted form, a curve which at the lowest temperature turned into a straight line, pointing to the absolute zero. The elusive phenomenon of gas degeneracy had been recorded in the laboratory.

The rest of the story is an anticlimax. I jumped into the next train to Prague to take my data triumphantly to my supervisor, Simon, who was attending the 1928 Physics Congress. He looked at the graph, took out a slide rule and then said sadly: 'The data are ten times higher than predicted by the Sommerfeld theory'. 'I know that', I had to admit, 'but it's linear'. This was, in fact, the only way I could have found it because, as I had realized since, the predicted value was at the very limit of accuracy that I could achieve. I never blamed Simon for refusing to announce the result. He was in line for a professorship and it would have been utter folly to prejudice his cause by a sensational discovery which was not in agreement with theory and had been obtained with an untried apparatus by an untried research student. And indeed a few years later the linear specific heat of the correct size was found at the Leiden laboratory on a sample of pure copper. There is, however, a postscript with a lesson to the story. Ten years later somebody recalculated the Sommerfeld formula with rather more refinement and found that for certain metals, such as iron, the specific heat should be much higher than indicated by the simple theory. A fresh measurement of iron was undertaken by a young Belgian research worker and completely confirmed my data of 1928. The lesson I learned was to believe in one's experiments first and foremost and in theory later.

The proof of Nernst's predicted gas degeneracy was only a small part of the rich harvest gathered from that *annus mirabilis* 1927. For the past decade there had been signs and portents of some tremendous development in physics of which Planck's quantum constant of 1900 had been the very first herald. Now, with the creation of quantum mechanics by Schrödinger, Born and Heisenberg, a new dawn had broken. The mist that had shrouded so many basic facts of physics in mystery began to lift and riddles that had puzzled man for thousands of years were suddenly solved in the space of a few months.

When four hundred years before Christ the school of Democritus postulated the existence of atoms, they provided them with little hooks and eyes to hold together. Since then the nature of these cohesive forces had successfully withstood all attempts at explanation. Unlike gravity, the cohesive forces must be of very short range. They will hold a piece of granite together with enormous strength but, once shattered, the fragments will never stick to each other again, however closely fitted. Evidently, the strong attraction that one atom exerts on another cannot reach much farther than to its nearest neighbour. Electrochemistry, to which Nernst had devoted so much of his early work, pointed to the electric nature of these forces but their operation remained obscure. Arrhenius' postulate of positively and negatively charged ions was, as we have seen, originally rejected because such a mechanism of separating electric charges on the atomic scale was equally inconceivable. Classical physics could find no reason why sodium and chlorine atoms dissolved in water should become electrically charged ions.

The first clue to the solution of this mystery was picked up in 1916 by Walther Kossel. He pointed out that in Bohr's quantized atomic model the sodium and chlorine ions, unlike their uncharged atoms, form smooth and symmetrical electron shells. Ten years later the Pauli exclusion principle and quantum mechanics provided a rigorous proof of the stability of these closed shells and for the first time it was understood what keeps a crystal of rock salt together. The explanation of the ionic bond between sodium and chlorine was the first step towards unravelling the mystery of the cohesive forces but in itself it provided no indication of how identical atoms such as those in a lump of copper or lead are bound together. Even the existence of simple molecules, each made up of two identical hydrogen or oxygen atoms, remained as puzzling as ever since their outer electrons should, according to classical concepts, repel and not attract each other. The quantum-mechanical solution of this problem was found in 1927 by two young co-workers of Schrödinger's in Berlin, Walther Heitler and Fritz London. It is significant that this solution of the age-old riddle of the cohesive forces cannot be explained in the language of classical physics; it has no counterpart in the macroscopic world of daily experience. In the hydrogen molecule, for instance, the two atoms share the electrons belonging to each of them and essentially it is the impossibility of distinguishing between the two electrons that is responsible for the binding force. This 'exchange' within the limits of the uncertainty principle is a quantum-mechanical interaction that is responsible not only for the cohesion of atoms in a molecule but also for the strength of metals.

With the elucidation of the nature of the inter-atomic forces, the dividing line between physics and chemistry had disappeared. Planck's prediction in the introduction to his classical paper of 1900 had come true; the quantum concept was revolutionizing not only physics but chemistry as well. Van't Hoff and Nernst had succeeded in expressing the old alchemists' concept of affinity in terms of free energy and entropy but these thermodynamical quantities gave no indication of the actual mechanism whereby certain atoms combine with those of some elements but not with others. Now the enigma of chemical binding emerged as a direct interaction of the Schrödinger wave functions and the Pauli principle. Almost overnight the practice of chemistry was changed into an operation of theoretical physics and the young chemists of the new generation had to be trained in higher mathematics for the mastery of wave and matrix mechanics.

The new dawn of modern physics, which in due course was to shed light even on the elementary structures of life, also broke for the study of that mysterious and elusive structure, the atomic nucleus. In 1905 Egon von Schweidler had recognized the strange fact that the time at which an individual radioactive atom will decay cannot be predicted, and seven years later Geiger and Nuttall had linked the probability of this decay with the energy of the emerging alpha-particle. These results were in complete contradiction to the concepts of classical physics and their interpretation appeared quite impossible. However, in 1928 a young Russian physicist, George Gamow, who had come to study in Goettingen and Copenhagen, attacked the problem with the newly developed armament of quantum mechanics. The assault proved a complete success. Gamow could show that in radioactive substances the wave function of the nuclear particles extended very slightly beyond the confines of the nucleus itself. In terms of Born's statistical interpretation this means that the particle has a small but finite chance of being found outside rather than inside the nuclear structure. Once an alpha-particle has 'tunnelled' quantum-mechanically through the barrier of the nuclear wall, it cannot return, since its own positive charge and that of the nucleus strongly repel each other. It emerges as the corpuscular radiation first observed by Henri Becquerel in February 1896.

The 'leaking out' of the wave function not only provided the explanation of radioactivity, it also opened a new and unexpected way for the investigation of the nucleus itself. If, Gamow argued, wave mechanics permits the rare event of a particle penetrating the nuclear wall from inside, it should also be possible for a bombarding particle to tunnel its way into the nucleus. Up to then all nuclear transformations had relied on using the highly energetic particles from radioactive decay as projectiles and it seemed hopeless with the available means to speed up any bombarding particles high enough artificially. Now Gamow had shown that such high speeds were not really required and that even a slow particle stood a finite chance of penetrating and transforming the atomic nucleus.

This quantum-mechanical consideration paved the way for the famous experiment of Cockcroft and Walton in which atomic nuclei were first split by means of a man-made device. From then on, quantum mechanics went ahead in giant strides in the exploration of the nucleus, culminating in the unlocking of the tremendous power reserve stored in the core of the atom. However, by then the German schools of science had been destroyed by the pied piper from Austria, who had declared their magnificent achievements as a rank weed of alien origin that had to be torn up by the roots. In this he succeeded within a year, and with the Germans following the piper's tune.

8. Heads Will Roll

During the 'twenties life in Germany had become tolerable and eventually comfortable. The Germans were used to working hard without complaining too much and in a remarkably short time after the inflation they were building the finest ocean liners in the world and were flooding world markets with the products of their chemical industry. In 1925 the leading chemical firms had decided that a cartell would be more profitable than competition and, under the chairmanship of Nernst's friend, Carl Duisberg, had combined into the 'Interessen Gemeinschaft Farbenindustrie'. With a share capital of 650 million marks I.G. Farben became the largest industrial combine in Europe. In the same year Paul von Hindenburg was elected President of the Weimar Republic. Seven years had been enough to forget the misery and losses of war and it was time for the army to reassert its old supremacy.

The intellectual life of the time was in strange contrast to this newly regained complacency of the large mass of the people. The young men and women who had grown up in the war and in the post-war years were an active and enterprising generation, free of all illusions but also without any ideals. The individual's effort was entirely devoted to personal interests in science, art, literature and similar pursuits. Politics was considered a mug's game and its practitioners were regarded as nothing better than the successors of the post-war *Schieber*. Political life in the Weimar Republic had successfully killed all active feeling for social improvement and those who, like myself, joined for a while one of the para-military organizations did so merely to combat the lunacy of Nazism rather than for any positive aim. As for the rest, we felt that mankind on the whole hardly merited an idealistic sacrifice and should be quite capable of looking after itself. In fact, we had created a world of intellectual achievement, accompanied by a sound cynicism on all emotional issues. The spirit of the closing years of that era has been preserved for posterity in the work of Brecht and Weill. Brecht's hard, ruthless and uncompromising lyrics in *Threepenny Opera*, *Mahagonny* and *Happy End*, were clothed by the composer in frivolous dance tunes and sweet, melting melodies. In one of the most haunting and longing tunes, the woman sings to her lover:

> 'And as you make your bed, so you will lie,
> Nobody is going to tuck you in,
> And if somebody kicks, it will be me,
> And if somebody gets kicked, it will be you'.

Again and again the truth is hammered home: 'We would so much wish to be good—but circumstance doesn't permit it'. Finally there is the warning: 'Don't get soft, for Heaven's sake, don't get soft'.

Then came the depression and as the number of unemployed rose to more than seven million, the strength of the Nazi Party, to whom the people were turning in despair, grew from day to day. At an election in the summer of 1932 the Nazis received 37 per cent of the votes but at the next one, in November of the same year, they lost ground and it seemed that the corner had been turned, especially as the world economic situation was now improving. The Germans heaved a sigh of relief. However, on the 22nd January, 1933, Ribbentrop gave a dinner party at his house for prominent Nazis and members of the old President's entourage. Later in the evening Hitler had a private talk with Oskar von Hindenburg, the President's son, lasting for a whole hour, from which the latter emerged extremely silent and thoughtful. A week later, on the morning of the 30th January, 1933, the old Fieldmarshal asked the Bohemian corporal to become Chancellor of the German Reich and to form a Government. Four weeks later Hitler was in power.

What exactly was said in the talk between Hitler and Oskar will never be known for certain, but all evidence suggests that the Nazis had come into possession of material which, if published, would ruin the Hindenburg family name for good and ever. There had been constant rumours that money provided by the Weimar Government under the name of *Osthilfe*, help for the eastern territories, had been misappropriated by the Prussian Junkers and that Oskar and the Hindenburg estate at Neudeck were deeply implicated in the tax evasions.

The history of Hitler and the Nazi movement has been established in much detail and with painstaking thoroughness so that it does not require repetition. However, almost nothing has been said about the manner in which the Nazis influenced German science and technology. Some eminent historians hold that Hitler was a genius, albeit an evil one. It is claimed that by clever cunning he was able to outmanœuvre every politician in Europe. If this was the case, his skill certainly did not extend to making use of Germany's immense scientific potential. Far from realizing its importance, the Nazis ruined it through quite unbelievable incompetence and stupidity. Their handling of the country's academic life provides a much better insight into their mental processes than do their political successes.

Right from the start, Nazification pervaded every aspect of life in Germany. It also extended, of course, to the universities, and immediately after assuming power Hitler appointed a Nazi Minister for Science and Education in Prussia, whose rule was extended in the following year to the whole of Germany. Like all the other key appointments, it was given to one of the old stalwarts of the early days of the Nazi Party. The man's name was Bernhard Rust and he was an elementary schoolteacher, who had been dismissed four years earlier in Hanover owing to 'mental instability'. It is significant that Hitler should entrust this important position to a hopeless moron whose only claim was that he had an early party-book and that he believed implicitly in Aryan superiority, of which he considered himself an outstanding example. It was a pattern that was repeated over and over again; ability counted for nothing and proven narrow fanaticism was the only important qualification. It is hard to believe that these appointments were the sign of political genius.

It was inevitable that the German universities now deteriorated at a breathtaking speed. Ten years later, on the 12th March, 1943, Goebbels wrote the following entry in his diary: 'The Fuehrer is an enthusiastic advocate of pure science—it was a great mistake that we failed to win science over to support the new State. That such men as Planck are reserved, to put it mildly, in their attitude towards us, is the fault of Rust and is irremediable.' Goebbels seems to have forgotten that, when in 1933 Hitler had been warned by Carl Bosch, a leading technologist, that his expulsion of Jewish scientists was ruining physics and chemistry in Germany, the 'enthusiastic advocate of pure science' had replied: 'Then we will do without physics and chemistry for the next hundred years'. Bosch, after this, was wise enough to send his own son to England for further study.

Nernst was made aware of the new state of affairs when one morning in the early spring of 1933 he was looking for his colleague, the famous spectroscopist, Peter Pringsheim, and was told that Professor Pringsheim, being a Jew, had been forbidden the laboratory. Nernst flew into a rage and demanded to know who had dared give such an order. It then transpired that the directive had come from his co-director, Artur Wehnelt. Wehnelt who was then in his sixties had once upon a time made some very outstanding technological contributions, such as the electrolytic contact breaker and the oxide-covered filament for radio valves which both bear his name. However, he had been a very sick man for a long time, possibly suffering from poisoning due to the inhalation of mercury vapour. The co-directorship had been bestowed upon him in recognition of his early researches and was not an active post. In fact my only recollection of Wehnelt is that he taught us glass-blowing in the practical course for beginners.

It is unknown whether the frustration over his illness had turned Wehnelt into an out-and-out Nazi or whether the Nazis had simply reminded him of the importance of his co-directorship. Whatever it was, Nernst was not in a mood to bother about Wehnelt's hidden motives and left him in no doubt about what he thought of him. The interview was not made easier by the fact that Wehnelt, instead of giving in, and conscious of his newly acquired power, became quite bumptious, lecturing Nernst on the need to throw out Jewish scientists. This was too much for Nernst; his reaction was quite unexpected but typical of his character. He left the laboratory, hailed a taxi and went straight to the Kaiser Wilhelm Institute for Physical Chemistry in Dahlem, asking on arrival to be shown into Haber's office. It may be remembered that, while there was never any open enmity between Germany's two top physicochemists, they had had their disagreements over the ammonia equilibrium and for years had not exactly sought each other's company. However, scientific argument was a thing that appeared justified to Nernst, particularly between men of equal rank, but stupid anti-Semitism was quite a different matter. The way in which Nernst now offered his hand and friendship to his great Jewish rival is interesting. He told Haber what had happened and that work at Nernst's laboratory had thus become impossible. Could Haber find a place for him at the Kaiser Wilhelm Institute?

There is no record of Haber's personal reaction but his answer was quite simple. He told Nernst that he could not offer his colleague a place, for the simple reason that he was leaving. In fact, he was just tidying up his office so that the Institute could be handed over to his successor, and then he would pack to leave Germany for ever. He was now 65, a tired and disillusioned man, who after the war had tried to pay Germany's war debts by gold, electrochemically extracted from sea water. After much effort, he had had to realize that the samples on which he had based his project were not representative and that the gold content of the oceans was much lower than that of the coastal waters which he had analysed. This failure had depressed him as much as his failure in personal relations; his second marriage had ended in divorce.

Haber's whole life had been devoted to Germany and there was no other scientist who had achieved as much as he for the benefit of his country in peace and war. He had never hidden or denied his Jewish parentage but he had certainly given it second place to his endeavour to be a German, a German with all his virtues—and with all his faults. Now, at the behest of the Bohemian corporal, his country had rejected Haber, an undesirable whose presence polluted the sacred soil of Germany. As his country turned him out, the enemy whom Haber had fought with poison gas and who had listed him as a war criminal, now offered him asylum and a place to work. Rutherford's laboratory at the University of Cambridge had offered him a position.

The Cambridge offer was in the same spirit as Nernst's handshake. It was not merely recognition of the achievements of a great scientist but a protest against Nazi barbarism with its ruthless contempt for learning and scholarship. The helping hand which the scholars of Britian, and later also of America, extended to the Jewish exiles has often been represented as a shrewd move on the part of these countries to secure for themselves first-rate scientists at low cost. Nothing could be further from the true facts and it is the duty of those who benefited by this manifestation of academic solidarity to repudiate this explanation emphatically. Nobody would expect men like Haber or Freud, who were both old and sick when they came to England, to make great contributions. Einstein, too, had passed the stage of his great achievements and the same was true for most of the scientists who already had a world reputation when they had to leave Germany. The great majority of the scientific emigrants were young and unknown people. Those who later made worthwhile contributions were able to do so because their host countries generously gave them the chance that Germany had denied them.

Hitler's flat refusal to Carl Bosch to reconsider the Nazi policy against Jewish scientists was repeated when the same suggestion was made by Max Planck. In the short note on this visit which Planck published after the war, he relates that Hitler, far from understanding the damage inflicted on the future of German science and technology, worked himself up into one of his anti-Semitic tirades, which Planck listened to in silence before he was permitted to withdraw. It is significant that Planck had not requested an audience with Hitler to discuss this problem but had made use of the official call which, as Secretary of the Prussian Academy of Sciences, he had to make early in 1933 on the new Reich Chancellor. Like all his colleagues in Germany, Planck had avoided a protest against Nazi policy and when he had received the Fuehrer's ruling, he abided by it.

Haber did not long survive the exile into which Germany had forced him. Accompanied by his sister, he arrived in England a broken man. He tried to regain his strength on a holiday in the South where he hoped to find a much needed rest. He died on his way, in Basle, on the 29th January, 1934. Max von Laue wrote his obituary in the journal *Naturwissenschaften* which earned him and the editor a severe reprimand with the threat of sterner measures. Haber had been a Member of the Academy of Sciences and Planck, as its Secretary, had agreed to speak at a memorial meeting held at Otto Hahn's suggestion at Haber's old institute at Dahlem. That the meeting took place at all, was probably due to a reluctance in the early days of Nazi rule to taking punitive action against Planck. However, Minister Rust who described it as: 'A provocation to the National Socialist State' forbade members of the universities and of scientific societies to attend. The organizers were also told that nothing about this meeting would be allowed to be published. This was the only little flicker of academic resistance to Nazism. It was not very strong and it passed unnoticed. The spirit of resignation was aptly put into words by Otto Hahn who, in 1966, said in his autobiography: 'As acting director I tried to soften especially harsh orders from the people in power, but of course I could not do anything about the general situation'.

There was one man who had the courage of his convictions, Erwin Schrödinger. As a pure Aryan he was perfectly safe in his exalted place as Planck's successor at the University of Berlin. Nevertheless, he had no hesitation in giving up his position and going voluntarily into exile, where, as he knew full well, no professorship was waiting for him. His action was in the first place a protest against the treatment of his Jewish colleagues, such as Einstein, Born and Franck, whose fate he preferred to share rather than to owe the safety of his job to an accident of birth. Secondly, he saw at this early stage and much more clearly than the rest of his German colleagues, that science in Germany had received a death-blow.

In their speeches and writings Hitler and the other leading Nazis had affirmed again and again that they would rid German intellectual life from all Jewish taints and from the theory of relativity in particular. Indeed, as we have seen, Einstein and his work had been the main target of anti-Semitic agitation for many years. The vanguard of the attack was now led by the two venerable cranks, Philip Lenard and Johannes Stark. As already mentioned, Lenard's anti-Semitism and Aryan superiority may have been overcompensation for his descent from Slovak-Hungarian merchants; it is more difficult to understand what was wrong with Stark. He may have been motivated by the fact that the explanation of the effect which he had discovered, and which earned him the Nobel prize, was provided by two Jewish scientists, Karl Schwarzschild and Paul Epstein. Moreover, Lenard and Stark had both been rejected in the choice for the Berlin physics professorship, to which Nernst was appointed in 1924, because 'their unusual views in theoretical physics would harm this school at Berlin'.

Stark had now been appointed president of the Physikalisch-Technische Reichsanstalt after the dismissal of its director, Paschen, who was a Jew. He lost no time in establishing truly Aryan physics by substituting for the 'Jewish dogmatic' concept of the electron a ring-shaped structure, and one of his scientific civil servants obediently provided the experimental proof for the director's theory. This was not difficult since he simply repeated a standard experiment for which he obtained the standard result. It had, however, nothing to do with the structure of the electron.

With one exception the world of international science passed over this piece of patent nonsense in icy silence. The exception was a Dr Madhavo Rao of Bangalore in South India. Rao first pointed out that he himself had hit upon the idea of the ring-shaped electron before Stark, but had shown by theoretical calculation that such a concept was untenable, basing his refutation on the work of the Jews, Heitler and Born. Stark was fool enough to treat Rao to a 3000 word reply with an appendix 'On the origin of physical discoveries' and winding up with a quotation from Helmholtz. He got back a much shorter answer, pithy and to the point, with an even better quotation from Helmholtz. Stark had evidently overlooked the fact that Max Born, in exile from Germany, was working at the time at Bangalore.

While Stark was going on to the bitter end with the Aryanization of physics based on bogus experiments, the other stalwart of Nazi science, Philip Lenard, was now over seventy and too old to conduct research. However, he enriched the scientific literature with four volumes of *German Physics*, a course of the subject which was freed from 'Jewish physics, a degenerate mirage of the basic Aryan physics'. The trouble with modern physics, as he pointed out in great detail, is the inability of the Jews to distinguish between truth and lies. Again Einstein was the archvillain from whose mental perversions the German people had to be saved.

The publication of this *magnum opus* was made the occasion for a treatise by a group of Nazi students, at the request of the Reich Studenten-fuehrer, on 'Lenard and his struggle for Nordic research'. It recalls the professor's courage when he expressed in the lecture room his satisfaction with the murders of Erzberger and of Rathenau and when he refused to have the institute's flag at half-mast on the latter occasion. Needless to say, the police of the Weimar Republic protected Lenard from the irate students of the day who wished to beat him up. In addition to these accounts of upright German heroism, the pamphlet contains a somewhat laboured paragraph, in small print, trying to establish Lenard's true Aryan descent, about which there seems to have been some doubt.

Stark and Lenard had not been taken seriously long before Hitler and were simply accepted as irresponsible but relatively harmless fanatics. A far more serious problem was the many second- or third-rate scientists who were quite sane but now saw a golden opportunity to get into positions which they would never have attained before Hitler. All that was now required of them was an Aryan pedigree and vociferous proclamation of racial superiority. One of these men, Professor Wilhelm Müller of Aachen, even scooped Lenard by bringing out a book on Jewry and science in which he described an international Jewish conspiracy to pervert science and ultimately destroy all true humanity. Fortunately, Adolph Hitler had arisen, in the nick of time, and of course Wilhelm Müller, to save mankind from the machinations of Jewish sub-humans.

Müller, the nonentity, was eminently successful with his scheme and was appointed professor of theoretical physics at Munich, in succession to the world-famous Arnold Sommerfeld. He celebrated his appointment with a theoretical physics colloquium given by the guest lecturer, Johannes Stark, who had chosen the scientific subject of 'Jewish and German Physics'.

While the main content of this lecture, featuring again the Aryan ring-electron, hardly merits repetition, a few introductory remarks are significant enough to be quoted verbatim. They deal with the dangerous breed of 'white Jews' among his German colleagues who, in his opinion, were sabotaging true German physics. 'Numerous men', Stark points out,

who taught in the Jewish spirit but were able to prove their Aryan descent have remained in office. Some have even adopted National Socialist guise but nevertheless continue in their propaganda work for Jewish-dogmatic theories. As late as 1936 Heisenberg wrote an article in the leading National Socialist newspaper *Voelkischer Beobachter* in which he declared that: 'The theory of relativity is the fundamental basis of future research'. Planck, who for years has supported Einstein and the Jewish influence, finds it possible, even today, to sponsor publication of scientific papers in the Jewish spirit. Sommerfeld, the chief propagandist of Jewish theories, was until recently, an academic teacher.

Stark then goes on reviling Sommerfeld, whose successor, the great Professor Wilhelm Müller, he was now inaugurating in office. Stark also had a few words to say about the renegade Schrödinger who, of course, had preferred voluntary exile to the blessings of German physics.

What really was happening is quite clear. The remaining German scientists of some standing were making a desperate effort to save a vestige of modern physics in their universities. Heisenberg, in particular, was trying to make the teaching of the relativity theory acceptable in the Third Reich by slipping a mention of its importance into the hallowed columns of the top Nazi paper. However, in the end it was all of no use. Mutilated German science failed to recognize nuclear fission when it had been discovered in a German laboratory and it equally failed to find the key to the atomic bomb. Rocket propulsion, the only field in which the Germans outstripped the allies, required no new ideas and it had been pioneered in Germany long before the Nazis came to power. Already in the 'twenties, Fritz von Opel had tested a rocket-powered motorcar and Hermann Oberth, at the same time, published his famous book on planetary rocket travel.

Nernst, too, was regarded as a white Jew. Two of his daughters had married Jews and there was even an attempt to doubt his own Aryan descent. This he never mentioned to his daughters, and the matter only came to light when after the war the university archives were scrutinized in East Berlin. Late in 1935 a student by the name of Otto Richter was working on a diploma thesis concerned with the genealogy of Nobel Laureates. It seems that Herr Richter got satisfactory replies to his detailed questionnaire with the exception of the Jews, Wallach and Willstaetter who, in any case, were beyond the pale and the frontiers of the Fatherland—and of Nernst. The latter, now in retirement, had returned the uncompleted form with a note that he had more important matters at hand. Richter, livid with venom, now reported this insult to the Ministry of Propaganda who, in turn, advised him to submit his complaint to the dean of the philosophical faculty, Professor Bieberbach.

Bieberbach, who had atoned for his decidedly a-Nordic appearance by describing Einstein as an 'alien mountebank', was a mathematician and therefore a kindred spirit to Richter, who was a mathematics student, researching into pedigrees. He promptly furnished Richter with Nernst's birthplace and date and with the good advice to obtain the genealogical information from the local church register. A cryptic note at the end of the dean's letter says that he himself would be much interested eventually to learn the result of this enquiry. That was on the 21st December, but in the peace of the Christmas holidays Bieberbach thought the matter over and decided that it was too promising to be left in the inexpert hands of Otto Richter. On the 30th December he asked Richter to send him Nernst's uncompleted pedigree form, which Richter submitted to him on the 4th January with the urgent request to let him have it back as soon as possible. It was indeed returned two days later, together with the 'confidential' copy of a report that Bieberbach had made to Rust. In it he drew the Minister's attention to Nernst's note which 'indicates that Geheimrat Nernst does not yet seem to have a correct appreciation of the basic tenets of the new Reich'. He also asks the Minister to empower him to force Nernst 'to fill in the great questionnaire (Form II, 64/65)', designed for professors suspected of non-Aryan descent. This request seems to have been granted to Bieberbach, since the correspondence ends with a triumphant letter from the dean to Otto Richter, dated the 29th February, and enclosing the completed questionnaire. It disclosed, however, the disappointing fact that Nernst was completely Aryan.

The incident is a typical example of the chicaneries that had become a dominant feature of academic life under Hitler. With the guidance of the new rector, a veterinarian, race studies had become an important subject in the university. In order to make quite sure that Nazification was thorough, the faculties were supervised by a *Dozentenfuehrer* whose activities corresponded to those of a Nazi Gauleiter. Professors and lecturers were acquainted with the true spirit of the Third Reich in courses at a *Dozenten-lager* to which they had to report, armed with a gym suit and a copy of *Mein Kampf*. Significantly, the overall command was in the hands of an S.S. Obergruppenfuehrer, who reported directly to the Minister—and, of course, to Himmler.

The tight control kept by the Nazis on academic appointments is illustrated by the case of one of my colleagues, a pure Aryan of right-wing political leanings, a good physicist but not a fervent Nazi. The faculty at Danzig offered him the chair of physics at their university and he accepted the post. A short while afterwards a party official called at his house and enquired about membership of Nazi organizations. The professor-elect offered membership of the Physical Society, a sailing club and a stamp collectors' association, all, of course, Nazified and each with its party secretary. The snooper raised his eyebrows in surprise, said this was a bit thin, and left. Needless to say, no further communication from the University of Danzig was ever received.

Not only Hitler but the Nazi leaders as a whole shared a thorough dislike of professors and intellectuals in general. None of their actions and pronouncements leave any doubt that they had not the faintest idea about the role of universities in the life of a country. They felt well satisfied with the brilliant forecasts of the great achievements of Aryan science to come, provided for them by men like Stark, Lenard and the surgeon Sauerbruch. The last had bolstered this prospect, by leading in the autumn of 1933, a deputation of 960 university teachers to take a solemn oath to support the Third Reich. Anyway, the Nazis would not know that most of these were third-raters, now looking forward to brilliant careers. Neither were they bothered by the fact that by 1939 the enrolment of science and technology students had dropped to less than half of the numbers in 1933. Official figures indicate that Rust dismissed almost 3000 university teachers for being non-Aryan or politically unreliable, a quarter of the total number. They were easily replaced by nonentities and cranks who had proved their worth by being fully fledged party members.

The utter lack of comprehension on the part of the new leaders is exemplified by a book called *Germany Speaks*, brought out by Messrs Thornton Butterworth in London in 1938. It consisted of a series of chapters, each written by a Nazi luminary for the express purpose of displaying to the British public the achievements and high ideals of the Third Reich. It features an article by Rust on education in which he points out that schools and universities had now been cleansed of 'Jews and others, animated by selfish motives or by international and anti-racial ideas'. These subversive elements had 'poisoned the healthy feelings of the nation by means of their educational policy'. Even more appalling is the chapter contributed by the Reich Minister of Justice,

Franz Guertner, in which he stated that: 'Under the present system of executing the sentences, the deterrent influence receives once more the recognition it deserves'. He further explained enthusiastically the operation of the new Special People's Courts and cites as a particular advance that forcible sterilization had, at last, become legally possible. Whatever may have been the motives of the publishers, it is hard to believe that, even in 1938, this can have been a line of propaganda particularly efficacious in Britain.

An even more glaring example of this crass stupidity is provided by a meeting to which all professors and lecturers were called in the great hall of Berlin University. The purpose had not been disclosed beforehand, but it had been made quite clear that attendance would be obligatory. It turned out that they were to be addressed by the Fuehrer's close friend, Julius Streicher. Strutting up and down the rostrum in jack boots and brandishing the horse whip without which he was never seen, he informed the professors where they really stood and that it was just as well for them to understand the blessings of the Third Reich. All their brains put together, he told them, did not amount to one-thousandth of the brain of the Fuehrer. He regaled them with accounts of the menace of the Jewish spirit and, being Streicher, he saw to it that the picture was filthy and obscene. The meeting had been arranged over the head of the university authorities and even over the Ministry of Education at the express wish of the Fuehrer. It was Hitler's own effort to win over the professors to the swastika banner.

Hitler himself resented education and background because he suspected it and it is significant that even among the Nazi hierarchy his closest friends were those who were the crudest and the most uncouth, without manners or breeding. These, in fact, were the only men whom he really trusted.

Neither Goering, nor Goebbels, and not even Himmler, are mentioned in *Mein Kampf* but he singles out Streicher and Esser as the true friends to whom he was deeply grateful. Like Rust, Streicher was a dismissed elementary schoolteacher. He was an extrovert sadist who issued a wildly anti-Semitic and openly pornographic weekly called *Der Stuermer*, and as Hitler pointed out, it was the one paper which he always read from cover to cover. Hermann Esser, a truculent Bavarian, was also a great Jew-baiter, who openly boasted that he was living off women and shared with Streicher a fondness for blackmail.

These were Hitler's closest friends with whom, however, the other Nazi leaders shared the distinction of being social misfits. Goering was a distinguished fighter pilot in the First World War but took to drugs. As a young man, Joseph Goebbels had tried unsuccessfully to get his articles accepted by one of the big newspapers and it is possible that being turned down by the Jewish-owned *Berliner Tageblatt* had tipped the balance towards anti-Semitism. However, his ego suffered far worse from the fact that he was a little man with a club foot and a singularly unattractive face. The great number of entries in his diary relating to love affairs make pathetic reading. Robert Ley, the Minister of Labour, was originally a chemist who had lost his job because of habitual drunkenness, a habit which grew worse as the years went by.

There remains the shadowy figure of Heinrich Himmler, the exterminator-in-chief of over six million people, head of the S.S. and of the Gestapo. The historians have astonishingly little to say about this mild-mannered, bespectacled poultry-breeder from Bavaria, except that, as every German knew, he was the most feared man in the Third Reich. In spite of his fiendish organization of torture and mass murder, there are no records of personal sadism, such as practised by Heines or Streicher, but of a single-minded devotion to the great task of cleansing the Earth of all Jews and white Jews. He firmly believed in the influence of the stars and was obsessed with the idea of the Germanic heritage. Even during the war, he would drop important business in favour of following up the rumour about an old woman in Friesland who still practised an ancient Nordic type of weaving. All information on such crafts, implements or customs were collected by the *Ahnenerbe*, Himmler's research institute for heredity. The same institution also required from the concentration-camp doctors the skulls of different ethnic groups, such as 'Jewish-Bolshevik Commissars', which had first, however, to be measured alive before being forwarded to the collection in hermetically sealed cans. In this single-minded obsession he was closest to Hitler who evidently for this reason entrusted Himmler with all those insane tasks that his own madness demanded. No record has been found of those long and frequent conversations 'under four eyes' in which the sordid details of mass murder were discussed. While Himmler saw to the actual operation of the plan, there can be no doubt that Hitler himself was the originator.

Hitler's ravings against the Jews in *Mein Kampf* are too well known to require repetition and all that interests us is whether they can be entirely explained as hatred engendered by his own feeling of inferiority and inadequacy. Perhaps there were deeper reasons for all this venom. Hitler graphically describes his first encounter with Jews during his nocturnal wanderings as a vagrant in Vienna's red-light district. In themselves these accounts of hook-nosed procurers of Aryan flesh hardly differ from Streicher's obscenities, but they might take on a different meaning when read in conjunction with Hitler's frequent mention of syphilis. There seems to be little reason to refer to this particular disease in a political manifesto but Hitler in *Mein Kampf* devoted page upon page to its ravages and later again he returned to the theme when he referred to failures to find a cure. Perhaps Hitler contracted the disease in his Vienna days under what he must have regarded as Jewish influence, and it is equally possible that it contributed to his mental derangement.

These then were the men who directed Germany's scientific and academic life throughout the thirteen years of the Third Reich and whose leadership remained undisputed to the bitter end. As the ghastly vortex of inhumanity and insanity spiralled faster and faster into mass torture and extermination, the German people remained loyal. Since it is inconceivable that a population of eighty million had become sadistic maniacs, the standard German explanation that people did not know what was going on is often accepted as the only alternative. However, since there were hundreds of camps with a personnel of tens of thousands of guards spread all over Germany, and as the cattle trucks carrying millions of victims moved along the railway system, this easy explanation is equally inconceivable. In any case, the Germans can hardly accuse Hitler of having kept them in the dark about his intentions. He had promised them the extermination of the Jews in 1923 and had reiterated his resolve since then innumerable times. Actually, his threatening and blood-curdling oratory had been a most important stock in trade. When he had shouted: 'Heads will roll in the sand', pleasant shudders crept up the spines of his audience. It was like a horror film.

When, after the war, I asked my German colleagues about the extermination of Jews, Poles and Russians, most of them admitted that they suspected horrible things were happening, but this was as far as they would go. And that is probably the key to the whole mystery of Nazi rule; the Germans all knew, but nobody looked and nobody questioned. After all, their State had been built up on the basis that 'an order is an order'.

Whatever they might have said later on, the generals supported Hitler to the full. For his promise of a war of revenge they had gladly sacrificed Kurt von Schleicher. Austria and Czechoslovakia were just manœuvres, but then, in 1939, their superb fighting machine swung into action against Poland, which was no match for it. Holland, Belgium and France were next on the list. The generals demonstrated to their Fuehrer that his army was invincible. Britain had been isolated and they drove into Russia, just as in 1914.

Just as in 1914, the generals did not see that again they had lost the war until it was far too late. Only when the enemy was closing in on the Fatherland in 1943 did the generals begin to wonder. They thought that it was time to find a scapegoat who could be blamed for their failure but the Jews were no good this time; they had been killed off already. There seemed to be little choice. Nevertheless, they procrastinated until on the 6th June, 1944, British and American troops landed in Normandy. Now something had to be done in a hurry.

In the evening of the 20th July a news flash came from the powerful radio station in Berlin, which within minutes was relayed to the remotest corners of the world; the generals had made an attempt on the life of Hitler. For a moment my heart stood still. Was it all going to happen again? Was the gallant army going to cleanse the sacred soil of Germany from that inhuman ogre whom they had served so faithfully for the past eleven years? Were the generals going to keep the Allied Forces out of Germany by offering them their clean hands in friendship, so as to be ready for the next war in twenty-five years' time? Then came the relief; Hitler was alive, and could be relied upon to deal with his faithful generals in much the same way as he and they together had dealt with the peoples of Europe. The end came in true Nazi fashion with hangings on piano wire and meat hooks, filmed in detail at Himmler's orders and shown to the Fuehrer after dinner on the same day.

One of the victims was Max Planck's son.

When the Third Reich perished in the final holocaust of 1945, Nernst was no longer there to see it. Neither did he take part in the degradation of Germany's academic life to which he had contributed so much. The ascent of Hitler coincided with the end of Nernst's official duties. Having reached retiring age, he gave up the Berlin professorship in 1933, a few months after shaking Haber's hand. That incident, as well as his row with Wehnelt, and other things he may have said about the new regime seem to have had an immediate effect. He was informed that in future his presence on the governing body of the Kaiser Wilhelm Institute was no longer required. It will be remembered that it was Nernst's influence with the Kaiser more than anything else to which this unique research institution owed its existence. He had always regarded the Institute with much affection and again after 1918 had seen to it that it received the necessary funds to continue and even expand its work. He therefore felt bitter about his dismissal from the Board but after the fate of Haber and his other Jewish colleagues Nernst was hardly surprised. A few years later he was to learn that this slight that he had received from the Nazis was considered a mark of distinction by his friends abroad.

It was time for Nernst to turn his back on the humiliations that had become the dominant aspect of German academic life, and on Berlin, the city whose sparkling and scintillating spirit had been snuffed out overnight. Suddenly he felt his age and he wanted to rest. He longed for the happy life of his childhood in the unending fields, forests and lakes of the East German plain.

When Nernst bought the estate of Rietz in 1907 he was at the summit of his career, a reasonably wealthy man who could well afford to indulge in mildly ostentatious living, so characteristic of the Wilhelminian era. The house had been built by a descendant of Frederick the Great's

Minister of Finance, who, however, had run out of money when constructing the top floor. Nernst had this part rebuilt and even added a
turret with battlements and a flagstaff. The idea was to have the flag
hoisted whenever he came into residence but, according to the testimony
of his daughter, this ceremony was usually forgotten. There had been
horses for the boys and a pony for the smaller children. Throughout the
summer there were guests and the highlight of Nernst's hospitality was
his shooting parties in the winter. After the death of his second son, these
memories became intolerable and Rietz was sold.

Zibelle was bought when Nernst was fifty-six and the affluence of the
pre-war days had given place to the scarcity and social insecurity of the
grim years after defeat. The changed circumstances were reflected in the
setting of his new estate. Nernst was now looking for peace and quiet
and for a place to which he would eventually retire. Although Zibelle
boasted the title of *Rittergut*, a squire's estate, it was in character a farm-
house whose garden opened on to the village street. There were nine
rooms altogether and a flat for the administrator. The cowshed, pigsties
and barn were close to the house, providing Nernst with all the aspects
of a farmer's life, which he liked. There were a thousand acres, partly
woods and meadows and partly fields with rye and oats and even some
wheat, for which the climate is a bit harsh. Other crops were potatoes,
clover and lupins. Lupin seeds were used for feeding the carp in which
Nernst took a particular interest.

A probably apocryphal story records Nernst's surprise on a cold winter
morning to find the cowshed pleasantly warm and wondering whether it
was heated. On being told that this was due entirely to the metabolic
heat of the cows, he sold the cows and invested the proceeds in carp since
he felt that he did not intend to spend his money on meat production
attended with so much waste heat when the same thing could be done
isothermally. Whatever the truth of this anecdote, Nernst forever
praised the thermodynamic efficiency of fish who were able to put on
weight at ambient temperature.

When Nernst bought the estate, he found that there were no less than
eighteen ponds and lakes of varying size covering altogether sixty acres,
which had probably already been used for fish farming. In addition to
providing him with an opportunity for swimming, which he liked very
much, the financial possibilities of breeding carp intrigued Nernst greatly.
He immediately immersed himself in literature on fish farming and then
set to work to have the ponds cleared and their water supply regulated.
It takes three summers and two winters to produce carp for the table.
In May the fish used for breeding are put into small ponds where they
must be left undisturbed and Nernst went so far as to set watchmen to
guard against any human or animal intruders during these critical weeks.

Once the fry are hatched, the small fish are transferred to larger ponds and again transferred every autumn so that the fish in each pond are of uniform age and size. Then, finally, in October, the ponds with the largest carp are drained and the fish are caught. It was a ceremony which Nernst liked to supervise personally. The fish were then sent alive and in special tanks, mainly to Berlin, where they fetched high prices as the traditional fare for Christmas and New Year's Eve. I remember one summer when, after a long dry spell, it started to rain, Nernst interrupted his lecture on general physics, to tell several hundred students that water in the carp ponds had been perilously low. It must have been very much on his mind. So much so that he had forgotten that his carp were a hundred miles away and possibly might not benefit by the downpour.

Before his retirement, Nernst drove out to Zibelle whenever he found time to spend the week-end in the country. In addition to his own wood-land he hired the shooting rights in some of the adjoining forests. As in his younger days, he was too impatient to spend hours in wait of large game and instead he went for hare, partridge and particularly snipe, which were plentiful by the lakes. Unlike Rietz, Zibelle saw no large parties. It was just the family or a few close personal friends who kept Nernst company in the country. Until his retirement the Nernsts enter-tained in their palatial official residences in Berlin, laid out by Frau von Helmholtz. From then on they lived at Zibelle, keeping only a small flat in Berlin which Nernst used when attending the weekly meetings of the Prussian Academy or when he had other business in the capital.

Nernst's seventieth birthday, in the following year, was celebrated in Zibelle with their closest friends, Max von Laue and his wife, the mathe-matician Erhard Schmidt and a few others. Hundreds of messages of con-gratulation poured in from all over the world and all the leading German newspapers marked the occasion with accounts of Nernst's achievements and career. Somewhat to the surprise of his family, Nernst was especially pleased with a letter from Hindenburg of whom he had been critical ever since his audience with the Kaiser. Perhaps he was pleased with the recognition expressed by the Head of State or he may have felt that, in spite of Hindenburg's past allegiance, the old man had served the Weimar Republic faithfully. Nernst knew nothing, of course, of the shameful manner in which Hindenburg had betrayed this trust by succumbing to Hitler's blackmail.

The seventieth birthday was the last time the Nernst family was to be together. A few days later, Hitler's liquidation of many of his old party members highlighted the ruthlessness of Nazi terrorism. Nernst shook his head and said that a regime in which one shoots one's best friends cannot last for long. However, he had no illusions about the immediate future. Above all, he was worried about the future of Hilde and Angela, who had Jewish husbands, and about their children, and he was far from complacent about the eventual downfall of the Third Reich. Dr Cahn, Hilde's husband, was trained as a chemist and, moreover, it was likely that his connection in international banking circles would help him find a new home outside Germany. Things were more difficult with Angela's husband, Albert Hahn, who was a judge whose professional qualifications would be useless abroad. The industrial holdings of the Hahn family had been taken over by the Nazis and there would be no money to fall back on. Nernst saw all this clearly and he advised Angela to acquire some skill by which she could earn money anywhere in the world. She took his advice and learned millinery, which was to help her over the worst in the difficult years to come.

Among the friends who came to see Nernst in his retirement was Lindemann, who was a great traveller and who dropped in whenever he passed through Germany. Unlike most Englishmen, Lindemann, from the beginning, had no illusions about Hitler's real aims. He knew German conditions too well to be bemused by the anti-Communist propaganda with which the Nazis tried to endear themselves to British public opinion. He was horrified by the insane destruction of German science and even more by the murder of Jews and political opponents, of which he had obtained information from reliable sources. In 1935 he requested an audience with Hitler. This was not granted and instead it was made clear to him that he was no longer considered *persona grata* and advised to leave Germany at once. His last evening was spent with the Nernsts in Berlin. It was a sad parting but, even if Lindemann could not come again to see Nernst in Germany, Nernst was clearly not too old to visit him at Oxford. Two years later they met again, but then it was for the last time.

The occasion was the conferment on Nernst of an Honorary Doctorate of Science by the University of Oxford in June 1937. The Oxford doctorate was the last of a long list of honours that he had received. In 1931 he had been elected as a Foreign Member into the Royal Society and he had become an Honorary Member of the Academies of Vienna, Oslo, Stockholm, Leningrad, Turin, Venice, Modena, Budapest and Munich. However, the trip to Oxford was different. It turned out to be a reunion with the former members of his scientific school who had been forced to leave Germany and whom Lindemann had brought to England. There was also another reunion, with his eldest daughter Hilde and her husband, who had by then emigrated from Germany and had settled in London. When Nernst went back to Germany after this visit, he did not realize that it was to be a parting for ever from his three grandchildren and their parents.

Angela's husband, the judge Albert Hahn, was dismissed in 1933, shortly after Hitler came to power. However, thanks to the fact that he had been baptized and in recognition of his war service, he was reinstated. Nevertheless, his position remained precarious and he lost his job finally in 1935 when the anti-Semitic Nuremberg laws were introduced which debarred not only Jews but anyone of Jewish descent from holding public office. For a while the Hahns stayed on in Germany, vainly hoping that things might improve, but after a renewed anti-Semitic drive in 1938 they left for good, first going to England and a year later to Brazil. In July 1939, before embarking for South America, Angela Hahn went back to Germany to wind up her affairs and to take their only daughter Ursula for prolonged medical treatment. It was the last time that Nernst saw his youngest daughter. On her way to Brazil she learned about the escalation in the European crisis preceding the war and telegraphed for her child to be sent immediately to her sister in London. Ursula got out of Germany just before Hitler's troops marched into Poland.

Nernst had always been fond of family life. Until his daughters left home, he had insisted on family meals so that he was sure to see them regularly and then he would discuss the day's events with them. When the grandchildren were born, he was delighted and lost no opportunity to share their company. Now the enforced separation and their fate in foreign lands affected him deeply and in May 1939 he had a severe heart attack. He never fully recovered.

His weekly visits to the Academy sessions in Berlin had ceased some time ago. Nernst detested the growing Nazification of all aspects of scientific life and there had been some serious unpleasantness when, on one of these occasions, he had refused to get up when the *Horst Wessel Lied* was played. From then onward Zibelle became his world, a tiny enclave of the past in which Emma retained the routine of their former life. She still got up every morning at six o'clock, supervising the household and going through the farm accounts with the administrator.

The only child left in Germany was Edith von Zanthier who lived in Kiel. Although the journey to Zibelle was a long one, taking from five o'clock in the morning until seven o'clock at night, Edith and her daughter always visited the grandparents in the school holidays. Her husband, too, came frequently because, like Nernst, he enjoyed the shoot. These journeys became increasingly difficult as the bombing of the German railways grew more intense and they often had to be interrupted for the passengers to take shelter. Even so, Edith not only kept up her visits but made every effort to see her parents more often. In 1941 she realized that the end was near and Nernst, too, wondered at each parting whether he would see her again, asking Edith to come back soon. Edith went on the grim journey every three weeks, usually staying a week in Zibelle.

F

Even worse than the separation from his daughters was for Nernst the inability to have regular news from them. For a while, friends in Switzerland helped to let him have news from the Cahns in London. Since Brazil was a neutral country communication was easier and Nernst wrote every week to his granddaughter. But this link, too, was to discontinue. His last letter that got through is dated January 25th, 1941, and in it he says 'We wish every day and every hour that you could be here with us . . .' From then on there was only sporadic and indirect news through the Berlin nuclear physicist, Lise Meitner, who had emigrated to Sweden.

Early in November the Zanthiers had been visiting Zibelle. Hardly had they returned to Kiel when, on the 15th, Emma rang her daughter, telling her that Nernst was sinking fast. Edith set out immediately but found her father already unconscious. He died in the morning of the 18th.

During the last days Emma had been sitting at his bedside, taking down notes during his moments of consciousness. The last of these was true to Nernst's whole character. He said: 'I have already been in Heaven. It is quite nice there but I told them they could have it even better.'

In 1943 Edith's husband died and Emma went to spend Christmas with her daughter in Kiel. In the first days of the new year the house was bombed while they were sheltering in the cellar and Emma went back to Zibelle. She was caught in another heavy raid in Berlin, all by herself, and sheltered under a railway arch, but eventually she got safely back to Zibelle. The bombing of Kiel continued and Edith, who could find no place to stay, later in 1944 joined her mother in Silesia. Life in the country was free from air attacks but soon a new danger was approaching.

There had remained a thin line of sporadic communication with Hilde in England. Through friends in Switzerland she told her mother and sister, late in 1944, that the Russians were likely to advance rapidly and she advised them to try to flee to West Germany. At the end of January 1945, relatives on their way westward from Poznan took shelter for a few days in Zibelle. Emma and Edith decided to join them and set out in a horse-drawn farm-cart in the icy cold of an East German winter. Emma was now getting on for eighty but her training in getting up every morning at six o'clock to a full day's work had kept her in good trim. She joined the others in telling anecdotes and reminiscences, whiling away the time of the long days of travel and keeping up their spirits. Edith wondered whether her mother realized that she had left her home for ever. After eight days they reached Halberstadt, where they stayed for a couple of days with relatives and where the railway westward was still running. They were lucky enough to get on a train to Goettingen, where they had spent happy years half a century earlier. There they awaited the end of the war.

In 1947 I was surprised to receive a letter from Emma which was posted in Wimbledon. She heard a radio talk which I gave on the B.B.C. about Nernst's work, and she clearly appreciated that her husband's achievements were not forgotten. A few months earlier, the physicist, Otto Hahn, had succeeded in getting a British visa for her, probably by appealing to Lindemann, who had become a powerful and influential man during the war. She now lived in Wimbledon with her eldest daughter and Lindemann visited her there in 1948. It was the last time that he saw Emma. She died in England on the 4th May, 1949.

After Nernst's death the urn with his ashes had been taken to Berlin, as had been his wish. He had objected to being buried in Goettingen because that university had become a citadel of Nazism. However, after their mother's death the daughters decided to bring both their parents' ashes to Goettingen. Times had changed and access to Berlin had become difficult. Nernst's ashes rest next to those of Max Planck and Max von Laue, three names that mark a unique period in the history of science.

An era had come to an end. Within a single life span, Berlin had been raised from provincialism to be the capital of a mighty empire and to become one of the great centres of science and learning. Now it was an empty shell, shunned even by its own dead. Those who had inherited its spirit carried it abroad, to the far corners of the world, and no less than fourteen of them collected Nobel prizes on the way.

9. Epilogue

When I woke up the sun was shining in my face. I had slept deeply, soundly and long—for the first time in many weeks. The night before I had arrived in London and gone to bed without fear that at 3 a.m. a car with a couple of S.A. men would draw up and take me away. Breslau, where I had a post at the university in 1933, was ahead of most German cities in establishing Nazi terror. In view of my record as a former member of a militant anti-Nazi organization, I considered it merely a question of time and statistics as to when my own turn for interrogation would come. This state of affairs was injurious to my nervous system and I began to sleep badly. It is quite a different thing to face your enemy with weapons in your hand from sitting helplessly in a cage, waiting for him to pounce. I had married a few months earlier and my wife was terror-struck when the police appeared at the door, just as I was expected back from work. It then turned out that they were checking on our landlady's passport, in spite of the fact that she did not have one. This was good enough and we decided to leave Breslau forthwith, ostensibly to spend Easter in Berlin. Being of mixed Jewish-German parentage and having had a Lutheran baptism I was, at that time, entitled to keep my passport, but I had no illusions that soon enough things would be less easy.

In Berlin I bought a ticket to London, leaving my young non-Jewish wife behind to wind things up in Germany before joining me in England. Having safely arrived in England, the next step was to go to Oxford and ask Lindemann for a job. I had first met Lindemann in 1930 in Berlin, when he was paying a visit to Nernst's old laboratory where he and his brother had been working for their doctoral theses. Those probably were the happiest years of his life and a strong nostalgic longing for his Berlin days remained with Lindemann throughout his life. As soon as he had been appointed to the Oxford professorship, he set out to create in his department a school of low-temperature physics similar to that of Nernst in Berlin. His first step had been to buy the Nernst–Hoenow hydrogen liquefier with the serial number 43 which has been mentioned in an earlier chapter. Two young research men spent a few frustrating years, only to establish beyond doubt that the machine would not work. It never did.

There is every reason to believe that the only example of this impressive serial manufacture which ever worked was the temperamental prototype in Nernst's own laboratory. When I went to the Berlin laboratory twenty years later the machine was still in use, having become even more eccentric through age, and still being operated by the trusted Hoenow. Hoenow, too, had become less tractable with advancing years and all research, including mine, was hampered and delayed by the insufficient and erratic supply of liquid hydrogen. Finally, Simon could not stand these frustrating conditions any longer and designed a more realistic type of machine which worked a good deal better. Following in Nernst's footsteps Simon, too, started on serial manufacture, employing Hoenow's brother for the job, an unwise step since it led to internecine strife in the Hoenow clan which almost culminated in fratricide. Old Hoenow suffered terribly under the handicap that, being the institute mechanic and thereby a Prussian State official, he could not engage in commerce. Finally Simon found a solution of Solomon; Hoenow's wife, Ida, was made director of the company. It proved a hollow victory since within a week of the announcement the new director received her first mail; it was an income tax demand.

Now Lindemann had come to Berlin to purchase a hydrogen liquefier which worked and it fell to me to demonstrate the machine to him. In the course of the trials we discussed outstanding research problems in the low temperature field and Lindemann suggested that I should come to Oxford. However, I had just accepted the job in Breslau and I felt it my duty to decline his offer. Lindemann installed the liquefier in Oxford where, to his delight, it worked. A little over a year later I suddenly got a letter from him to say that he wanted to extend the work to helium temperatures, suggesting that I should build a small helium liquefier to work in conjunction with the hydrogen machine. He also invited me to go to Oxford and set up the helium installation at the Clarendon Laboratory. This I did in the Christmas holiday of 1932 and the first liquid helium in England was produced within two weeks of my arrival at Oxford.

Only later did I learn why Lindemann had been so much in a hurry with this project. In the traditional rivalry between Oxford and Cambridge, the latter university had been leading in physics for many years, getting all the money for the Cavendish Laboratory while the Clarendon was fairly destitute. In particular, Rutherford's immense prestige had succeeded in getting funds from the Royal Society and from Robert Mond to build a splendid low temperature laboratory of which Kapitza was made director. Much was made of the novel helium liquefier that was under construction there.

Now Lindemann had scooped Cambridge, Rutherford, and especially Kapitza in the most dreadful manner. When announcing the success at the Clarendon in the columns of *Nature*, Lindemann took particular care to rub salt into the wound by pointing out the low cost of the Oxford installation. To make things even worse, Lindemann's announcement was printed next to a picture of the impressive new—but as yet empty— laboratory at Cambridge. When I visited Kapitza in Cambridge a year later, I found him strangely formal and reserved and it was only then that I got the true background of my visit to Oxford. However, when Kapitza learned that I had been completely unaware of the plot, his attitude changed completely and we have been very good friends ever since.

Before I returned from Oxford to Breslau in January 1933, Lindemann had applied to the Rockefeller Foundation to give me a grant to work for a year at the Clarendon, starting in October. Hardly was I back in Germany when Hitler came to power and I felt that October was rather a long time off and a lot of unpleasant things might happen in the meantime. Fortunately, my mind was made up for me by the Rockefeller Foundation who, with the peculiar wisdom that characterizes this type of institution, had declined to give the grant. They did not quarrel with my qualifications but, as they pointed out, the basis of the grant had changed since the original application. It was their rule that scholars, receiving a grant, should return to their original place of work and, since Hitler had now come to power I would be unlikely to go back to Breslau. Accordingly, their rules required that I was to stay in Nazi Germany.

Fortunately Lindemann, who knew Germany well and who had no illusions about the shape of things to come, took a more realistic view when late in April I turned up uninvited on the doorstep of the Clarendon. However, he still had to find a job for me. The Clarendon Laboratory, housed in a small chalet of Venetian Gothic, had two demonstratorships and no earthly hope of getting more. Moreover, Lindemann realized that the cause of the displaced scholars who were bound to turn up in numbers would be prejudiced by putting them into competition for regular positions. Somebody had to be found who was prepared to spend money on foreign scientists. He approached an old friend of his, Sir Harry McGowan, Chairman of Imperial Chemical Industries, who in turn persuaded his directors that the money would be well spent. It was typical of Lindemann that he avoided an appeal on humanitarian grounds. It also was typical that he got results quickly. My contract with I.C.I. dated from the 1st May, 1933, and it was the first of many.

As the year wore on, the stream of refugee scientists became a flood. The new Diaspora had begun. On the 22nd May an appeal for funds, signed by eminent British scholars in all branches of learning, was launched. Under the presidency of Rutherford they formed the 'Academic Assistance Council' which, at this early stage, saw clearly the danger which fanaticism and intolerance were to bring upon the world in the next decade. If the foresight of these scholars had been shared by the politicians of the day, untold misery might have been averted. In this appeal the following passage was significant:

> The issue raised at the moment is not a Jewish one alone; many who have suffered or are threatened have no Jewish connection. The issue, though raised acutely at the moment in Germany, is not confined to that country. We should like to regard any funds entrusted to us as available for university teachers and investigators of whatever country who, on grounds of religion, political opinion or race, are unable to carry on their work in their own country.

This remarkable gesture on the part of the British scholars long preceded efforts on behalf of the refugee scientists in America or any other country. There can be little doubt that Lindemann's initiative and his vigorous approach to I.C.I. had a decisive effect on the early action taken in Britain. For two years the Royal Society provided offices for the Academic Assistance Council and for another eighteen months hospitality was provided by the London School of Economics. Money came in through individual subscriptions and from the universities. In some of these the whole staff unanimously gave up a percentage of their salaries to help their colleagues whom Hitler had driven out of their home country. While the world was trying to shut its eyes to the growth of totalitarianism, the scholars of Britain set up a silent monument in honour of the achievements of the human mind. But for their understanding and willing sacrifice, the heritage of German science and learning might have perished without trace.

The money collected by the Council was used to create temporary jobs for the refugee scholars and it provided the necessary breathing space until most of them could find more permanent positions and the majority could be gradually absorbed into the life of other countries, especially America. The Council and its successor, the Society for the Protection of Science and Learning, eventually had on their books the records of no less than 2600 refugee scholars, which is almost equal to the total number of university teachers dismissed by the Nazis. Of these 500 remained in England. Of the 200 scientists among them 50 were later elected into the Royal Society and eight received knighthoods.

As soon as it became clear that the Nazis meant business and, apart from 'eliminating' all Jews, were also going to drive out any physicist who believed in the theory of relativity, Lindemann swung into action. He now suddenly saw the possibility of realizing his great ambition: to create in Oxford a worthy continuation of the Nernst school. He made frequent trips to Germany, offering positions to scholars whom he wanted to collaborate in setting up such a centre of research and study in Oxford. It was a relatively easy thing for young scholars, who had their career still before them, to leave their country and take new roots abroad. For men like Simon and others who already held professorships in Germany, the decision was much harder. Many educated Germans felt at that time that the madness of Nazi rule could not go on for long, that either Hitler would fall or that he would be tamed by big business. It might, they argued, be all over in a few months and it was folly to leave their positions. Most of them were to pay for their indecision in the extermination camps. Few of the scientists, however, succumbed to this form of reasoning and they left while it was still possible. Simon gave up his professorship and came to Oxford. Nicholas Kurti and Heinz London, who had been working with him, followed. Heinz was joined by his brother, Fritz London, Schrödinger's co-worker, and when Schrödinger resigned, he too, was attracted to Oxford by Lindemann. Imperial Chemical Industries, at Lindemann's behest, provided salaries for all of them. Lindemann was happy in this new world of old memories which he had built around himself at the Clarendon. He did everything to encourage the Nernst atmosphere but, wisely, he never assumed any form of scientific direction.

Once upon a time Nernst had said to Lindemann: 'If your father were not such a rich man, you would become a great physicist'. As so often, Nernst had been right. The man who in 1933 set out to continue the Nernst tradition was now very different from the Secretary of the famous Solvay Congress of 1911. Holding that secretaryship jointly with the Duc de Broglie had been the apex of Lindemann's career as a research scientist. To the end of his days, the photograph taken at that memorable meeting in Brussels, hung over Lindemann's desk, showing Nernst, Rutherford, Planck, Einstein, Sommerfeld, Jeans, Poincaré, Mme Curie and other great scientists of that time. He himself, a tall, dark and handsome young man, stood respectfully in the last row. In the years to come, Lindemann would rise to the exalted position of being Winston Churchill's closest friend and adviser, feared and hated by many, loved by very few, immensely powerful and completely withdrawn.

Even his biographers could do little to make him more than a gifted but distant and shadowy figure. Their attempts to attribute human qualities to him were limited to a catalogue of foibles, idiosyncrasies and acts of kindness to servants and animals. Even to them Lindemann remained 'the Prof' with his bowler hat, umbrella, grey suit in summer and dark one in winter, and his Rolls. The latter, incidentally, was changed for a Packard, when one day the prince among motorcars let him down on a trip to London and Lindemann, bowler hat and all, had to be rescued by a junior research worker, driving an open three-wheeler.

Lindemann's transformation from Nernst's enthusiastic research student into an unbending Victorian gentleman had taken place during the First World War. He had been born into a world where you could travel throughout Europe without a passport, and thanks to his parent's wealth and connections he did this extensively. They were bent on giving him a good international education and sent him to the *Gymnasium* at Darmstadt from which he passed to the technical university at the same place. They gave him an introduction to the Grand Duke Ernst Ludwig who appreciated the young man's ability at tennis and arranged for him to play with the Kaiser and the Czar. For the quieter moments of his life, he played the piano with almost professional virtuosity and Bach was to become the solace to which he turned under the strain of later years. In this civilized world at the turn of the century, Lindemann's mother thought nothing of travelling to Baden-Baden for the cure at a time when she was pregnant, failing to appreciate the trouble that the future Viscount Cherwell would have in hiding this fact in his entry in *Who's Who*.

This comfortable world came to a sudden end in August 1914 Lindemann had to get out of Germany in a hurry, leaving the tennis tournament at Zoppot which he had hoped to win. Almost overnight, his Darmstadt schoolmates and his Berlin co-students had become the hated 'Huns' and there was poor Lindemann, with a Hun name, a Hun education and, worst of all, even a Hun birth certificate. It was inevitable that most people with whom he now came into contact should regard him as a German and some of them were convinced that he was a German spy. In a rather pathetic letter to the Army Command, Lindemann affirmed his British nationality, explaining laboriously the accident of his own German birth and that of his father, citing as head of the family the Comte de Lindemann in France. The letter, dated in 1915, was an application for a commission, which was not granted. Lindemann, at that time, was at the Royal Aircraft Factory at Farnborough, where he remained throughout the war.

The transition from a rich young tennis champion, who enjoyed the hospitality of princes, to a suspect outcast, had a profound influence on Lindemann. He became withdrawn to avoid exposing himself to slights and insults. Secretiveness about his personal life developed into a mania and he discouraged personal approaches by a stand-offishness which was easily mistaken for arrogance. Possibly without realizing it himself, Lindemann now followed Nernst's example of playing a role on the stage of life, wearing a mask to protect his real self from a hostile world. Indeed, the mask which he chose, emphasized his resentment against the commission that had been refused. His country had decided to relegate him to civilian status; so let it be: he was going to be the most civilian civilian in the war. It was at this time that Lindemann decided on the bowler hat, the long dark coat and the rolled-up umbrella.

He would arrive on the runway in this regalia, walking up to the 'plane and only then changing into flying kit. Bowler hat, coat and umbrella were carefully stowed away under the pilot's seat. On landing, the reverse process was gone through and he would not leave the aircraft until his metamorphosis was completed. This was at the time when he carried out the near-suicidal tests in which he landed safely after first having put the 'plane into the dreaded tail-spin. He demonstrated to his own, and he felt to everyone else's, satisfaction that a civilian with a German birth certificate could serve his country with the same cool courage as any British-born soldier.

Perhaps the break due to the war was strong enough to prevent Lindemann returning to the life of an active research scientist. We will never know, because the next phase of his life, the professorship at Oxford, proved to be less favourable to a modern scientist than one might have thought. Except for a short period before the Restoration, when Oxford became the cradle of the Royal Society, the university was never able to rival the impressive scientific tradition of Cambridge. Possibly as a result of this failure, Arts subjects, and Classics in particular, came to be held in inordinate esteem and were considered the only worthwhile avenue of first rate scholarship.

Lindemann probably thought that, by appointing him, Oxford was trying to encourage modern science but he was soon to learn how completely he had misjudged the original intention. The chair of physics had become free and a professor had to be appointed. The renown of the university required that this should be an outstanding man but the appointment did not imply that the illustrious School of Literae Humaniores would regard experimental philosophy as a worthwhile field of study. If the new professor held a different opinion it would be just as well to guide him on the correct path at an early date. Roy Harrod has given a vivid account of a lecture given by Lindemann at the invitation of the Jowett Society shortly after coming to Oxford. Its subject was the theory of relativity and he imagined that his audience would expect the new professor to give a lucid account of this important development which had been much in the news. Had his parents sent him to Oxford instead of Berlin, Lindemann would have known that, at this time of the day, entertainment was expected rather than instruction. The evening was saved by the locally famed logician, H. W. B. Joseph of New College who, by shrewd exercise of his craft, proved conclusively that Einstein was wrong. He thereby scored an impressive victory for the Oxford Humanities School over the new science professor. Lindemann, who was brilliant in repartee, was poor in verbal argument and felt that he had been made to look a fool. He hated this more than anything since it undermined the image that he had chosen to create for himself.

Oxford provided him with further incidents of this kind and he became more and more resentful. He began to escape into the two worlds in which he had found a place before the war; gracious living and the memory of the Nernst school. Lindemann soon discovered that his visits to stately homes and their charming hosts and hostesses evoked sarcastic comment in the parochial environment of Oxford dons into which he had been cast. He also realized that their disdain sprang partly from envy of his acceptance into circles that remained closed to them. This gave him considerable satisfaction, particularly since he met there people of real influence in the country's affairs. It was at a week-end spent with the Duke and Duchess of Westminster in June 1921 that he first met Winston Churchill. The two men, so different in background and character, took to each other immediately and their acquaintance soon turned into a close friendship.

Recovering the lost world of the Nernst Laboratory took much longer. Lindeman's efforts to get money out of the university for the Clarendon Laboratory proved extremely frustrating. He succeeded in bringing A. C. (later Sir Alfred) Egerton, an old friend from his Berlin and Farnborough days, to join him at Oxford and we have already mentioned his abortive attempt to get a hydrogen liquefier going. His real chance came only with the refugee scientists from Germany in 1933 and he took it with both hands. From then on all his efforts were directed towards establishing in Oxford the kind of scientific atmosphere which he had enjoyed to the full in Berlin. He was eminently successful and when he retired twenty-three years later he had, despite the interruption of the war years, given to Oxford a large and flourishing school of physics.

Lindemann's nostalgic attitude towards his Berlin days resulted in a personal relationship with the members of the old Nernst school which was quite different from the distant reserve with which he treated his other acquaintances. In fact, I did not become aware of Lindemann's cold and unbending image until after I arrived at Oxford. In Berlin I had found him a warm-hearted and eminently approachable elder colleague, always ready for a joke and full of entertaining anecdotes about his days with Nernst. Even in Oxford this personal attitude never changed and it became very pronounced in his later days after he had returned from exalted Government office. Then, in the middle of summer when he was not burdened with administrative work, he would sometimes ask me to come to his office. The reason given was invariably trivial and disposed of in a few minutes. What he really wanted was to chat about the old days in Berlin, talking about all the fun he had had then and about the thrill of discoveries in those days. As often as not, he would slip into German, feeling that this evoked the atmosphere of the past more thoroughly. There was a curious air of confidence, almost of conspiracy, in his conversations with the German scholars of the Nernst school. Talking about English habits and customs, he would always refer to them as 'they' and never as 'we'. One summer evening Sir John Cockcroft, who was then director of the Atomic Energy Research Establishment at Harwell, gave a party at his house and after dinner the guests trooped out on to the floodlit lawn, doing and watching Scottish folk-dancing. Only two dissenters, the South African scientist Basil Schonland and I, remained in the drawing-room, thumbing through magazines, when a late guest was shown in: Viscount Cherwell. He looked out on to the lawn and then turned to us, saying: 'A curious race, the British'.

It is sad that his biographers should have overlooked the immense influence which his Berlin days had on Lindemann. They have found his tendency to tell smutty stories or use coarse expressions incongruous but they would have found the source of this habit, had they listened to his conversation in German. Remarks of this nature often occurred in Lindemann's quick repartee which also was a legacy of the Nernst days. On the morning after the Munich Pact some of us were discussing its implications in front of the Clarendon when the Packard drew up and the Prof emerged looking very serious and tense. We asked his opinion and whether he thought that Chamberlain had something up his sleeve. 'No', Lindemann growled, 'something down his pants.'

In science, the years before the war yielded a rich harvest at the Clarendon. With the helium liquefier that I had built for Lindemann in Breslau and installed at Oxford in January 1933, I could get to work immediately after arrival and the first interesting results started to come in after a few months. When Simon and Kurti arrived in Oxford in the summer, they brought further equipment with them and settled down to work in the very low temperature region which had recently been opened in Leiden and California by using a magnetic cooling method. Their elegant development of this method soon brought Oxford into the forefront of this type of research. My own research group was concerned with the strange properties of superconductivity and superfluidity and we were lucky enough to discover some interesting and also pretty spectacular new effects which helped to make the Oxford low temperature school known throughout the world. At the same time the brothers Fritz and Heinz London developed an electrodynamical theory of superconductivity, solving an important problem that had eluded many. Schrödinger took a lively and active interest in both the theoretical and the experimental work. He was not a man who suffered fools gladly and could be extremely impatient with people who, he felt, were wasting his time. However, it was different with the young Oxford research school to whose members he became not only a brilliant adviser but also an exuberant personal friend.

Lindemann, of course, was delighted with the new spirit that pervaded his laboratory and he redoubled his efforts in getting money for equipment and supplies from industry or from benefactors. He knew people who had or managed money and he was most skilful in getting them to part with it.

One of the scientists who came for a while to Oxford was Leo Szilard, a Hungarian who had been working in Germany, and who later, even before the discovery of fission, took out a patent for a nuclear chain reaction.

The day after I arrived at Oxford, Lindemann presented me, rather diffidently, with the copy of a book that he had recently written on the physical significance of the quantum theory. It was an attempt to analyse the basis of the theory as well as the developments which had occurred in the long years that had passed while he was not in direct touch with the relevant research. Many of his deductions are interesting and some of the proposals show imagination and originality but they reveal that to some extent he had lost touch with current trends. I always suspected that Lindemann, by writing it, had convinced himself of this fact. He was too good a physicist to delude himself and he never attempted to insist on his views when we discussed current problems. This he liked to do, usually contradicting my own opinions vigorously, calling them heretical and unnecessarily abstruse. One day, when I insisted that the treatment of gas degeneracy required the use of the momentum coordinates, he ended his own dissertation on the subject by saying: 'And don't talk to me in momentum space!' It seems that he savoured these discussions as a reminder of his days with Nernst rather than as an attempt to make a serious scientific point. Sticking obstinately to his ideas did not prevent him from submitting my papers, unopposed, for publication to the Royal Society.

Just like Nernst, Lindemann made inspired guesses and many of them turned out to be correct. He could also sometimes be very wrong, and being obstinate, he did not like to change his mind. Still at Berlin, he asked my opinion on profitable lines of applied research and I suggested work on rockets, basing my views on a book by Oberth—now very famous —that had recently been published but had elicited little enthusiasm. Lindemann told me that during the First World War they had made experiments with rockets at Farnborough which had convinced him that rockets were useless and none of my arguments cut any ice with him.

Lindemann had also hoped to gain Einstein for Oxford. Thanks to his efforts Einstein had been invited to Christ Church in 1931 and the College had made him a Research 'Student'—which is their name for a Fellow—after his visit. Accordingly Einstein visited Oxford for short periods in the two following years. When he left Nazi Germany, he seriously considered making Oxford his home and he began to visit the Clarendon. However, the long arm of Nazi terrorism was now reaching out to German refugee scholars of note and Professor Theodor Lessing who had fled to Czechoslovakia was murdered by Nazi thugs in Marienbad. A price had also been put on Einstein's head and a friend of Churchill's,

Commander Locker Lampson, overacted slightly by having his picture taken, guarding Einstein with a rifle. This seems to have worried Einstein seriously. Unfortunately, Lindemann with whom Einstein could have discussed the matter rationally, was abroad at the time and Einstein left for America where a position had been offered to him.

The great event for the Oxford low-temperature group was, of course, Nernst's visit in 1937. Not only had Nernst retired but he saw clearly that science in Germany was, more or less, finished. He was therefore pleased to see the continuation of his school which Lindemann had established in Oxford. Nernst was delighted when I introduced my research students to him as his scientific great-grandchildren. He was now seventy-three but still in great form, bubbling over with anecdotes and his usual caustic remarks. When told that J. J. Thomson had just published his reminiscences, Nernst asked in his usual surprised manner whether Thomson had anything worth while to remember. Nernst evidently recalled very well the tiff they had had forty years earlier over the discovery of the electron.

The hospitality Lindemann gave his adored teacher was lavish and he knew that Nernst appreciated this to the full. It was Nernst's last excursion into the wide world which he liked so much. The heart attack that was to chain him to Zibelle came about a year after the Oxford visit. Sandwiched between his reminiscences and his outrageous indiscretions there was deep apprehension about the future of his grandchildren. He told us that he was converting his assets by spending all his money on buying woodland. War, he said, might destroy cities and lay waste the land but the trees would keep growing, steadily and undisturbed, to yield timber for the grandchildren when all the trouble was over. For once he miscalculated. The trees are now growing in Poland.

Lindemann had various infallible ways of making enemies and, being rich and independent, he rarely bothered to curb this faculty. He derived a certain satisfaction from being hated by people he disliked. It was inevitable that during the war, and in high office he should make even more enemies than normally. Some of these were distinguished colleagues who were shocked by his high-handedness. One of his failings was not to turn up personally at meetings but to send a representative who would expound the professor's point of view without having a brief to accept changes. The real reason for this apparent arrogance was that Lindemann was convinced that his view was correct but knew that he was poor in verbal debate and might not be able to refute criticism.

It is deplorable that these disagreements, particularly with Lindemann's old friend Henry Tizard, were exploited after his death in a highly dramatized form by the Press. Most disgusting to my mind was the appearance of Lindemann's face on giant hoardings, advertising this story for one of the large newspapers. Throughout his life Lindemann had most assiduously avoided all publicity and had never posed for a Press photograph, but this wish was clearly not to be respected when his face might bring increased sales.

No provision had been made for retirement in the old statute under which Lindemann had been appointed. It gave him pleasure to announce in Christ Church Senior Common Room that he had no intention of retiring and in fact would prolong his life with implanted monkey glands, so as to be with them for a very long time to come. As he kept the date of his birth a closely guarded secret, we did not know how old he was. Then, out of the blue, he announced his retirement in 1956 because he was now seventy and wanted to make room for a younger man. He seemed relaxed and in good spirits when I saw him at the Vice-Chancellor's garden party in June 1957 but he was shocked when I told him that at the week-end I was flying to Moscow and would see Kapitza there. It was just after the 'thaw', and trips to Russia were still a great novelty. Lindemann considered my decision to accept the Soviet invitation an act of utter folly, pointing out that the 'Bolsheviks' had kept Kapitza and would certainly keep me as well. As usual, he remained stubborn when I told him that the times had changed then dismissed me by saying: 'All right, have it your own way. But I warn you, if you go to Moscow, I shall never see you again.' In a macabre way he turned out to be right. Ten days later, between conference sessions at Kapitza's laboratory, a message from the British Embassy in Moscow was handed to me. Lord Cherwell had suddenly and unexpectedly died.

When Lindemann became professor at Oxford, the Clarendon Laboratory resembled inside and out a stage decoration for Goethe's *Faust*. When he retired, it had become one of the largest and most flourishing physics departments in the world. That his plans for safeguarding the future of his low-temperature physics school were not accepted, was a tragedy for Oxford. Whether he was disappointed by the subsequent developments is difficult to say. Lindemann was not the kind of man who would show his feelings. However, he changed his will two days before his death, not leaving any part of his considerable fortune to the Clarendon.

Oxford may have been the first place where German refugee scientists found an opportunity to continue their work; it did not remain the only one. The new Diaspora covered the world. From England to Australia, from America to India, there was hardly a university which did not give shelter and a place of work to the displaced scholars. They, in turn, did all they could by teaching and research to repay the hospitality they were receiving. Around groups of them, or even individuals, there sprang up new schools, recruited from the local students who, in turn, carried forward the heritage of all that had been good and useful in German academic life. Far from destroying the spirit of German scholarship, the Nazis had spread it all over the world. Only Germany was to be the loser.

The most momentous advance of our century, the release of atomic energy, can serve as an example. In the 'thirties the discovery of the neutron opened a new and exciting prospect to nuclear physicists. By shooting a neutron into the nucleus of the heaviest known element, uranium, it might be possible to create a still heavier atom, a new element which did not exist on Earth. It was this particular challenge which dominated the efforts of the nuclear laboratories throughout the 'thirties.

The original idea of creating such 'transuranic' elements was first proposed by the Italian physicist Enrico Fermi and he immediately set to work in his laboratory at Rome. It seemed to be a relatively simple experiment but the results obtained were strangely confusing. Instead of the expected one or two nuclear species, an enormous number of them made their appearance. In fact, the experiment turned out to be far too successful for any rational interpretation. Other groups than Fermi's were working in this exciting field and their experiments, too, suffered from the same *embarras de richesses*. These researches continued through most of the 'thirties.

Among the teams engaged in this work, there was also a German team working at the Kaiser Wilhelm Institute at Dahlem. Unlike the French or the British, the Germans had a poor start in radioactive research. Emil Fischer, Germany's great chemist at the turn of the century, was quite uninterested in this new branch and did nothing to encourage it. In fact, Germany's foremost radiochemist, Otto Hahn, first came in touch with his subject during a study visit to Ramsay's laboratory in London. In 1905 he went to work with Rutherford in Montreal and then returned to Germany to try to continue his research. He was joined a year later by a shy young woman colleague with an immense crown of black hair and huge dark eyes. Her name was Lise Meitner. The daughter of a Jewish lawyer from Vienna, she had studied physics and now had come to Berlin to learn about the new quantum theory from Max Planck. Lise Meitner was also intrigued by the work of Mme Curie on radio-activity and, finding that Planck's lectures did not occupy all of her time, she decided to try her hand at experimental research.

In 1935, Hahn and Meitner began experiments on neutron bombardment of heavy elements similar to those initiated by Fermi one year earlier. They used thorium as well as uranium, getting further vexing results. The most surprising result, obtained early in 1938, yielded in addition to various 'transuranic' elements also radium. In the summer of 1938 they planned a crucial experiment involving a very careful chemical separation in order to identify these decay products. However, when a few months later this experiment was carried out, she had left Germany.

Lise Meitner was fortunate in having retained her Austrian citizenship throughout her thirty years of work in Germany. She was therefore not affected immediately by Hitler's anti-Semitic laws and, for the time being, the Nazis were careful not to infringe Austrian rights. Her life became unpleasant but she was still able to carry on with her work, to which she was completely devoted and which meant everything to her. Then things changed with the annexation of Austria in 1938 and she was not allowed into the laboratory. Neither was she allowed to leave Germany. Carl Bosch, who with Haber had perfected the nitrogen fixation process, was now President of the Kaiser Wilhelm Society and he applied for an exit visa for her. It was not granted. As in so many other cases, the scientists in countries outside Germany extended their help. Through the intermediacy of the Zürich physicist, Scherrer, the Dutch scientists Coster, Fokker and de Haas were approached and they, in turn, persuaded the Dutch Government to admit Lise Meitner without an entrance visa. She escaped to Holland and from there went to Sweden where through the efforts of Niels Bohr and Siegbahn a position was found for her in Stockholm.

The results of the experiment planned in collaboration with Lise Meitner were published by Hahn early in 1939 together with another co-worker, Fritz Strassmann. They disclosed the surprising fact that the nuclei resulting from the bombardment of uranium with neutrons were not radium but barium, an element of only about half the weight of uranium. This was the discovery which was to provide the key for un-locking the energy stored within the atomic nucleus, but Hahn and Strassmann completely failed to grasp its meaning. It was left to Lise Meitner, who had planned the experiment with them and who now lived in exile, to find the correct solution.

Hahn had sent a copy of the report which he submitted for publica-tion to Lise Meitner in Stockholm. It arrived when her nephew, Otto Frisch, had come over from Copenhagen for a visit. Frisch had studied in Berlin in the late 'twenties, had then worked with Otto Stern in Hamburg and had emigrated to England in 1933. He was now working with Bohr in Copenhagen. Frisch and Meitner, reading Hahn's report, immediately realized what had happened in the Berlin experiments. On being hit by the bombarding neutrons, the uranium nucleus had broken up into two fragments and the barium atom observed by Hahn and Strassmann was one of them. They explained this new phenomenon which they called 'fission' on the basis of a theory advanced three years earlier by Niels Bohr.

In his autobiography, Otto Hahn has given a most interesting account of why he and Strassmann failed to understand the true meaning of their own results. It shows that they were completely out of touch with current nuclear theory. Hahn was a brilliant radiochemist but he was now working in isolation. It required an expert nuclear physicist, or preferably a team of them, to grasp the significance of the barium nuclei that he and Strassmann had chemically isolated. However, Lise Meitner had left, and even before her Frisch and many others, with whom Hahn could have discussed his results. The destruction of German science by the Nazis now made itself felt. Fission, the key to the release of atomic energy, was first observed in Germany but its true nature was only recognized by two refugee scientists. Their discovery set in progress a rapid sequence of events which led, on 16th July, 1945, to the detonation of the first atomic bomb at Alamogordo Flats in New Mexico. It was an event which changed the course of history and the refugee scientists cast out by Hitler had done much to bring it about. But science in Nazi Germany had had no part in it.

Twelve years earlier, on the 30th January, 1933, Hitler had made a scathing speech in which he ridiculed England and other countries which were giving shelter to refugee scientists. 'How grateful', he jeered, 'they must be that we are releasing these precious apostles of culture, and placing them at the disposal of the rest of the world.'

Volume 143, 1939 of *Nature* makes epic reading. Following the letters of Meitner and Frisch, there is an avalanche of reports, confirming and extending the discovery of nuclear fission. The large amount of energy which is liberated in the form of the speed with which the fission fragments fly apart had already been noted in Frisch's experiment. Now another refugee, Hans von Halban, working with Joliot and Kowarski in Paris, showed that not only kinetic energy but neutrons too are ejected at the fission of a uranium nucleus. These free neutrons, they pointed out, might enter other uranium nuclei to cause them, in turn, to fission, leading to an energy avalanche of tremendous dimensions. What is required for such a chain reaction is, of course, that more than one neutron should be emitted from each fission and this the Paris team had shown to be likely. A few weeks later Halban again returned to the chain reaction which, he said, might develop into an explosion.

Uranium metal had first been prepared more than a century earlier and lumps of uranium had been peacefully lying about in cupboards and drawers of many laboratories without exploding. Moreover, none of the samples bombarded with neutrons in the experiments of Fermi, Hahn and others had gone up in smoke. Some further piece of information was evidently missing to explain this failure. The answer to this riddle was given by Bohr early in 1939, at the same time as the experimental results on fission were coming in. It was based on his theory of the atomic nucleus.

It had been known for a long time that atoms of the same chemical element can have different weight. These are the so-called isotopes. The liquid drop model of the atomic nucleus which Bohr now extended with his former pupil J. A. Wheeler predicted very different behaviour for the uranium isotopes under neutron bombardment. Both the common isotope, U238, and the rare one, U235, would undergo fission when hit by very fast neutrons but only the latter would break up under bombardment with neutrons of any speed. Moreover, the U238 nucleus would capture any bombarding neutron, except the very fastest and the slowest ones, without undergoing fission. Bohr's prediction also indicated that any chain reaction would have to rely on making use of the small U235 content of the metal.

One of the teams thinking on these lines were Szilard, now in America, and Fermi, who in the meantime had also become a refugee. Mussolini, while failing to understand the importance of science, had not very seriously interfered with it. However, with the Nazis coming to power in Germany, anti-Semitism was becoming an export article and Fermi had a Jewish wife. It was Fermi who, under the grandstand of the Chicago stadium, built the first nuclear reactor, piling up an ever-increasing number of graphite blocks, interspersed with uranium ingots. On 2nd December, 1942, the pile had reached its 'critical' size and a controlled, self-sustaining chain reaction set in. Man had liberated atomic energy. The agreed code message was sent to Washington. It read: 'Italian navigator has reached the new world'. The acknowledgement from Washington came in the form of a question: 'Are the natives friendly?' They were; the reactor operated smoothly with no danger of explosion.

The realization, in 1939, that a nuclear chain reaction using uranium would have to rely on slow neutrons had a most important bearing on the question of a possible atomic bomb. Any explosion is a reaction developing heat and this heat has the effect of driving apart the exploding substance. In a nuclear bomb this will stop the reaction unless it has been fast enough to proceed to its end before the driving apart has gained momentum. Rough calculations soon showed that fission by slow neutrons would not be fast enough and that instead of a detonation there would only be a 'fizz'. The whole problem was summarized by Frisch in the winter 1939–40 in an article in the *Annual Reports of the Chemical Society* when he wrote with regard to atomic bombs: 'Fortunately our progressing knowledge of the fission process has tended to dissipate these fears and there are now a number of strong arguments to the effect that the construction of such a super bomb would be, if not impossible, then at least prohibitively expensive, and furthermore the bomb would not be so effective as was thought at first'.

Five years later, after Hiroshima, a British statement on the bomb was released which contains the following sentence: 'At the beginning of 1940 Dr Frisch and Professor Peierls of Birmingham University, and Professor Sir James Chadwick of Liverpool University, independently called attention to the possibility of producing a military weapon of unprecedented power'. R. E. (now Sir Rudolf) Peierls was also a refugee from Germany.

In view of the closeness of the dates, one might suspect that Frisch's earlier statement had been a blind to mislead the Germans. However, he assured me that this was not the case. What had happened was that, with war now in progress, scientists began to think about projects which were so gigantic that they would never have been considered in peacetime. It was the tortuous passage through the moderator, required for the avoidance of U238, which prevented a fast neutron reaction. However, an explosion might still be obtained if U235 only and fast neutrons were used. Nevertheless, the immensely difficult and costly separation of sizeable amounts of the rare isotope had deterred scientists from thinking in these terms. Now, Frisch and Peierls calculated what, if it were feasible to obtain pure or highly enriched U235, the fast neutron reaction would look like. Basing their calculation on the assumption that any neutron hitting a U235 nucleus would cause fission, they saw to their surprise that the critical size of the uranium bomb would be quite small. This meant that the reaction could proceed fast enough to be explosive and also that the total amount of U235 was much smaller than they had anticipated. Even so, they made a slight miscalculation by saying that the plant might 'cost as much as a battleship', a statement which Peierls later described to me as 'a substantial underestimate'.

The rest of the story of the development of the bomb and of the truly fantastic effort involved has been told often enough not to require repetition. In their own way the Nazis helped it along. After their occupation of Denmark, life for Niels Bohr, who had a Jewish mother, was likely to become difficult and he, too, became a refugee scientist and left secretly in a fishing boat for Sweden. From there he was flown in a Mosquito aircraft to England and later went to America. Under the name of Nicholas Baker, he then spent some time at the Los Alamos Laboratory and in Washington. When in 1940 the problem of obtaining pure U235 by isotope separation was discussed, Bohr had rejected its feasibility, saying: 'You would have to turn the whole country into a factory'. Now, four years later, Bohr was told about the atomic bomb development and he was shown the immense separation plants. 'You see,' he said, 'I was right. You *did* turn the country into a factory.'

Throughout the war there had been the uneasy fear that the Germans might use the atomic bomb as the ultimate weapon. When at the end of hostilities the ALSOS mission was rushed to the German nuclear research establishments, its members saw how thoroughly unjustified this apprehension had been. The Germans were still at the stage of progress at which Frisch's report of 1939 had left them. They had never even reached the idea of a fast neutron reaction and their attempts at producing a weapon had remained in a sadly neglected exploratory stage. If any of their scientists had, indeed, repeated something like the calculation of Frisch and Peierls—and for this we have no evidence—they must have burnt the piece of paper without showing it to their rulers.

As long as the threat of an ever-increasing Nazi terror had been hanging over the world, the scientists engaged on the bomb project, far from having doubts about its ethical justification, had considered the perfection of the weapon as their prime duty. New problems, however, arose with the collapse of Germany when, quite apart from the question whether the new weapon should be used on Japan, the wider issue of international control arose. The refugee scientists in particular, whose personal experience of violence and of political adventurers was more acute than their colleagues, were worried. Fear and dismay that their achievement might bring more misery to a war-torn world were voiced by Einstein, James Franck, Szilard and many others. Among these were Bohr who, with the help of Lindemann, obtained an interview with Churchill, whom he tried to convince that Russia should be informed about the bomb before it was used.

For the next ten years the world, busy with the repair of war damage, lived blissfully unaware through a period which may eventually be recognized as the time of greatest danger for mankind. In those years adventurous politicians or trigger-happy generals could have waged a nuclear war, possibly under the flag of saving mankind from Communist domination. It was a danger which was bound to recede with Russian possession of the bomb and with the build-up of the nuclear arsenals on both sides. It is a testimony to the basic sanity of man that this critical decade passed without accident.

The years of waiting were cut short by an event which took place at dawn on 1st March, 1954, at the Bikini atoll in the Pacific Ocean. It was the successful test of the first hydrogen bomb, a weapon immensely more powerful and destructive even than the fission bombs exploded over Hiroshima and Nagasaki. The basic principle involved is simple and straightforward. It had long been known that the combined mass of two individual protons and two neutrons is somewhat larger than that of a helium nucleus which is made up of these four particles. The explanation of this discrepancy is provided by Einstein's law of the equivalence of mass and energy which is a consequence of the theory of relativity. The mass that has disappeared when the four separate particles combine to a helium nucleus simply represents the energy which is liberated at this fusion. It is a very large energy per particle. Fusion never takes place under ordinary conditions because the nuclei remain separated from each other by the surrounding electrons and also by mutual electric repulsion.

Only under conditions of very high temperatures and densities can such nuclear fusion reactions take place. Such conditions obtain in the centre of the stars and some years ago Hans Bethe, a pupil of Sommerfeld's and also a refugee scholar, showed how this fusion occurs in the interior of the sun. It was a brilliant piece of research which earned him the Nobel prize. It will be remembered that Nernst, too, had predicted nuclear energy as the source of solar radiation but he lacked the necessary data to suggest the detailed scheme of such a process.

The virtue of Bethe's theory is to have discovered the fairly complicated mechanism by which in the sun the conversion of hydrogen into helium proceeds at a steady and non-explosive rate. However, it is clear that the fusion reaction can also proceed with explosive violence and that, in principle, this mechanism could be utilized as a weapon. Its initiation would require temperatures of many million degrees, which cannot be attained in the laboratory, but the successful development of the fission bomb lent an entirely new aspect to the possibility of such a scheme. At the explosion of a conventional atomic bomb, temperatures of many million degrees do indeed occur, though only for a very short time. Nevertheless it seemed not impossible to initiate a fusion reaction by using a fission bomb as a 'fuse'.

However, between the rather trivial suggestion of such a device and a realizeable scheme to bring it about, there is an enormous gap and for a time the considered opinion among experts was similar to what it was at the early stages of the uranium bomb: that the creation of such a super-bomb was impossible, or at least prohibitively expensive. Among those who held this view was the leader of the bomb project, J. R. Oppenheimer. Neither he, nor most others, could have foreseen then that a manageable scheme would be found for a hydrogen bomb and it is shameful that, a few years later, American politicians should have construed this error of scientific judgement as an act of disloyalty, or even of treason.

The man who with single-minded determination believed in the possibility of a hydrogen bomb was another refugee scientist, Edward Teller. Born in Hungary of Jewish parents, he came to Germany to study, obtaining a doctorate in theoretical physics at Leipzig in 1930 under Heisenberg and then going to Goettingen where Max Born was professor of theoretical physics. When Hitler came to power, Teller went for a year to Copenhagen and then became a lecturer at London University. Working during the war at Los Alamos on the bomb project, Teller became absorbed in the possibility of the fusion reaction and from then on pursued it with great determination, suggesting various schemes for its realization. Finally, the successful one was worked out together with a refugee scientist from Poland, Stanislaw Ulam. Teller and others have pointed out that the immense explosive destructive power of the hydrogen bomb can be further enhanced by creating in the explosion long-lived radioactive nuclei, such as cobalt. Deposited by the original explosion over a wide area, it can make large tracts of land uninhabitable for many years. All in all, mankind now had a 'doomsday machine', the means to destroy itself and, if required, most other forms of life quite efficiently.

The detailed mechanism of the hydrogen bomb is a closely guarded secret which, however, has not prevented other nations from developing and successfully testing similar devices. This is as it should be to safeguard the future of mankind. With the possession of the doomsday machine by more than one great power, the traditional manner of solving human conflicts by recourse to major wars has become useless. For many years now the stage has been reached at which the world can indulge in only one more major war. Since this would certainly end civilization and possibly most human life, the contemplation of the problem presented by such a war is necessarily profitless and only the alternative of peace can be of interest to us.

The abolition of major war does not necessarily presage an easy future. On the contrary, the sudden and unforseen impossibility of settling our affairs in the traditional manner, practised for several millennia, is bound to force us into a complete reassessment of our customary codes of behaviour and misbehaviour. Rethinking is always a slow and painful process and we will be reluctant to dispense with usages which so far have been regarded as honourable and indispensable. However, the signs are there, for everybody to read. War as such has not yet been abolished but it has ceased to be a total threat to highly developed forms of society. Instead, it has been reduced to a form of ceremonial combat in carefully preselected and fairly underdeveloped regions of the globe. Its spread is almost clinically controlled by precisely measured doses of non-nuclear arms shipments, suitably apportioned to the contestants. This may go on for quite a while but the inability of escalating them into full-scale nuclear war may, in due course, take much of the ancient glamour out of these contests and will ultimately fail to ensure their continuance.

No doubt, many more and extremely difficult problems lie ahead. A world lifted off its hinges by the abolition of war will probably be as turbulent for the individual, or even more so, than one traditionally regulated by warfare. There is setting in a twilight of the politicians who can no longer threaten war and who will have to find novel methods or even give way to some new profession, possibly one with accredited qualifications, which learns to conduct human affairs otherwise. It will be a long and irritating time before mankind, irrespective of colour, creed and prejudice, will, as it eventually must, find the means of sharing this world peacefully. Even so, the beginning has been made and it is a comforting thought that a new generation associates the name 'Bikini', not with an immensely horrifying weapon, but with a rather pleasing item of feminine attire.

Whether we like it or not, science has forced man into an entirely new phase of his history. Five hundred years have passed since the little ships of the Portuguese set out to conquer the world, spreading the gospel of their new and terribly efficient experimental philosophy, nowadays called science. They were guided by the mathematicians of Prince Henry's secret research establishment at Sagres who taught them how to navigate on a globe and in this way to make poor little Europe richer than the great civilizations of the East. Since then there has been no halt, and we have been taken from the age of mechanics to the ages of steam and electricity with ever-increasing populations to be controlled by ever-increasing wars. Now, we stand at the threshold of an entirely new era into which science has taken us unawares. In one way or another German science has played its part in bringing this about.

Index